CRITICAL THINKING
FOR
WORKING STUDENTS

CRITICAL THINKING
FOR
WORKING STUDENTS

MICHAEL ANDOLINA

SUNY—Empire State College

CHAPTER CONTRIBUTOR:

MARY S. ANDOLINA

The Evans Library
SUNY Fulton – Montgomery Community College

DELMAR

THOMSON LEARNING ™

Australia Canada Mexico Singapore Spain United Kingdom United States

DELMAR
★
TM
THOMSON LEARNING

Critical Thinking for Working Students
by Mike Andolina

Business Unit Director:
Susan L. Simpfenderfer

Executive Editor:
Marlene McHugh Pratt

Acquisitions Editor:
Zina M. Lawrence

Editorial Assistant:
Elizabeth Gallagher

Executive Production Manager:
Wendy A. Troeger

Production Editor:
Elaine Scull

Executive Marketing Manager:
Donna J. Lewis

Channel Manager:
Wendy E. Mapstone

Cover Design:
Kristina Almquist Design

Illustration:
Don Almquist

For permission to use material from this text or product, contact us by
Tel   (800) 730-2214
Fax   (800) 730-2215
www.thomsonrights.com

Library of Congress Cataloging-in-Publication Data

Andolina, Mike.
    Critical thinking for working students / Mike Andolina.
        p. cm.
    Includes bibliographical references and index.
    ISBN 0-7668-2253-2
    1. Critical thinking. I. Title.

BF441.A56 2001
160—dc21   00-047474

NOTICE TO THE READER

Publisher does not warrant or guarantee any of the products described herein or perform any independent analysis in connection with any of the product information contained herein. Publisher does not assume, and expressly disclaims, any obligation to obtain and include information other than that provided to it by the manufacturer.

The reader is expressly warned to consider and adopt all safety precautions that might be indicated by the activities herein and to avoid all potential hazards. By following the instructions contained herein, the reader willingly assumes all risks in connection with such instructions.

The Publisher makes no representation or warranties of any kind, including but not limited to, the warranties of fitness for particular purpose or merchantability, nor are any such representations implied with respect to the material set forth herein, and the publisher takes no responsibility with respect to such material. The publisher shall not be liable for any special, consequential, or exemplary damages resulting, in whole or part, from the readers' use of, or reliance upon, this material.

Dedication

To Mary, Kerry, and Kate

Contents

Preface

*E*ngaging traditional-aged college students in the practices and techniques of critical thinking can be exciting and rewarding. But engaging students who bring substantial life and work experience to the subject can be one of the most challenging and gratifying experiences a teacher can have. Even after twenty years of interacting with nontraditional students—working students, students re-entering the workforce or planning to enter it—I am always surprised at the insights, creative applications, and diverse perspectives they bring to the study of critical thinking.

According to the 1999 Chronicle of Higher Education Almanac, *46.5 percent of all students are 25 years old or older, most of them working.[1] Yet, few, if any, critical thinking texts on the market today address the specific needs, interests, and special circumstances of working students. What makes this even more surprising is that management associations, labor unions, human resources managers, and CEOs have been claiming that there is a significant unmet need for employees who can assess information, critically evaluate new data, reason and write in a logically coherent way, develop effective strategies for problem solving, and forecast relevant consequences of their decisions. In short, the increasing complexity of the workplace requires workers who can think critically. This text is intended to address this growing need.*

CONCEPTUAL APPROACH

Most education experts agree that when students are engaged in educational material directly related to their interests and particular circumstances, with clear applications, their comprehension and retention increase dramatically. When practical, concrete examples that integrate and build on their experiences are added to this approach, the groundwork is laid for lifelong learning. This text is designed to promote lifelong learning.

This text also includes three special chapters devoted to working students that are not found in most critical thinking texts: Critical Thinking: Information Literacy and Research, Critical Thinking and Moral Reasoning, and Applying Critical Thinking to Management Decision Making.

Moreover, the text is self-reflective in a way that clearly establishes connections among the chapters. There are numerous examples and exercises in which students are reminded of the applications and relationships of the parts to the whole, reinforcing what was learned in earlier sections. In this sense, much of the book is cumulative.

ORGANIZATION

The general tone of the text is informal and readable at the introductory college level. It provides an ample number of examples that relate to experience. The level of difficulty of the reading and the exercises increases as the student progresses through the book. Almost every chapter concludes with a writing exercise in which the student must integrate the topics in the chapter by creating an essay drawn on personal experience.

The text begins with an extensive definition of critical thinking and introduces many of the concepts explored later in the text. Chapters 2 and 3 focus on clear, precise, coherent, and effective communication. Chapter 4 examines the language in which communication becomes clouded and confused by emotively charged and misleading language.

Chapters 5 and 6 focus on the nature and underlying structure of arguments. They attempt to "distill" ordinary language into a format that allows students to trace the logical flow of ideas and the connections among premises and conclusions. Chapter 5 examines the fundamental structure of fairly simple arguments, whereas Chapter 6 examines more complex arguments and provides strategies developing logically coherent and convincing arguments. The arguments are based on examples from work- and home-related contexts. The exercises provide opportunity for students to create their own examples and exercises.

Chapter 7 is devoted to fallacious, misleading, circular, and confusing reasoning encountered in ordinary experience. Several patterns of fallacious reasoning are identified and evaluated. The chapter also offers strategies for avoiding fallacies.

Chapters 8 and 9 investigate empirical and scientific reasoning. Chapter 8 introduces inductive generalizations, reasoning by analogy, inductive arguments, and fallacies in empirical reasoning. It includes criteria for evaluating inductive arguments. Chapter 9 distinguishes inductive generalizations from causal connections and causal arguments. It provides criteria for evaluating causal analyses and suggests strategies for developing sound, empirically based arguments.

Chapter 10 focuses on developing strategies for efficiently locating, prioritizing, evaluating, and organizing sources of information, including electronic sources. The chapter presents a thorough examination of information literacy and its application to problems at work and at home.

The primary focus of Chapter 11 is the application of the principles of critical thinking to moral dilemmas at work and at home. In a nutshell, it is critical thinking integrated with business ethics. Students explore moral dilemmas in the workplace and apply critical thinking strategies to "real-life" situations. Once again, students have an opportunity to create or re-create examples from personal experience.

Chapter 12 is a "capstone" review of the material in the text. It applies the strategies and techniques learned throughout the text to management decision making. The chapter presents four complex case studies in which students must analyze and apply various critical thinking strategies. The first case focuses on how problems in communication contribute to ineffective management, exacerbating an already difficult situation. Case 2 presents four styles of management supervision in a large distribution center and then applies empirical reasoning strategies in identifying obstacles to efficiency and productivity. Case 3 applies the strategies and techniques of information gathering to develop a knowledge base on which a complex business decision is formulated. The final case focuses on the "logic of consequences" or "best alternative" theory in developing a strategy for implementing a major staff reduction plan.

SPECIAL FEATURES

The text contains several cartoons and "light" examples to supplement its informal tone and to offer some comic relief. Important concepts (Key Terms) are highlighted in color and boldface type. Several exercises also ask students to work independently with the material outside the classroom setting. For example, the exercises ask the student to practice the strategies and techniques at home and at work with friends, coworkers, and family.

To gain the most from the text, students are continually encouraged to consider the application of the ideas and techniques to their personal circumstances. The text reinforces the notion that the ideas do indeed have practical value.

About the Author

*T*he author is an associate professor in philosophy at the State University of New York—Empire State College, the nontraditional college of the State University system. He has taught both traditional and nontraditional students for over twenty years. The last sixteen years have been spent developing pedagogical tools to improve the teaching of critical thinking. He has published articles on teaching critical thinking and has led faculty seminars on teaching critical thinking across disciplines. He holds an AB, an MA, and a PhD in philosophy.

Acknowledgments

*T*here are several people who made this text possible. Dr. Craig Tunwall, associate professor in management at Empire State College, provided invaluable advice and counsel on topics in management. Numerous examples and exercises are a direct result of his input. Nearly the entire chapter on information literacy was written by Ms. Mary S. Andolina, assistant professor/librarian at Fulton-Montgomery Community College. Her practical guidance on navigating the sea of information will serve students well in all aspects of research. Ms. Paula DeSantis provided outstanding clerical support and editorial assistance. Dr. Andrew DiNitto provided encouragement and advice. And Delmar Thomson Learning editorial assistant Ms. Elizabeth Gallagher's publishing patience and guidance made the project a reality.

Readers' suggestions, corrections, ideas, and comments are welcome. Please e-mail them to mike.andolina@esc.edu.

The author and Delmar Thomson Learning wish to express their sincere appreciation to the following reviewers:

Charles K. Fink, PhD
Miami-Dade Community College
Miami, FL

David Peterson
Santa Rosa Junior College
Santa Rosa, CA

Matthias T. Schulte
Montgomery College
Rockville, MD

TOPIC COVERED IN THIS CHAPTER

• The importance of critical thinking

• Critical thinking defined

• Truth and objectivity: Preliminary definitions

• Separating fact from opinion

• The decision method criterion for truth

• Critical thinking in settling disputes: Preliminary discussion

• Emotions and bias in critical thinking

Chapter 1

WHAT IS CRITICAL THINKING?

Emerging trends in Total Quality Management and collaborative decision making have necessitated training in [several] areas. Without an understanding of critical thinking and the ability to assess one's own reasoning, these requirements remain difficult—if not impossible—to reach.

–AMERICAN MANAGEMENT ASSOCIATION, TRAINING MANUAL

The Importance of Critical Thinking

In everyday situations, critical thinking can make the difference between success and failure in any given task.

Critical thinking has long been recognized as an essential skill to participate wisely in a democratic society. It also has been championed as a necessary skill for success in the modern business world. Employers seek college graduates who are able to analyze, synthesize, evaluate, and interpret information rather than merely apply technical abilities. Those who can think critically are the ones who will be successful in the global marketplace. These skills become more crucial as more and more decision making is spread across the hierarchy of an organization.

Yet despite the need to develop critical thinkers, we rarely reflect on the critical thinking process itself, nor do we fully discover the power of its usefulness for resolving conflicts, solving problems, communicating effectively, and developing lifelong learning skills. This text is devoted to learning those skills and applying them to real-life contexts at work and at home. It assumes that by careful analysis of the thinking process and by working through several challenging exercises, you can improve your ability to think critically and ultimately become better citizens and employees.

One further note on the text: As students, either currently engaged in the workforce or about to enter or re-enter it, you have a significant advantage, because skills acquired through practice and careful analysis apply directly to work experience. These skills, we hope, will make work experience more interesting and practical. Just as important, however, is the advantage you have of building on and integrating the knowledge and skills you already possess. Both should help in retaining and in establishing lifelong learning skills. You are therefore strongly encouraged to experiment with the ideas and exercises in this text at work and at home.

Critical Thinking Defined

Most of us have some understanding of what thinking is in general. The fact that you are now reading this text presupposes that you are engaged in a mental activity, or thinking process, and that you have some reason for doing so. Thus it is commonly held that thinking in general is a purposeful mental activity that is performed naturally and without much effort.[1] It is distinguished from mere daydreaming and simple reflex actions, and from rote mechanical activities such as typing on a keyboard. Thinking is generally described as a higher order human mental skill that also entails some kind of underlying logic and coherence. However, to perform it well, to think *critically*, requires concerted effort, a good deal of practice, and diligence.

The word "critical" in critical thinking is less abstract and easier to define than thinking in general. Often, "critical" implies *criticism*, which carries a negative connotation and casts a disapproving or unfavorable light on an idea, theory, or action. Used in this way, it is seen as an attack, an unconstructive evaluation. In this text, the word will not be used in this way; rather, it will have a much more positive connotation, one that is closer to the concept of a *critique*. In addition to pointing out weaknesses, a well-constructed critique *summarizes* main themes, *offers constructive comments* in the form of suggestions to improve or expand on ideas, *establishes connections* to other related concepts, and *enumerates possible consequences*. This is the sense of "critical" intended here. We appreciate it when others evaluate our work by outlining its strengths and suggesting ways to correct deficiencies. However, we do not appreciate direct, destructive criticism without a rationale and suggestions for improvement, which in the long term is less effective for obtaining results we prefer and for moving our organization forward.

The following description of critical thinking is adapted from an American Management Association training manual. It captures our intended meaning in plain language.

> Critical thinking, or the art of reasoned judgment, is really little more than thinking about how we think in various aspects of our lives. For example, we can shop critically or uncritically. Uncritical shoppers buy what they don't need and pay too much money. Critical shoppers, on the other hand, think about **how** to shop, their past errors, buying patterns, and impulses. They use their critical thinking skills in a specific way to intervene in their decision about shopping. Similarly, uncritical voters have no criteria to use in evaluating candidates and ideas. The critical voter focuses on issues, analyzes them, is skeptical about propagandistic appeals and soundbites, has reflected on the nature of the offices and ideas, and has clarified criteria for rationally assessing candidates and issues. Critical thinking entails a coherent plan and a test for reasonableness that can be applied to life's various decisions.[2]

Critical thinking then is much more than *any* purposeful mental activity and more than criticism, although it sometimes includes both. **Critical thinking** is a process whereby you evaluate ideas and information and the sources that provide them, arrange them in a coherent way according to their reasonableness and coherence, make connections to other ideas and information, consider alternative sources, and assess them for their implications. However, memorizing this definition will not necessarily help you understand critical thinking or guarantee that you will become a critical thinker. In order to appreciate its power and application fully, you will need to practice it. You will need to remind yourself to sort out information and not accept it at face value merely because it is in print, or simply because it is familiar. As Vincent Ruggiero, a leader in teaching critical thinking, puts it, "Don't settle for shallow thinking."[3]

This definition does not deny or underestimate the role of emotions, bias, and perspective in thinking, including critical thinking. These factors are significant and are dealt with later in this chapter and again in Chapter 4.

Moreover, intelligence alone is not the sole requirement for critical thinking. Even the most seemingly intelligent and reasonable people do some amazing things without thinking about them critically. Just turn to a typical television program that exploits human frailties, such as "T.V. Bloopers" or "Funniest Videos," to find humorous examples of uncritical thinking. And, we all know voters who vote for the "good-looking" candidate, or shoppers who buy a "family size" quart of soft drink thinking that it actually contains more than 32 ounces simply because the ad says that it was made for the *entire family*. Let's not leave out the bank robber who gave the bank his identification number to cash a check before proceeding to rob the bank. So, intelligence alone does not ensure critical thinking. But with practice and some guiding principles and strategies, this text will help make sense of the world and better prepare you to cope with its complexities and challenges.

Truth and Objectivity

It would seem that the first and most obvious place to start in making sense of the world is with a set of true statements, a collection of facts that are known objectively to be true. But as we shall see, truth and **objectivity** are not easy concepts to nail down. To appreciate this requires some critical thinking.

Let's begin with a basic definition of a statement then establish some criteria for a *true* statement. A statement is any expression whose main purpose is to convey information. It expresses a purported fact or opinion about the world and is judged as either true or false. If there is insufficient evidence, judgment is suspended as to its truth or falsity until more information is provided.

One extreme methodological approach to establishing truth was offered by French philosopher René Descartes in his *Discourse on Method*. Descartes argued that to arrive at objective or absolute truth, we must begin with a set of rules. He says, "The first [rule] was to accept *nothing* as true which I did not clearly recognize to be so."[4] He then proceeded to doubt *all truths* so that he could build a solid foundation from his comprehensive, systematic doubt. On the other extreme from Descartes is the view that *everyone's* beliefs are true, or anyone's belief is at least as true as anyone else's belief. Because previously held "truths" or matters of fact were later shown to be false and/or value-laden, it is argued that *all* statements are only matters of opinion;

purely objective truth or absolute truth is elusive. According to this view, matters of opinion *are* truths for each person; truth is purely subjective.

Somewhere between these extremes are principles that guide us in separating mere opinion from established fact, even if the statements expressing the facts are later shown to be false. Determining the difference between fact and opinion is an important first step in critical thinking. Deciding whether to accept a statement as true, reject it as false, or suspend judgment about it, is a foundation for critical thinking.[5] Without these determinations, our reasoning will always lead to questionable results.

OPINIONS AND FACTS

As the British philosopher John Wisdom once said, philosophy is not "knowledge" of new facts but "new knowledge of fact"— it is a deeper, more profound understanding of the facts we already have.

Opinions are statements of *belief* that are open to questioning, evaluation, and analysis; their truth is not obvious. Statements of fact are not open to such questioning. For example, "there are five chairs in this conference room" states a fact that is accepted as true once we count the chairs in the room. The statement "The upcoming merger should boost corporate morale" is an opinion subject to questioning and further analysis. "You are now reading this book" states a fact. "This is the most interesting book on the market" states an opinion. Unfortunately, most statements are not that easily characterized as fact or opinion. Some opinions are more reasonable than others, some elicit more confidence than others, and some fall in the gray area between establish fact and mere opinion.

In fact (pun intended), many beliefs that were once considered to be true are now considered confused and false. For example, in the thirteenth century many people believed that the earth was flat, that the sun revolved around the earth, and that human fluids were life-spirits coursing through one's body. Today we hold a different set of beliefs and no longer accept the earlier statements as an accurate (i.e., true) description of our world. That truth is elusive, particularly given human beings' limited abilities and knowledge, should not surprise us. The search for truth is an age-old quest and philosophical problem that has perplexed humans for generations. Achieving it is a goal we can only all strive for. However, let's set aside for now a philosophical debate about the nature of absolute truth and accept that some statements are indeed true and that some are mere opinions. We will return to the thirteenth century in a subsequent exercise.

Let's consider the following statement: "The company's merger resulted in a net increase in profits." In order to determine whether this statement is true, we begin with an accepted procedure for checking certain pieces of information (e.g., balance sheets, profit statements, expenditure vouchers, payroll, ledgers, etc.). Although there are many factors needed to be considered in verifying this statement, there are standard methods for doing so. These procedures have in the past produced satisfactory results and have been accepted as reasonable criteria. Once the method reaches these results, we generally accept the original statements as true.

Statements referring to historical events are also evaluated on the basis of standard criteria for establishing their truth and credibility. The claim "The industrial revolution in the early part of the nineteenth century led to centralization of goods and services, which in turn led to urban growth" can be verified in a way similar to the way we verify the statements about profits.

The process and methods for accepting these statements can be very complex, a topic we will examine closely throughout the text, but however complex they might become, they can be applied with a reasonable degree of success and consistency. Let's call this approach the **decision method criterion** for the truth of statements and accept it as a basic principle.

Although the method may not lead to an actual determination, the method assumes that it is at least possible to apply it consistently and within reasonable expectations. In our simple example, the method for counting the number of chairs allows us to come to some kind of resolution. But most processes are much more complex than this. Compare, for example, the procedure for checking the truth of "The merger should boost morale." In this statement, words like "should," "boost," and "morale" can be vague and ambiguous. Applying the decision method may never lead to satisfactory results and will remain open to questioning and analysis.

A second principle we can adopt now is **the law of contradiction**, which asserts that no statement can be both true and false at the same time (in the same way). If you assert "there are five chairs in this conference room" is true, you cannot assert at the same time that "there are not five chairs in this room" is true. Contradictory statements *must* have opposite truth values. Sometimes called the principle of consistency, it requires that true statements describing the same subject must be consistent with each other if asserted at the same time. For example, it could be true that the merger should boost morale and it could also be true that it should not boost morale. It also is possible that the merger will actually do both, depending on an employee's personal circumstances. But it is not possible, given a specific decision method, for the company to show a profit and not show a profit at the same time.

EXERCISES

1 . List five areas in which critical thinking plays an important role at work or home. Describe two ways in which critical thinking helps resolve a problem at work.

_____

_____

_____

_____

_____

2 . List four key elements in the definition of critical thinking.

_____

_____

_____

_____

3 . In the context of this text, provide a definition of a statement.

_____

_____

4 . Which of the following are fact? Which are opinion? Which could be both? If you are uncertain about a specific question, explain your answer.

a) The parking garage is too small for the number of people who drive to work at this location.

_____

_____

b) Employees are expected to arrive at work no later than 8:00 A.M.

_____

_____

c) Not all employees are on time every single day.

_____

_____

d) There are 1,200 employees in this company.

_____

_____

e) Cancer is a preventable disease.

_____

_____

f) The department manager will probably offer you a raise next month.

_____

_____

g) The company really needs to provide for a day care center.

_____

_____

h) Anyone who thinks that the office manager is lenient doesn't know her well.

_____

_____

i) Teenage girls are harder to raise than teenage boys.

_____

_____

j) Greed is good.

_____

_____

k) In the movie *Wall Street*, Michael Douglas said, "greed is good."

_____

_____

l) Money is the root of all evil.

_____

_____

m) The company should provide a day care center.

_____

_____

5. Consider the following statements expressed in the thirteenth century. How would you analyze them today?

a) The earth is flat.

_____

_____

b) The sun revolves around the earth.

_____

_____

c) Many people in the thirteenth century believed statements 1 and 2 above were true.

_____

_____

Settling Disputes and Controversies

Distinguishing between fact and opinion can play an important role in resolving disputes or controversies. For example, determining whether a conflict is really a disagreement about the facts or about opinions or about judgments regarding the facts, affects the way we approach a resolution to the conflict. If we determine that the dispute is factually based, we can then proceed to isolate which *specific* facts are in conflict (i.e., are inconsistent) with each other, which in turn will move the discussion forward by following the decision method of accepted procedure. We can change people's opinion but not the facts once accepted. We don't want to waste time and energy making decisions based on unrelated facts or irrelevant information, or attempt to accommodate contradictory statements. Changing people's opinions is another matter.

For example, two people may disagree about a supervisor changing her position in supporting a new project. They may agree that the change in position did occur, but disagree on whether the change was a step forward or a step backward. Employee A might say, "Ms. Florio's most recent memorandum shows real foresight in taking the company in a positive direction," whereas employee B might say, "Ms. Florio's memorandum shows the same old lack of leadership. We are in the same situation now that we were in last year." The issue here is not whether the supervisor changed her position but whether the position taken by her is a good one; it's an issue of approval and disapproval, a matter of opinion, and an interpretation of *what the facts mean*.

> In resolving disputes we must first ask, Is this really a dispute or disagreement over certain facts? or, Is it about how we interpret or feel about the facts? or, Is the dispute really only a matter of differing opinions?

Emotions and Bias

Helping you achieve a degree of objectivity and reasonableness in applying critical thinking skills is one of the most important goals of the text. However, this does not mean that you will always be able or want to rule out emotions and feelings in many of the decisions you make in everyday experience, including work experience. The importance of emotions to decision making cannot be underemphasized. It is often reasonable and necessary to take them into account in the critical thinking process, particularly when you take into account the implications of your decisions. But as rational human beings we also strive for the highest levels of reasonableness, especially as critical thinkers. As critical thinkers you will develop skills for determining *how* and *when* emotions cloud objectivity and reasoning (the subject matter of Chapter 4) and be better able to detect how and when emotions bias your judgments and judgments of others. Just knowing these factors is important to the process when emotions are involved. And knowing our own values, biases, attitudes, and perspectives as well as others' is essential to becoming a critical thinker.

Summary

IN THIS CHAPTER WE:

- Discussed the importance of critical thinking as it relates to work, family, and all aspects of informed citizenship

- Defined critical thinking and gave examples of how it is applied to work-related situations

Exercises

1. Explain how critical thinking can contribute to conflict resolution at work. Provide a specific example where you have used this skill in resolving an actual conflict.

2. List three key differences between fact and opinion.

Writing from Experience

1. Describe a specific situation where you will use critical thinking skills as described in this chapter in resolving an actual conflict at work.

2. Using the definitions in this section, list the facts, opinions, and the method you will use to resolve the conflict.

TOPIC COVERED IN THIS CHAPTER

- Clear thinking and communication are integrally connected.

- Ambiguity is an obstacle to clear thinking and clear expression.

    - Semantic ambiguity results from confusing at least two possible meanings of the same word or phrase.

    - Syntactic ambiguity results from incorrect or unclear sentence structure.

    - Grouping ambiguity results from unclear reference for a word or phrase.

- Vagueness is an obstacle to clear thinking and clear expression.

    - Vagueness is the result of imprecise, indefinite, or unclear language.

    - Vagueness is a matter of degrees.

    - Some words are inherently vague.

- Strategies for removing these obstacles are discussed throughout.

CLEAR COMMUNICATION IN PROBLEM SOLVING

KEY TERMS

grouping ambiguity

semantic ambiguity

syntactic ambiguity

vague statement

Communication is essential to rational choice.

– JEROME D. BRAVERMAN[1]

Unclear language leads to confusion, misunderstanding and, ultimately, conflicts or problems. In this chapter we will show how clear, precise language is the key to effective communication. We will also examine ways in which we can use language as a tool to clarify thinking.

Clear Thinking and Clear Expression

Failure to communicate your precise meaning in both oral and written expression is at the root of many conflicts at home and at work. Clear expression, which presupposes clear thinking, helps avoid or resolve conflicts and is an important tool for problem solving. Deliberate and careful consideration of effective communication skills not only allows us to be better understood but also helps us in clarifying our own thinking. Because language and thinking are so closely related, most would say *integrally related*, how well we perform in one process affects how well we perform in the other. The processes are interactive: unclear thinking results in unclear writing and oral communication; unclear writing and oral communication confuses clear thinking. When we are unable to express ourselves effectively, it may mean that we have not thought through completely what we want to communicate. Using words in an ambiguous and/or vague manner can lead to misunderstanding, confusion and, ultimately, conflict. Whether in an office memorandum, a written report, a résumé or job application, or an oral presentation or interview, we should ask ourselves, "How should I communicate my ideas and experiences so that they are as clear as possible?" This forces us to think more carefully in choosing the right words and correct mode of expression so that we prevent misunderstanding before it occurs.

SEMANTIC AMBIGUITY: DIFFERENT MEANING OF WORDS

It depends on what is, is.

– PRESIDENT BILL CLINTON

One common obstacle to clear communication originates with confusion over the meaning of certain words in the English language. Because most words in English have more than one meaning, it's a wonder that there isn't more confusion in communicating with one another. These *ambiguous* words or phrases result in misunderstanding because they allow at least two possible interpretations of what is conveyed. The specific meaning of these words is determined only in the context of other words in an entire sentence or in the context of other sentences. For example, consider the various meanings of the word "work" in the following sentences. The probable intended meaning is in parenthesis.

1. He is going to work. (place of employment)

2. The fax machine does not work. (function improperly)

3. He will work on the scheduling project tomorrow. (perform a function on an assigned task)

4. The work of Adam Smith is still important to modern economists. (perhaps a volume of writing)

5. The auditor's work is done. (a set of tasks)

6. In 1999 the New York Yankees made short work of the World Series. (colloquial expression for winning easily)

7. We still need to work out the budget details for the proposal. (to balance or to calculate numbers)

Each of these sentences expresses a different meaning of "work." To add to the confusion, every profession, trade, or business has *specialized* meanings for certain words in addition to their common meanings. For example, in computer jargon we hear the expression, "cold-boot your system." Despite the interesting image it creates, the phrase has little more meaning than the commonly understood phrase, "Start up your computer all over again." *Jargon* can lead to ineffective communication or misunderstanding.

> The more precise we make the context, the easier it is for others to grasp the intended meaning.

Consider, for example, the sentence "The work of Adam Smith is still important to modern economists." It could refer to the entire volume of his writings or to the objects that he produced at work, depending on the context in which the statement was uttered. Without clarifying context, the sentence is ambiguous. Had the sentence read "The ideas expressed through the writings of Adam Smith are still important to modern economists," potential misunderstanding could be avoided.

In an ambiguous statement, each word has a clear and distinct meaning (as in the various meanings of "work"). We just don't know which meaning to accept as the intended one. In the sample sentence, "The auditor's work is done," the speaker could mean that the entire audit has been completed or the auditor is done for the day and is going home. Here both "work" and "done" must be clarified. Had the speaker said, "The auditor's review of the accounting records is complete for today," the potential confusion would be eliminated. Ambiguity in meaning, called **semantic ambiguity**, can be avoided by substituting an unambiguous word or phrase for the ambiguous one. Or, the semantic ambiguity can be explained away by providing clarifying information that makes only one interpretation possible. For example, we could avoid the ambiguity by saying, "The auditor's work is done. He does not need to come back until next year." The additional context avoids the ambiguity.

Thinking about the precise way in which we express our thoughts is of the utmost importance in avoiding misunderstanding. As we shall see in Chapter 11 on moral reasoning, unclear language can lead to ethical conflict simply because the speaker was not careful in choosing the precise language to convey his ideas.

AMBIGUITY: RELATIVE WORDS

There is an additional type of ambiguity worth mentioning that arises with the use of words that express a relation or comparison. "Relative" words, which also have different meanings depending on their contexts, are used to express comparisons or connect two related objects or ideas. Relative and relational terms such as "tall," "short," "to the left of," "above," and so on, create special problems because their precise meaning can be determined only by their context. A short list of tasks is short only in relation to other lists. A tall oak tree is tall only in relation to other oak trees; a stair is above or below another stair only in its relation to others in the entire flight of stairs. Confusion occurs when we use a relative term in place of a word that has a fixed meaning, and the resulting substitution allows us to infer two possible separate meanings. For example, a 3-ton mature whale is a large animal, but in normal contexts even a baby whale is a large animal when compared to most other animals. So, if we argued that Baby Shamu is a whale, and all whales are mammals, therefore, Baby Shamu is a mammal, there wouldn't be a problem. But if we argued that Baby Shamu is a baby, and all babies are small, therefore, Baby Shamu is small, we might cause confusion. A baby whale is far from being a small animal, at least in normal contexts. In the first version of the argument, the property of being a baby was not ambiguous, but in the second version, the property of being small is. As we said earlier, the meanings of most words depend on their context; with relative terms, the meaning of the terms *derives* from their context. Without sufficient context, the reader or listener can misunderstand the intended meaning of the sentence. Here's another example of a relational word where the perspective is unclear. "The photocopies are below the file trays on the copier." The phrase "below the file trays" is ambiguous because we are not sure whether the copies are directly beneath the file trays or somewhere else below the file trays.

Whenever you use relative terms to describe an event or object, remember to provide sufficient context (including perspective for phrases like "to the left of") so that the reader cannot misinterpret your meaning.

EXERCISES

I. Identify the ambiguous word or phrase in the following sentences.

1. He made a good presentation at the job fair.

_____

_____

2. The glasses left on the table belong to Jose.

_____

_____

3. The calculator is to the left of the coffee mug.

_____

_____

4. Security on the job is necessary for productivity.

_____

_____

5. A poor security guard can create a hazardous work situation.

_____

_____

6. No single person can do the job well.

_____

_____

7. My desk is before the first row of file cabinets.

_____

_____

8. The supply budget is meager.

_____

_____

9. Women in difficult labor say that relief in effort should occur more frequently.

_____

_____

10. Foreign markets are easier to do business in if you are multilingual.

_____

_____

11. The new Plan of Action for dealing with cases of office violence was distributed to newer employees only.

_____

_____

II. Rewrite the sentences above in unambiguous language.

1. _____

2. _____

3. _____

4. _____

5. _____

6. _____

7. _____

8. _____

9. _____

10. _____

11. _____

········WRITING FROM EXPERIENCE········

1. Provide four examples of ambiguous sentences from a work-related situation. Use an office memo, company policy, ethics code, report, or some other document for examples. Show how you would change each sentence by either substituting nonambiguous words or phrases or adding clarifying context to eliminate the ambiguity.

_____

_____

_____

_____

_____

_____

_____

_____

2. Select three examples of ambiguous language in a newspaper article or television program. Translate the example into unambiguous statements.

_____

_____

_____

_____

_____

_____

_____

_____

SYNTACTIC AMBIGUITY

Another common obstacle to clear expression is **syntactic ambiguity**. This type of ambiguity occurs when the *structure* of a sentence leads to misunderstanding and/or confusion (Figure 2-1). Often it is the grammatical construction, or loose or awkward wording of a sentence that leaves the reader with at least two possible interpretations of its meaning. For example, here is a caption from a company newsletter:

> Mr. Jacobi, Assistant Vice President/Marketing, shown here, describes what he learned during a training seminar at a workshop on Saturday.

Grammatically misleading sentences containing misplaced modifiers or "dangling participles" can cause confusion because the structure of the sentence leaves us with two possible interpretations. In the above caption, is Mr. Jacobi describing the learning that took place some time ago in the training seminar, or is he describing what he learned in a workshop that took place Saturday? "Mr. Jacobi, shown here at Saturday's workshop, is describing what he learned in last month's training seminar" is less likely to be misunderstood. Consider

FIGURE 2.1 *"We unpacked the files from the file cabinets and then threw them out."*

this syntactically ambiguous sentence:"He erased the file on the diskette with his new invention." Did the file contain information about a new invention or did the new invention provide a more efficient way to erase files? Had we said, "He mistakenly erased the data about his new invention. The data were saved on this diskette," the meaning would be unmistakably clear.

Sometimes an uncertain reference causes confusion of this sort. For example, "He gave him his letter of recommendation" is ambiguous because we are not certain whether the person is giving his own letter of recommendation to someone else or is returning a letter of recommendation that belongs to someone else. "Mr. Munez gave the supervisor his letter recommending Mr. Wallace" is clearer. Another error of reference is committed in the following: "The account supervisors follow all international routing calls until they come to a dead end." It is not clear whether the calls or the executives come to a dead end. Usually, the only remedy for this type of confusion is to start fresh and rewrite the sentence. For example, "The account supervisors follow all international routing calls until each call leads to a dead end" is clearer. Sometimes ambiguous reference leads to rather absurd or humorous situations like the one quoted at the beginning of this section.

> In rewriting, editing, proofreading your written work, or practicing a speech, look for sentences where the intended meaning cannot be misconstrued or misinterpreted by your audience. Eliminate all ambiguous references by substituting nonambiguous words or references or by writing the sentence with clarifying information (Figure 2-2).

FIGURE 2.2 *Demonstrating your meaning too clearly? (Cartoon from B.C. By permission of Johnny Hart and Creators Syndicate, Inc.)*

EXERCISES

1. *Identify the syntactically ambiguous words or phrases in the following sentences.*

1. One way to tell if the supervisor is upset is to see if she talks to her secretary. But her secretary also knows when to keep a low profile. In fact, she never talks to her when she is irritated.

   _____

   _____

2. Let's have the boss for dinner tonight. She's really a sweet person.

   _____

   _____

3. Ms. Boris is promoting cross-functional working teams. This means that she wants people to be trained in several tasks so that they will have a broader view of various operations in the department and be able to fill in for coworkers in case of emergencies. She is going out on a limb in promoting this. Some employees say it violates contractual agreements between management and employees. Upper management says the idea might not work in practice. They are going to wait to the see details before supporting it.

   _____

   _____

4. Ms. Gaines exposed herself again to the radiation treatment.

   _____

   _____

5. Ms. Siad criticized the new employee over the computer.

   _____

   _____

6. She asked for time off to perform community service but was refused. They said there wasn't enough for her work to do.

   _____

   _____

7.   The group got together at the Downtown Pub almost every Friday after work. After a few cocktails they would leave their drinks at the bar for some pool and darts.

_____

_____

8.   The company decided to install video cameras and one-way mirrors on the second floor to monitor employee performance and to enhance security against theft. The practice is paying off already. Two people were caught on tape in some very awkward positions.

_____

_____

II. Rewrite the sentences above in clear, unambiguous language.

1.   _____

2.   _____

3.   _____

4.   _____

5.   _____

6.   _____

7.   _____

8.   _____

GROUPING AMBIGUITY

There are occasions when ambiguity in reference is the result of uncertainty in whether an intended referent (the object being referred to) is an *individual* or a *group* made up of several individuals, each of which is considered separately. This type of ambiguity occurs when a class (group) of objects is confused with its individual members (Figure 2–3). The following is an example of a **grouping ambiguity**. "In an old manufacturing plant, factory line workers can earn more money than supervisors." This is unclear because we are not certain whether the sentence refers to *all* factory workers, taken as a

FIGURE 2.3 *"Manufacturers are leaving for foreign markets to seek cheaper wages."* Senator John McCain in a campaign speech.

whole, or to some factory workers taken as individuals. The speaker could be saying that the total payroll for all factory workers exceeds the total payroll for all supervisors. But then again, in a long-standing factory, given seniority raises and special incentives, factory workers, as individuals, might earn more money than individual supervisors. Clarifying context is needed to avoid the ambiguity and ensuing confusion.

Sometimes it is extremely difficult to determine whether a group or an individual is being referred to. For example, "The cost of company-sponsored child care for last year was several hundred thousand dollars" probably means that the entire cost to the company for all children in the child care program was several hundred thousand dollars and not the cost per child. But, "The children like to play for hours at a time" is not as clear. It probably means that each individual child likes to play for hours, but it could also mean that as a group, that is, children in general, like to play for hours at a time. Only more contextual information will clarify which meaning is intended.

> When you intend to refer to a group or class of individuals, make sure that your meaning cannot be misconstrued to refer to each individual member of the group or class.

•••••••••••••••••••••••• **EXERCISES** ••••••••••••••••••••••

I. Identify the ambiguous words or phrases in the following sentences, then rewrite each sentence in a clear, unambiguous language.

1. Public employees make millions of dollars a year in public service.

   _____

   _____

2. Employees at Logical Services Company enroll in the payroll deduction program each year.

   _____

   _____

3. Laptop computers are lighter than portable typewriters.

   _____

   _____

4. All clerical staff must report to the director of human resources between 10 A.M. Tuesday and 4 P.M. Wednesday.

   _____

   _____

5. Manufacturers are leaving for foreign markets to seek cheaper wages.

   _____

   _____

6. Human resource managers oversee the enforcement of the company's ethics code.

   _____

   _____

7. Whistleblowers undermine company morale.

   _____

   _____

8 . The company's security policy covers all employees except outside contractors.

_____

_____

II. List five sentences you have encountered at work in which ambiguous language led to confusion or misunderstanding. Ask associates, coworkers, or family members for additional examples.

_____

_____

_____

_____

_____

III. Locate a report, memorandum, or other written document at work or at home in which the language is ambiguous. Discuss in class how you would reword the document in unambiguous language.

Vagueness

By the explication of a familiar but vague concept, we mean its replacement by a new exact concept.

–RUDOLF CARNAP[2]

The problem of vagueness should be distinguished from the related problem of semantic ambiguity (Figure 2–4). In the latter case, the meaning of a sentence is unclear because it could be confusing with at least two separate but clear meanings or interpretations of a word. In a **vague statement**, the intended meaning of a word or phrase is imprecise, unclear, indistinct, or indefinite. Both vagueness and ambiguity lead to misunderstanding, but in

FIGURE 2.4 *"What goes up must come down."* Jesse Ventura referring to recent
gains in the stock market.

order to achieve clarity and avoid confusion, we need to know what is at the
root of the problem. If ambiguity is causing confusion, then providing clarifying context or substituting a nonambiguous word will prevent misunderstanding. A similar line of reasoning applies in avoiding vagueness, except that
vagueness is a matter of degrees. To avoid vagueness, substitute a more precise word or phrase for a vague one, or provide specific information, including concrete examples, that supply clarifying context.

As we describe the world around us and try to make sense of it all, we often
use language that we assume communicates a clear picture of what we are
thinking, feeling, or experiencing. However, later, after careful analysis, we discover that we are not as precise as we could be in conveying our ideas. When
we use language in this vague way, we not only risk being misunderstood, we

leave the impression that our thoughts themselves are not clear, distinct, or precise. Consider the following:

1. The memorandum arrived *some time* ago.

2. That was an *interesting* idea.

3. His children do *reasonably well* in school.

4. The company's safety policy is *rather dated*.

5. There were a *number of* clerical staff at the meeting.

6. The company has *too many* locations for its distribution capacity.

The problem with the italicized words is that they do not provide a clear and precise description of the thoughts the speaker or writer intended to convey. Let's consider some of the statements above. In statement 1, do we have a clear idea of when the memorandum arrived? "Some time ago" could mean any time early in the same day, or it could mean weeks or even months ago. A vague expression such as this should be clarified by providing more specific information, such as a brief time span that would help express the thought more precisely. Because vagueness is itself a relative concept and is subject to a matter of degrees, some words and phrases are more or less vague than others. However, the more precise the language, the better the understanding.

Example 2 about an "interesting" idea is a disappointing response for a teacher to hear in response to a question about a certain text or passage in a text. The ideas are interesting in what way *specifically?* Similarly, when a supervisor or manager asks you for an opinion about a new product, policy, or proposal, the response should provide specific relevant reactions, including some examples of possible outcomes. In general, almost any additional information is better than merely saying it is "interesting."

Another vague phrase that has crept into common usage in the past few years is mentioned in number 5 above. This usually unhelpful phrase is imprecise because it does not provide any information as to what number the person has in mind. Even "in the past few years" mentioned in the previous sentence is more precise than "a number of years ago," even though "the past few years," too, is vague and should be replaced with a range of years, say four to five years. Although an approximate number is still somewhat vague, it is better than no number at all.

There are occasions when a nonspecific term or phrase is the best you can do. For example, the sentence, "there are billions, perhaps trillions, of stars in the visible universe" does not provide precise information. But more precision is impossible given the current state of our knowledge of astronomy. Yet, it is still more precise than "there are a whole lot of stars in the visible universe." Note also that "some time ago," as stated on page 23 in describing Mr. Jacobi, is vague because no specific time frame was provided. The example, however, required a vague expression because the exact time was indeterminate.

Relative terms and general terms of measurement like big, tall, heavy, and so on, discussed earlier not only lead to ambiguity but can also lead to vagueness. For example, when we compare a tall building to other buildings, we know its general context for comparison, thus removing the ambiguity. But we still don't know how tall the building is. So even when we eliminate ambiguity, vagueness can remain a problem.

EXERCISES

I. Evaluate the following in terms of vagueness:

1. There are billions, perhaps trillions, of bytes of storage memory in the new generation of computer chips.

   _____

   _____

2. The national debt is measured in the trillions of dollars.

   _____

   _____

3. The total gross national product of the island of Tobago is less than the gross revenues for one year of General Motors Corporation.

   _____

   _____

II. List three situations in which a general term is as precise as it could be yet is still not precise. Explain your answers.

_____

_____

_____

_____

_____

_____

_____

_____

Abstract Words

If I am asked "What is good?" my answer is that good is good, and that is the end of the matter. If I am asked "how is good defined?" my answer is that it cannot be defined."

–GEORGE EDWARD MOORE[3]

Some relative words that express abstract concepts are difficult to make precise due to the very nature of the ideas expressed. For example, "good," "bad," "moral," "ideal," "reality," and "human rights," are abstract concepts that have puzzled philosophers and other thinkers for centuries. Their meaning is the subject matter of volumes of books. However, in most cases a degree of clarity can be achieved by providing specific examples to help clarify the meaning when a substitute word or phrase is inappropriate.

Consider the following expression uttered in the context of a business ethics course.

> It is always morally wrong to fail to report to the CEO each time you discover that in your opinion one of the products your company produces is defective.

The meaning of concepts like "morally wrong" seem clear in most contexts. After all, many of us already know right from wrong. However, in the context of a business ethics course, for example, the concepts of right/wrong and moral/immoral are the very concepts under examination. In these contexts, morality is the subject matter we are trying to define. For situations involving inherently abstract words and contexts, the best approach is to define what you mean by way of specific examples. In addition to providing depth to your writing, specific examples not only make your writing and thinking more concrete to the reader and to yourself but more interesting as well because they establish connections to other ideas or experiences the reader can relate to. The sentence above could be made clearer by providing specific examples of what the author means by "always morally wrong" (also see Figure 2-5).

FIGURE 2.5 *Adding clarifying information in everyday experience. (Cartoon from B.C. By permission of Johny Hart and Creators Syndicate, Inc.)*

Summary

IN THIS CHAPTER WE:

- Demonstrated how clear thinking is integrally related to clear expression

- Examined two major obstacles to clear thinking and clear expression: ambiguity and vagueness

- Discussed three types of ambiguity and the problems in communication associated with them

- Discussed three aspects of vagueness

- Developed strategies for removing ambiguity and improving on vague statements

- Practiced critical thinking skills in achieving clear thinking and clear expression

Exercises

> **I. In the following paragraph there are at least seven vague phrases (not a few, several, or "a number," but seven). The vague words are in italics.**

MEASURES OF SERVICE

The Office of Quality of Health Services has developed *a number of* indicators to monitor health and safety measures in public offices in the State of New Texas. Among the indicators are: *the large amount* of cleaning products used, the compliance with legal restrictions governing smoking in the workplace, the total number of written and phone complaints received, and *several aspects* of services related to the time it takes to respond to a problem. These indicators are seen by people in *various levels* of the organization as inadequate measures. *Many say* that the Office of Quality of Health Services requires fewer new measures than the measures implemented last year when the organization was required to police itself. There was *more* complience and more service. *They said* that OQHS should be *doing even more* to protect its workers, although they liked *many of the things* the office has done recently.

This passage doesn't provide much specific information and, therefore, does not successfully communicate precisely the ideas of the author.

1. Is the phrase "the total number of written and phone complaints received" vague? Explain or defend your answer.

2. Is the phrase "health services require fewer measures" vague? Explain or defend your answer.

3. Replace the vague phrases in italics with precise language or add examples that will clarify their precise meaning.

4. In a brief essay describe how you would react to this report if it came to your attention.

Writing from Experience

1. Develop a brief paragraph of about seventy-five words in which you give precise directions to someone who is completely unfamiliar with your town or city how he or she should travel to meet you at your place of work. This person will be arriving by car on the nearest expressway from at least 100 miles away.

2. In an essay of about fifty words, describe your work setting. Exchange this description with a colleague and compare how he or she would describe the same setting.

TOPIC COVERED IN THIS CHAPTER

• The importance of definitions to critical thinking

• The relationship between words and concepts

• Three functions of definitions

> • set boundaries
>
> • summarize properties
>
> • articulate relation between concepts

• Ways to define words and concepts

> • by example
>
> • by synonym
>
> • by genus and species
>
> • by analogy

• Rules for good definitions

Chapter

3

DEFINITIONS

Definitions serve as a starting point for much of
human reasoning.

– Diane Romain[1]

....

Clarity Through Definitions

In Chapter 2 we examined how clarifying information eliminates ambiguity and vagueness, obstacles to clear thinking and clear communication. In this chapter we will discuss a specific type of clarifying information—definitions—as a way to reduce vagueness, avoid ambiguities and, hence, prevent misunderstanding.

Definitions play an important role in alleviating potential conflict by specifying the *precise* meaning of a word or phrase and by explaining concepts in unambiguous and familiar language. For example, consider the following statement: "We will evaluate Ms. Montell's *performance* in the next few weeks." Uttered in certain circumstances, "performance" can be taken two ways. The first assesses the quality of her current and past work on the job, whereas the second assesses the quality of how well she performs in a public arena. The latter is concerned with her method of delivery in communicating, the former with her accomplishments at work. However, as we saw in the previous chapter, if you provide additional information, such as a definition of the word in question, adding, "by 'performance,' I mean her accomplishments in her *role* as line supervisor" to the sentence, the ambiguity is removed. The additional clarifying information defines which sense of "performance" is intended. Defining your terms, especially in the beginning of a discussion, establishes the intended meaning and sets boundaries for what you are attempting to communicate. In all forms of communication, the old adage "First define what you mean" is in fact good advice. As stated earlier, the English language can be confusing and misleading; achieving clarity through definitions is an effective strategy to add to our repertoire of critical thinking skills.

Words and Concepts

Words form the vocabulary of language. They are the main vehicles through which we communicate our thoughts, feelings, and experiences. However, a mere string of words is inadequate for communicating these experiences in an intelligible way. We need to organize experience under general ideas so that the listener or reader can fully understand what we are trying to convey. Concepts perform that function. *Concepts* are general ideas that bring order and intelligibility to our experience. They group things together into classes or categories based on similarities among the things with which we are concerned. The concepts themselves are grouped into more general categories based on similarities with each other and on their connections to other concepts. Critical thinking involves developing expertise in the conceptualization process—forming new concepts from experiences and bringing familiar ones together under general connecting ideas. Only then can we apply general concepts to particular experiences in a coherent and informative manner. One of the most important ways to engage in this process is by defining clearly and distinctly each word and concept. In this way, definitions not only give the meaning of words, they also *explain and explicate* the concepts we use in communicating our thoughts and experiences.

Three Functions of Definitions

A good definition is often the only way to begin a discussion, particularly when you introduce new ideas as the result of new terminology. Definitions of words whose meaning is yet to be established are sometimes called **stipulative definitions**. For example, if you wanted to explain a concept called "outsourcing," you would begin by providing a clear definition of what you mean by that word. You would state the essential properties of the concept and then give specific examples, describing certain instances when the practice of outsourcing has been and/or should be put into effect. You would mention, for example, certain aspects of the company's work-related activities that are normally performed by your organization that will now be performed under contract with another organization. You could continue by outlining how this will be accomplished and provide specific examples of projects that have been or will be "outsourced." Of course, a rationale, explaining why, when, and by whom the practice will be carried out should accompany the definition. By defining the concept clearly, your audience will have a better understanding of it and how it can be applied.

SETTING BOUNDARIES

In defining a new or well-established concept, you create a category or class for which the concept applies. The category is identified by its *essential* properties or characteristics, and the definition *sets boundaries* for the use of each word in the category. A major function of definitions is to tell us what is and is not included in each category. The definition sets the conditions that must be met for something to be considered an example of the concept. For example, it tells us what should and should not count as outsourcing.

Although the boundaries are sometimes "fuzzy," and the meaning of words changes over time, the essential characteristics identifying the use of a concept remain fairly fixed and constant. (We will discuss essential characteristics in the next section.) The important point is that the definition helps you become more precise by limiting the discussion to relevant topics. It sets parameters for the application of concepts, even when we think we already know what it means.

Consider this example: You are at a meeting and someone announces that the new Employee Training Program should now be treated as a department resource available immediately to all employees. Someone asks, "What do you mean by 'a department resource'? Define 'resource' for us." First, you would need to enumerate the characteristics of the things that should be included in that concept. Identifying the main characteristics and specifying those that are *common* inform us as to which objects or things *belong* to the concept. For "resource," they should include the following.

1. Something that can be ready or available for our use

2. An asset

3. Something that can be drawn on immediately or in the future for aid

4. An aspect of wealth

All of the objects that have these properties fall under the general concept of a resource; they belong to that class or category. More specifically, the following things belong to this class: monies allocated in the form of a department budget; all physical assets appropriate to perform department functions, including equipment and employees (human resources); technology and technical support; office and building space; investment monies; and so on. All the things that are available for use by a department are examples of things that fit into this category. These examples expand, clarify, and supplement the definition. In understanding the definition, its requirements and boundaries, you know to which things the concept can be applied. That is, you know what belongs to the concept of a resource in the form of an employee training program.

SUMMARIZING

Another function of definitions alluded to earlier involves their role in synthesizing information. A good definition *summarizes* the collection of objects that the concept refers to. This function informs us about each object in the category by synthesizing the knowledge we have about them and labels them according to their most common properties. So rather than providing example after example to determine what "resource" means, the second function of a definition *organizes* this knowledge, giving us just the *key* elements, the essence (i.e., essential properties) of the concept. For general, complex, or abstract concepts like "business," which can include anything from financial management to consumer buying patterns to international trade laws, and much in between, a list of all the relevant characteristics would be impractical. A good definition will provide a unifying explanation that gives the most important characteristics of the things in the class, identifying what is *essential* to the class rather than having an exhaustive list.

RELATIONSHIP TO OTHER CONCEPTS

A third function of definitions is to clarify where a concept "fits" in relation to other concepts. Complex concepts are generally defined in relation to other concepts; they are not understood in isolation from each other. That is, they *derive* their meaning in the context of other concepts.

Consider the word "corporation." The general concept expressed by this word is not easily defined because you cannot simply point to some object as its referent, or provide a list of examples, or offer a single word synonym. Because it is an abstract concept, one that captures several simple and complex ideas, it is understood only in relation to several other concepts. For example, as you define it, you immediately begin to organize your thoughts and begin to picture in your mind the various objects, ideas, buildings, persons, and so on, that fall under the general concept. In addition to the objects, people, and equipment, you would also need to think about other abstract ideas, such as "an *organization* with a hierarchy," a "*legal entity* formed for profit," a "legal entity formed for a *social purpose* without profit," "an *association of individuals* with powers to function independently from its members," and so on. All of these (italicized) phrases, which express abstract concepts themselves, help explain and define the concept of a corporation. As we organize these ideas into some kind of rational order, the concept becomes clearer in our mind, allowing us to apply it in various contexts. If we don't understand any of the associated concepts, or can't follow their connections to the original concept, then we really don't understand what a corporation is at all.

EXERCISES

I. Consider this definition of rationality. It is offered as part of an explanation of the "Rational Choice Theory of Management."

Like many commonly used words, 'rationality' has come to mean many things. In many of its uses, 'rational' is approximately equivalent to 'intelligent' or 'successful.' It is used to describe actions that have desirable outcomes. In other uses, 'rational' means 'coldly materialistic,' referring to the spirit of values in terms of which an action is taken. In still other uses, 'rational' means 'sane,' reflecting a judgment about the mental health displayed by an action or procedure. Heterogeneous meanings of rationality are also of the literature on decision making. The term is used rather loosely or inconsistently. [2]

1. Identify the different functions of definitions used in this explanation of rationality.

_____

_____

_____

_____

_____

_____

_____

_____

2. Evaluate the definition in terms of the three functions discussed earlier. How would you improve on this definition?

_____

_____

_____

_____

_____

_____

II.

1. Provide three definitions of each of the following terms. In each definition explain how you incorporated the three functions discussed earlier.

    Compensation

    Commuter

    Retirement benefit

_____

_____

_____

_____

_____

_____

_____

(continued)

2. Select three abstract terms you use in everyday communication at work. Define these terms using each of the functions cited above.

_____

_____

_____

_____

_____

_____

_____

_____

_____

_____

_____

_____

_____

_____

_____

_____

_____

_____

_____

_____

·········WRITING FROM EXPERIENCE·········

In a brief paragraph, describe an incident in which providing a clear definition would have either improved communication or prevented miscommunication.

_____

_____

_____

_____

_____

_____

_____

_____

_____

_____

_____

_____

_____

_____

_____

_____

_____

_____

_____

_____

Four Ways to Define Words and Concepts

If you want to define a word, why not just use a dictionary and be done with it? Dictionaries are a good place to start but are inadequate for the standards we set for critical thinkers. In most cases, dictionaries provide nothing more than a synonym, and rarely provide a full context that helps explain the *concept* expressed by the word. Moreover, if you don't understand the concept at all at the outset, the synonyms will provide no additional understanding of the original concept. For example, according to Webster's *New World Dictionary,* the word "leader" is defined as "one who leads" and "perspicuous" as "demonstrating perspicuity." For the standards of clarity and effective communication required for critical thinkers, you therefore need to go beyond dictionary definitions.

However, having said this, it is important to note that even though synonymous definitions have limited explanatory power, synonyms *can* be useful, especially as a starting point. A synonymous definition is provided when you offer another word, whose meaning is already understood because it is familiar to you, and that word has (roughly) the same meaning as the word being defined. So to begin, you might use a dictionary as a starting point, but remember to follow up with one of the following types of definitions to promote a clearer and more thorough understanding.

FIGURE 3.1 *A definition by example.* (Cartoon from B.C. By permission of Johny Hart and Creators Syndicate, Inc.)

DEFINITION BY EXAMPLE

Understanding any specific decision in a specific situation requires a great deal of concrete contextual knowledge.

– JAMES G. MARCH[3]

Providing examples is often the easiest and best way to define words and concepts, particularly abstract ones (Figure 3-1). To define concepts such as "business," "corporation," "capitalist," "harassment," "entrepreneur," "subordinate," "performance," "slacker," "economist," "outsource," and "integrity," it is best to paint a mental picture, a descriptive story about the kind of specific things you want to include in the definitions. A particular example of a well-known capitalist, say Andrew Carnegie or John D. Rockefeller, conjures images that allow us to make informative connections to a variety of ideas that define the word. A reference to *a particular* person of integrity, or a description of a specific relationship between a boss and an employee brings to mind what we mean by "integrity" and "subordinate," respectively. Specific examples give *concreteness* to your writing and thinking, helping you clarify the precise meaning in your own mind as well as in the minds of others. Equally important, a definition with specific examples avoids the problems with vagueness, which was discussed in Chapter 2.

Also called **denotative definitions**, definitions by example bring to life images that allow your audience to expand their thinking beyond immediate experience. The "real-life" examples bring abstract concepts down to earth, when expressed in familiar terms, producing a richer understanding of the concept. Thus, it is useful to give a variety of examples (as many as are practical) and to include ones that your audience will not expect you to give. Both strategies call on your audience to think in new ways. Including unusual examples demonstrate the boundaries of the definition and delineate the scope of what you are talking about, as well as spark attention in your audience. Denotative definitions correspond to the first function of definitions because they enumerate the things that should be listed under the general concept.

Let's reexamine the concept of a leader as an example. After stating the essential characteristics of a leader (the unifying function of a definition) we should provide a list of things that define that concept. The list could include famous political leaders, such as George Washington, Franklin Delano Roosevelt, Abraham Lincoln, Margaret Thatcher, Jesse Jackson, Geraldine Ferraro; religious leaders such as Jesus Christ, Buddha, Ghandi, Mohammed, Martin Luther King; social movement leaders; or business leaders. The list could go on and on. But you might also cite some people who normally would not be on the list, like a coach, who leads a team yet does so stoically from the sidelines; an effective manager, who performs best "behind the scenes"; a rowing captain, who leads from the "back" of the scull; or a spiritual leader, who silently conveys leadership qualities through deeds and meditation. *Adding* these unusual examples will stick in the minds of your readers and make for more interesting reading and listening. As long as they are not *substituted* for familiar examples, they are useful in expanding a concept's application.

A specific type of definition by example is the **ostensive definition**. You provide an ostensive definition if you say, "This is what I mean by a file organizer," and then you point to the actual file organizer, a type of Rolodex® for manila file folders. When you actually point to the objects named, everyone usually knows what you mean immediately. When you say, for example, "here's what I mean by a..." and point to the object, you can't miss being understood as to which things the word applies. However, ostensive definitions are useful, obviously, only when you are in position to actually point to the things being defined. Even then, your audience still might not know what a file organizer is unless you explain or show what it does. (A definition of a word that describes what its referent is used for, that is, what it does, is called a *functional definition*.) Moreover, ostensive definitions cannot help us with general concepts that you cannot easily point to, like corporation, profit margin, integrity, entrepreneurship, or resource. It would be quite difficult in any circumstance to define what you mean by a corporation by simply pointing to some objects. What would you point to? the buildings, which might be in several cities? the corporate officers? the company logo?

When the referents themselves are not immediately present, it is useful to provide a pictorial *representation* of the objects. For example, visual aids are useful tools that will help you define concepts. Visual presentations such as overhead projectors, power point presentations, flip charts, pictures, and physical samples are effective in conveying your ideas and defining precisely what you mean.

CONNOTATIVE DEFINITIONS: THE "SENSE" OF A WORD

As you can see, definitions by example have drawbacks. Providing an exhaustive list of examples can be an inefficient use of time and space (for written examples), particularly for complex concepts, and might turn out to be impossible for some, depending on your creativity and imagination. Moreover, the list could offend some people because their favorite examples were left out, or the list did not include certain groups that are clearly representative of the class but were omitted. To avoid these problems, it is useful to rely on the second function of definitions: summarizing the common characteristics of the examples to which the concept refers. Definitions that organize several common characteristics of the objects referred to are called **connotative definitions**. A good dictionary definition is often connotative. In addition to giving a synonym they usually also give common usage or "connotation" of a word, often called the "sense" of what a word means. For example, the *Random House Dictionary of the English Language* defines management as, "1. the act or manner of handling, directing, guiding or controlling of persons or affairs of others, 2. the act of managing an institution, business, organization, etc."[4]

Now compare the dictionary definition of management with the following quotation from a text in management decision making.

> Some management theorists define management as a process of getting things done through people. Others define management in terms of the functions a manager must perform, such as planning, staffing, directing, controlling, and organizing.[5]

DEFINITION BY GENUS AND SPECIES

Sometimes called "analytical definitions" or "conventional definitions," definition by genus and species is one of the most common types of definition among all types. To understand definition by genus and species, we must introduce the concept of a *class*. Membership in a class is determined by the attributes or properties that an object has. The properties it shares in common with others are the ones that place them in the *same class*. Most objects belong to more than one class, and most classes have more than one subclass. The complexity of the properties of an object determines the classes to which an object belongs.

The term "genus" is used to describe the class whose membership is divided into subclasses, and the subclasses are the "species." As *relative* concepts, genus and species can be subclasses to each other. Just as children can be offspring to parents, those parents can be offspring to their parents. A genus can be species of a larger genus; a species can be genus to a subclass. For example, a General Motors car can be a member (a subclass) of all station wagons (the genus, or larger class). A Chevrolet can be a member of both, a subclass of GM products and station wagons. However, a Cadillac does not have the property of being a station wagon and cannot belong to that class, even though it is a GM product.

Although these distinctions may seem overly confusing and merely academic, defining concepts by genus and species makes complex relationships clear by differentiating a concept from other concepts and from other species. This corresponds to the third function of definitions. The species distinguishes the objects from other members of the same genus. Think of the genus as the general name, or the generic name. The species' properties are the distinguishing characteristics that separate the individuals that have the same generic name. For example, "Kennedy" is the family name of the former president of the United States. The first names John, Joseph, Rose, Robert, and Edward distinguish the members of the Kennedy family from one another. If we wanted to distinguish them further, we would add middle initials, and/or generation indicators such as "junior" or "senior," or "the second," "the third," and so on. In a similar way, "station wagon" distinguishes certain types of cars in the same class from other types in that class, such as convertibles. The distinguishing characteristic that identifies the species tells us *what kind* of thing is being referred to. In this sense it *qualifies* the genus name as it defines what kind of car it is. For example, in the sentence, "Humans are rational animals," the species rational animal tells us what kind of animals are under discussion. Rational animal partially *defines* humans by genus and species. The Aristotelian notion of essence was the forerunner, no doubt, of the modern notion of intension or meaning. For Aristotle, it was essential in men to be rational, accidental to be two legged.[6]

EXERCISES

I. Consider the following quotation defining managerial decisions. Explain how it uses the method of genus and species.

What is a managerial decision?

What is the difference between a managerial decision and those common everyday decisions made by managers and non-managers alike? Managerial decisions are complex decisions that have a significant effect on some organization. In business organizations, the effect of managerial decisions is generally monetary. The crux of the definition of managerial lies in the complexity of the decision situation and the significance of the result to the organization. We make the distinction between managerial and nonmanagerial decisions simply to eliminate the trivial and unimportant. For example, a decision about carrying an umbrella ... would not normally be considered a managerial decision. But who can tell? Under certain circumstances even decisions such as these might have significant consequences to the organization. [7]

_____

_____

_____

_____

_____

_____

_____

_____

_____

_____

_____

_____

_____

DEFINITION BY ANALOGY

A multinational corporation is like a giant octopus. Its tentacles reach all over the globe, but its heart is its headquarters. This **analogy** (more precisely, a simile and a metaphor) *defines* a concept by comparing it to something else. In this case, an interesting image is created that allows you to define an abstract concept in a way that examples and genus and species cannot.

Consider the following.:

> How do I define good management strategy? Good corporate management strategy is a road map that takes the company into the future. Each turn in the road leads to new markets, new opportunities. With a good map we can achieve our goals in the most successful way possible.

Here, a **metaphor** is used to accomplish similar results: an interesting image that will capture the attention of your readers and listeners. Denotative and connotative definitions provide clear, concrete, and fairly precise definitions that serve a definite purpose. But sometimes a little creativity with analogies and metaphors will go a long way in ensuring that your audience will remember the definition later on.

> Caution: Use analogy and metaphor only when you have already provided one of the other types of definitions.

Since analogical definitions do not give the literal meaning of a concept, the *precise* meaning is open to interpretation. Metaphors and analogies used alone might actually confuse your audience if they allude to unfamiliar context or if the primary purpose of the communication is to convey precise information. For example, in a factual report, comparing a corporation to an octopus might mislead more than help. Metaphors are vague but colorful uses of language. Use them cautiously. And remember to provide clear definitions first and, perhaps, leave your audience with a metaphorical or analogical definition last.

Rules for Good Definitions

A DEFINITION SHOULD NOT BE TOO BROAD OR TOO NARROW

A definition is too broad if it includes objects that do not belong to the concept being defined. In other words, the definition exceeds its intended scope. Consider this definition of virtue. "Virtue means maintaining good habits." This may seem like a reasonable definition of a standard ethical term. However, there are things that we might consider good habits that are not, in an ethical sense, virtuous or nonvirtuous. For example, habits like placing your car keys in a safe place at work, avoiding deserted parking lots at night, and locking your desk drawer every evening, are all good habits to maintain. But they have little to do with virtue, at least in an ethical sense. As in defining humans as two-legged creatures, broad definitions include members outside the scope of your definition, such as birds and apes.

Conversely, a narrow definition does not include members in the class that should belong to it. In other words, the concept refers to fewer objects than provided for by the definition. For example, let's define a file cabinet as a piece of furniture with sliding drawers that stores folders. However, there are other types of furniture that store folders and include sliding drawers, such as office desks, large bookcases, or revolving file holders. Narrow definitions exclude referents that you *want* to include in the class being defined.

The problem with both narrow and broad definitions is that they exceed or overly restrict their intended scope of application. In these definitions, the relationship between the concept being defined and its referents is inaccurate, which leads to confusion and imprecision. One way to tell if your definitions are too broad or too narrow is to try to think of *counterexamples*. If your definition is too narrow, providing one example of an object that obviously fits the definition but is excluded by it demonstrates its narrowness. Conversely, a counterexample of a referent that is included in the definition but should not be demonstrates its excessive scope.

A GOOD DEFINITION MUST STATE THE ESSENTIAL PROPERTIES

As stated earlier, one of the primary functions of a definition is to summarize information by capturing its key elements or properties. These fundamental properties constitute the criteria for deciding which objects belong to the concept. They are also the properties that *best explain* the concept as well as provide links to other properties of the concept. They are the necessary properties that make the object what it is. For example, a local area network (LAN) system for your computer has the property of being managed by centralized operators. However, that is not its most important or necessary property, nor is it the property that distinguishes it from other systems with a centralized operator. The ability to communicate from various locations on a single networked system is of the utmost importance. Without including that key (i.e., essential) feature, we would not be able to explain accurately what a LAN is.

A DEFINITION SHOULD NOT BE CIRCULAR

*I tell you, once and for all,
that by sensible things I mean only those which are
perceived by sense.*

–Bishop George Berkeley[8]

As we saw earlier, defining the word "leader" as "one who leads" is not very helpful. The problem with this definition is that it uses the word "leads," a form of the word we are trying to define, in the definition itself. This *assumes* we already know what the concept means. Instead of *explaining* what it means to be a leader, providing examples and essential properties, the definition turns on itself and becomes circular. The quotation at the beginning of this section is a good example of a circular definition.

However, not all circular definitions are this obviously flawed. Synonymous definitions, for example, provide a word with a similar meaning that does provide some additional understanding of the concept being defined, provided you already understand the meaning of the synonym. This type of definition, however, can be circular as well. For example, if we define a "merit wage increase" as a "raise based on accomplishments," we might know a little more than we did before defining the concept. But it would be better (i.e., more effective) to define the concepts of merit and wage in the ways described earlier, in addition to providing the synonymous definition. More synonyms such as compensation, reward, benefit, and perk, for a job well done, can be added later in a list of words that will be familiar to as many people as possible.

WHENEVER POSSIBLE, STATE DEFINITIONS IN THE AFFIRMATIVE

Suppose we define "robotic assembly line" as "a process for piecing products together without human involvement." This reasonably good definition does provide information that helps explain the concept. But the definition is about what is *not* involved in piecing together (assembling) products. There are many other aspects of an assembly line that do not involve human intervention. None of them helps much in explaining what a robotic assembly line is. This rule complements the rule requiring us to state the essential properties of concepts. If we define a term by what it is not, that is, the properties it doesn't have, we will never identify the essential properties it does have.

Here is another example: A management confidential worker is defined as someone who is not paid on an hourly basis. A better definition would explain the main responsibilities that define a management confidential employee.

Summary

IN THIS CHAPTER WE:

- Discussed the importance of definitions in critical thinking

- Defined the relationship between words and concepts

- Explored the three major functions of definitions

- Demonstrated four ways to define words and concepts

- Examined rules for good definitions

Exercises

I. Evaluate the following definitions according to the Rules for Good Definitions.

1. What is meant by 'steadfastness'? Certainly not a moralizing 'rigidity,' a stubbornness of the 'in the no other way' kind; certainly no holding on to outdated positions, no love of self which indulges in favorite habits. What is it then?

2. "A liberal arts education is fundamentally non-technical and non-vocational."[9]

3. A shift worker is basically any hourly employee who changes the times of the shifts he or she works.

4. We should let our management trainees develop new program initiatives. After all, isn't a management trainee anyone who wants to enter a management program?

5. We should let our management trainees develop new program initiatives. After all, a management trainee includes only those people who received extensive preparation for the job.

6. A customer service person is someone who delivers services to clients and customers.

TOPIC COVERED IN THIS CHAPTER

• Definition and role of "emotive force"

• Persuasive language and its uses

• Specific examples of five persuasive techniques

Chapter 4

USES AND MISUSES OF PERSUASIVE LANGUAGE

KEY TERMS

emotive force

euphemisms

hyperbole

innuendo

loaded question

persuasive comparison

slanters

stereotyping

Emotive Language

I am firm; you are obstinate; he is a pig-headed fool.

–Bertrand Russell

As we have seen, the English language can be quite complex and confusing. Its many functions and modes of expression, which include commands, exclamations, emotive expressions, and questions, are rich in communicative powers that move, inform, direct, and query, as well as mislead and misinform. However, in this text we are concerned primarily with only two fundamental purposes of communication: to convey information and to persuade or influence others. Some might argue that even the informative function is really intended to persuade others to accept the "objective" information you are presenting. This chapter is concerned with the persuasive function of language.

The most common way to persuade others is through argumentation. Arguments persuade by producing evidence and support for the truth of a statement, which is the argument's conclusion. However, not all methods of persuasion are this formal in structure. Other methods make minimal use of evidence and support and rely more heavily on the **emotive force** of words and phrases. This type of communication emphasizes the *feelings* your words elicit or express. The emotive aspect of language should not be underestimated, even in the most apparently "objective" contexts. The impact your words have on an audience often depends on their emotive force.

In this chapter you will develop skills in recognizing these special words and phrases, not for the purposes of eliminating them, but to be proficient in detecting them and their specific uses. Only then will you be able to measure their impact and assess the *underlying messages* they convey. When reading reports and proposals at work, for example, being able to distinguish the emotional appeals from factual information is essential for evaluating *all* aspects of the message.

Consider the italicized words in the following questions. Did the department head *delegate* responsibility or *pass the buck*? Is the new employee drug testing policy an *effective screening measure* or an *intrusive test*? Was the workforce *reduced* or was it *slashed*? Each word or phrase you choose to communicate your messages will have a different emotive impact, depending on its emotive force. Recognizing that factor is an important first step toward better understanding and effective communication.

This skill will also help you in writing your own factual reports, whose primary purpose is to summarize data or convey factual information. In these situations, you would want to be sure that your language is as *emotively neutral* as possible in order to ensure its objectivity.

Nonetheless, there are times when you will *want* to use persuasive language to get your point across, which in many cases is perfectly appropriate, depending on the context. The main point is that you should be aware that these *rhetorical devices* are powerful tools that can also *disguise hidden agendas, mislead, misinform, cloud communication*, and *artificially support implausible or irrelevant data*. Distinguishing factual information and well-supported reasons from linguistic techniques of persuasion will help you evaluate arguments and identify points of view. In other words, it will strengthen your ability as a critical thinker.

Let's turn now to some specific linguistic expressions that rely on emotive force for their persuasive power.

Persuasive Devices

EUPHEMISTIC LANGUAGE

Euphemisms are used when you substitute a more pleasant or neutral word for one that either carries a negative connotation or provides a bluntly direct statement or both. For example, the statement "She *rescinded funding* for the project" is not as blunt as "She *killed* the project." The statement "This *less expensive* machinery includes *pre-owned parts*" sounds more positive than "This machinery includes *used parts*," and even more positive than saying "This machinery includes *cheap used parts*."

Most often, euphemistic language is chosen with good intentions. Used in this way, the language is intended to avoid potentially embarrassing situations or to ease someone through a difficult situation. "The boss's husband croaked yesterday" will offend many and cause embarrassment when overheard by the boss and those dear to her and her husband. "The boss's husband passed away yesterday" will be less offensive and more sensitive to a difficult situation. The department title, *Health and Wellness Center* is less frightening than the *Company Infirmary*, and the *Corporate Dining Facility* is more appealing than the *Cafeteria*. And finally, hearing that your daughter's grades *need significant improvement* will lessen the shock when you find out she *flunked* the course. The euphemistic language, which a critical thinker should be able to detect, lessens the impact of the underlying message.

Sometimes, blunt or negative language (Figure 4-1) is used deliberately to evoke an emotional response to show that the neutral language masks the sig-

FIGURE 4.1

nificance or urgency of the particular situation. Thus, there are cases in which emotively charged language is preferable to neutral language. Pointing out that "She is padding her expense sheet" may actually be preferable language for "She is embellishing the cost estimate of the trip." A *revenue enhancer* may be easier to accept from politicians than a *new tax*, but we should not be deluded into thinking that the added revenue will not cause some pain for taxpayers.

Thus, in certain circumstances, emotively colored language is preferable to neutral language, whereas in other circumstances, neutral language is preferable to emotively charged language. Critical thinking is required in recognizing cases in which the most appropriate linguistic phrasing should be used.

Euphemisms Taken to the Extreme?

The following "euphemisms" are taken from the *Official Politically Correct Dictionary and Handbook*.[1]

To fail = Achieve deficiency

Overweight = Possess an alternative body image

Bald = Hair disadvantaged

Fired = Selected out or negative employee retention

Mature = Experientially enhanced

Lazy = Motivationally deficient

EXERCISES

1. Identify the euphemistic expressions in the following paragraph.

    The upcoming merger of our two companies will make us more attractive to stock traders. We will assume all their operations nationally and streamline the personnel side of the budget. Overseas, we will expand manufacturing in low production cost countries and re-evaluate our overhead in U.S. plants. We will have an eye to less demanding overhead encumbrances and look to "downbuild" the outdated ones.

    _____

    _____

    _____

    _____

    _____

2. Rewrite the above sentences in non-euphemistic language.

    _____

    _____

    _____

    _____

    _____

3. Select an article from a newspaper, magazine, or trade journal that contains emotively charged language. Rewrite those phrases in neutral language.

    _____

    _____

    _____

    _____

    _____

_____

_____

_____

_____

_____

4. Describe a recent disagreement you have had with any member of your family or a coworker. Now translate that description so that an impartial audience will be unable to tell which side of the disagreement you were on.

_____

_____

_____

_____

_____

_____

_____

_____

_____

_____

_____

STEREOTYPING

At one time or another probably all of us have been the object of **stereotyping**. Whether it is being labeled according to our profession, gender, ethnic group, lifestyle, or work habits, most of us as individuals have been lumped together under one name, description, or group label. Some of these labels are more insulting than others, but all categorize people under a generalization without sufficient evidence for the descriptor or without proper attention to individual differences. Being labeled by colleagues as a nerd, techy, bottom-liner, or number-cruncher might not be offensive, depending on contexts and circumstances. But being labeled by others who *assume* certain characteristics based solely on certain job skills ignores other important qualities a person might have, not to mention the negative associations these labels imply.

More serious are those stereotypes that are based on race or ethnic origins, religion, gender, sexual preferences, class status, and so on. They will not only offend but also lead to incorrect errors in judgment and fail to appreciate the real merits, strengths, and weaknesses of the individuals. To assume that a female manager will be more emotional than a male, a male accountant better at numerical calculation than a female, a feminist supervisor more likely a man-hater, a gay male employee effeminate, a southerner a bigot, or a white Anglo-Saxon male unemotional, is to stereotype others. Statements that categorize people by stereotypes foster unthinking attitudes that lump people together with unsupported and misleading or misinformed judgments—additional obstacles to clear and critical thinking—not to mention possible legal action (Figure 4–2).

FIGURE 4.2

EXERCISES

1. Identify the stereotypes in the following sentences. (Note: Some sentences may not contain a stereotype.)

    a) The comptroller is a typical number-cruncher. He doesn't understand that we are in a period of transition. Our cash-flow problems always straighten out by the end of the year.

    _____

    _____

    b) He must think he's quite a real macho lady's man. Look, he has a vowel at the end of his last name.

    _____

    _____

    c) He must think he can push us around. He's a former football star and thinks we are all going to jump when he speaks.

    _____

    _____

    d) Why do they always say it's OK when a working mother is late for work but get upset when a working father is late?

    _____

    _____

    e) I guess the new manager must be ok to deal with. As a woman with her own children, she will be more compassionate and caring.

    _____

    _____

2. Where possible, rewrite the sentences above by eliminating the stereotypical language.

    a) _____

    _____

b) _____

_____

c) _____

_____

d) _____

_____

e) _____

_____

3. Explain how the author of this letter uses emotively charged language and stereotyping in her characterization of a fellow driver. Discuss whether the author is guilty of her own stereotyping.

After visiting a friend in an upscale neighborhood, I came out of her apartment building and found one of those conspicuously huge SUVs parked behind me in a way that left only a narrow space to pull out of my parking place. I finally managed to maneuver out of the space with my old beat-up, dented compact. I exited carefully so I wouldn't scratch his brand new tank of a car. As I was exiting, I noticed a well-dressed man sprinting down the road toward me shouting something. Wary of his intentions, I sped away from the parking spot so he could not approach me. When I looked in the rearview mirror I saw the man inspecting the SUV for dents and scratches.

I was outraged that he would assume that I had touched his precious car! He was obviously so taken with his new trophy car and so prejudiced against people with cheap cars, that he assumed someone like me would not have been careful to avoid hitting his car. He probably also assumed that someone with a standard shift, especially a woman, couldn't maneuver out of such a tight spot without bumping into something.

Although I am not rich like him, I have things he will never have: selfrespect, integrity, social consciousness, and respect for others. His obnoxious behavior and his values are demeaning to people like me, a person with social awareness and a conscience.

_____

_____

_____

_____

_____

_____

_____

_____

_____

4. Select a letter to the editor in your local newspaper in which stereotyping was used. Translate the stereotyping phrases into neutral language.

_____

_____

_____

_____

_____

_____

5. Explain how grouping individuals under a general name is helpful but avoids the negative aspects of stereotyping. Give an example.

_____

_____

_____

_____

_____

_____

WRITING FROM EXPERIENCE

Describe an event where you have been the object of stereotyping. Explain how the situation could have been avoided.

_____

_____

_____

_____

_____

_____

_____

_____

_____

_____

_____

_____

_____

_____

_____

_____

_____

_____

_____

_____

_____

_____

_____

PERSUASIVE COMPARISONS AND PERSUASIVE DEFINITIONS

Comparisons

Although we have already discussed analogies and definitions in earlier chapters, we will now turn to the persuasive function of those linguistic tools. A **persuasive comparison** expresses attitudes or influences others by relying on emotively charged language as the basis for the comparison. For example, you could compare a supervisor's management style to an authoritative one, saying she is like a captain leading her troops. Or, you could compare her management style to an authoritarian one, asserting that she is like a dictator controlling her underlings. Both comparisons have emotive force, but the latter is much stronger and probably should be spoken out of earshot of the supervisor.

In another example of a persuasive comparison, your daughter might tell you that the new security policy in the school cafeteria makes school seem like a prison, the principal like a prison guard. She is using a persuasive comparison. When the purchasing agent of the company compares the vendors to sharks or barracudas, he or she is making a persuasive comparison.

Definitions

Similarly, persuasive language creeps into definitions when certain words that express or elicit strong emotional responses are included in providing the meaning of a word or concept. These words or phrases, called **slanters**,[2] influence your audiences by providing *biased* or *"loaded"* meanings of words. For example, you could define *affirmative action* as "a policy designed to correct past discriminatory hiring and personnel practices. It encourages organizations to seek qualified employees from specific groups who have been underrepresented in certain positions." A slanted definition of affirmative action could be "a bureaucratic policy that gives jobs to unqualified minorities and women at the expense of white men. It sets arbitrary hiring and promotion quotas for those least qualified for the job."

Another way to slant definitions is to provide meanings of words by selecting *only* examples that are biased toward a particular point of view. These prejudicial examples will influence your audience but at the expense of objectivity and impartiality. Moreover, these selective examples are not only unrepresentative but they also give an incomplete picture of the entire message. They often express a predetermined evaluation of the facts and advocate for a specific position. Recognizing their biases is just one more strategy in critical thinking.

Another point to remember is that the examples do not necessarily express falsehoods or partial truths. They simply do not include the *full range* of activities or events we want to describe. What's included and omitted makes a big difference in whether we convey a complete representative picture or an incomplete slanted view.

As we mentioned earlier, spicing up your communication with words that elicit or express emotions can add color to your communication. However, when it clouds communication, angers or elates the listener, or misdirects the intended message by focusing on the feelings created instead of the ideas you want to convey, then you risk being misunderstood or not heard at all.

EXERCISES

I. Evaluate the following definitions according to their emotive force.

1. a) Abortion is the clinical procedure for terminating a viable fetus.

_____

_____

   b) Abortion is the murder of an innocent baby.

_____

_____

2. a) How would I define the telecommunications tax? It is the government's way of invading the last bastion of doing business without its intrusion.

_____

_____

   b) The telecommunications tax is a way to equalize and standardize sales taxes across state borders for trading over the Internet.

_____

_____

3. a) The concept of strategic sourcing avoids the drawbacks of outsourcing and allows management to plan more effectively for change.[3]

_____

_____

   b) The concept of strategic sourcing is nothing more than a new gimmick to hire more consultants. It is essentially the same concept as outsourcing, with a few minor restrictions.

_____

_____

4. a) Welfare means the programs that provide a basic income to those who qualify as "needy."

_____

_____

   b) Welfare means giving hard-earned tax dollars to those who do little to earn them.

_____

_____

II. Analyze the following letter to the editor. Discuss how the author uses persuasive comparisons to make her point more forceful.

The big superstores are becoming monopolies that force out "mom and pop" stores and other small operators. We all like cheaper prices but this is outrageous. It can't be good for America. A "world economy" is a lot of hogwash. Just look at what NAFTA and the WTO are doing. Our local industries, farmers, and small merchandisers are not prospering. They are losing jobs. Multinational conglomerates and mega-stores are killing our economy.

Has congress been bought by big interests, big octopus-like companies with more inter-weaving connections to other monopolies, and corrupt foreign governments?

_____

_____

_____

_____

_____

HYPERBOLE

We have been discussing emotively charged language, loaded language, and biased language as a way to slant the communication to influence others, often at the expense of clarity and objectivity. One type of persuasive device that makes use of exaggeration to distort communication is called **hyperbole**. A good deal of the language used in the persuasive comparisons and definitions above could also be categorized as hyperbole, depending on the emotive force and extent of the exaggeration. For example, a definition of affirmative action policy as "the fuzzy headed thinking of bleeding heart liberals" is exaggerated (and slanted) to an extreme. But an even more blatantly distorted and absurd use of language would be involved in labeling women supporters of affirmative action as "femi-nazis." When exaggerated language expresses sentiments that exceed reasonable boundaries of emphasis, taste, or enthusiasm (not to mention offensiveness), the language contains hyperbole.

Consider this example: The CEO of your company provides innovative leadership, and the value of its stock hits an all-time high. It would probably be a well intended exaggeration to say that she is the best president the company has ever had and *ever* will have. Likewise, if the CEO takes drastic steps to reduce the workforce by over 20 percent, saying that she is a ruthless fascist, the worst we have ever had, would be hyperbole.

When exaggeration becomes distortion (depending on degrees), the real message can be lost and the originally intended meaning manipulated beyond recognition. This, of course, can lead to misinformation and confusion, further obstacles to clear thinking.

INNUENDO

When you use language to insinuate something without actually saying it directly, you are using **innuendo**. This type of language relies on implication, suggestion, and implicit messages. For example, someone says, "Did Helen remember to drop off her children at the sitter's before work?" You reply, "Yes, she did, *this time*." Your response *suggests*, without saying so, that Helen *has forgotten* to leave her children in the past. The insinuation is clear. When someone questions whether the new project director possesses the most qualified background for this particular project and you reply, "Yes, *for the most part*. She does have *some* good qualities," you are using innuendo. Here, "for the most part" insinuates that there are weaknesses in her background,

EXERCISES

1. Explain how the following letter contains hyperbole.

   The recent decision by the Kansas school board to eliminate evolution from the school's curriculum is a major step backward to the Dark Ages. To deny evolution is to deny all major sciences, from geology to biology to astronomy. Even other scientific studies such as plate tectonics, ice core samples, to even the study of tree rings mean absolutely nothing. (*The Recorder*, Amsterdam, NY)

   _____

   _____

   _____

   _____

   _____

   _____

   _____

   _____

   _____

   _____

   _____

   _____

   _____

   _____

   _____

   _____

   _____

and "*some* good qualities" implies that she has at least one, but not many good ones, or has insufficient skills for the task. When the language asserts *faint praise*, which "some good qualities" does in this case, the underlying message will negate the positive associations that that phrase might contain. Innuendo is a powerful tool that can be damaging without providing evidence or support for the negative assumptions entailed in the expressions. Public figures, especially politicians and performers, can attest to the damage achieved through innuendo in the press.

LOADED QUESTIONS

A **loaded question** is another type of linguistic persuader, a version of innuendo, that also makes use of implicit assumptions. The question, "When did you stop cheating on your spouse?" makes it clear without specifically saying so, that the person had cheated in the past. Another obvious example of a loaded question is "Did you always resent that long commute to work?" Loaded questions assert assumptions already contained in the question itself, no matter what the actual answer to the question is. In fact, most answers, including a simple "yes" or "no," probably will be irrelevant to the *underlying message* contained in the question. Sometimes called *rhetorical questions* (loaded questions that do not require an answer at all), these inquiries can be as damaging as innuendo. Like innuendo, they rely on *unwarranted* or *unfounded* assumptions. The assumptions, although not explicitly stated, can influence others without adequate support or justification based on fact or sufficient evidence. They can not only cloud and misdirect a discussion but also import misinformed accusations. The underlying statements must be made explicit in order to be assessed for their credibility and relevance. As critical thinkers, your first step is to recognize them for what they are, then transform them into explicit language. Assessing their credibility is a challenge that will be examined in a subsequent chapter.

HEDGING YOUR BETS

Phrases that qualify statements so that they are protected from potential criticism and leave open a way to evade an attack are called "hedgers." For example, when you say, "Most people questioned about their benefits package preferred to remain with their existing health care provider for now," you are "*hedging your bets*." The qualifier, "most people questioned," does not tell us what percentage of the total number questioned responded in favor of keeping their provider, nor does it tell us what percentage of the total number of employees were actually questioned. Perhaps the percentage is 50.01 percent of a large number of respondents or a larger percentage of only a few people surveyed. If 3 of 5 who were questioned agreed but they represent only 5 out of 500 employees, we would question the results. The phrase "for now" implies that they might change their minds later or that they gave an answer based on incomplete information. In any case, the statement is weakened as the result of the hedging phrases. (The pitfalls in statistical reasoning will be examined in greater detail later.)

Having said this, we should also note that qualifiers make a statement more difficult to disprove. For example, it is difficult to challenge a claim that says, "Some of the people tested sometimes prefer brand X." If *only one person* who, *on occasion*, preferred brand X, the statement would be confirmed as true. Conversely, and obviously, the more qualified the statement is, the easier it is to defend. Statements with specific information are clearer but require more work to prepare and to defend. Arriving at an exact percentage is more difficult than finding some people (at least one person) of an unspecified number.

The more qualified a statement is, the less force it has, and the less information it conveys. The qualified statement about brand X tells us very little because the hedgers water down the impact of the statement.

Other types of hedgers include the following expressions: "it seems that," "it appears that," "it seems to me," "I feel that," among others. (Do you only *feel that* the outsourcing strategy is shortsighted or *do you have evidence* that it is shortsighted?) Although these phrases are well suited for certain contexts and may be unavoidable, use them sparingly and only when necessary; they water down the forcefulness of your message and can lead to confusion.

EXERCISES

I. Identify the implicit assumptions in the following questions. Then rewrite them eliminating the innuendo.

1. Have you completed all your homework?

    _____

    _____

2. Don't you really care about your grades?

    _____

    _____

3. Are you really going to work overtime? Do you need the money that badly?

    _____

    _____

4. Ms. Diaz is a thoughtful supervisor. Doesn't she make you feel that your work is valued?

    _____

    _____

5. You heard about Ms. Faust? She's the one who took her grievance to the H.R. office. Don't you think she should have gone to her supervisor first?

    _____

    _____

    _____

II. Evaluate the following for all types of loaded language.

1. Now environmentalists want to hold up construction for a butterfly! That's ridiculous. Do you believe that our tree-hugging friends want to stop a project that will bring jobs to our area and

supply needed housing? That's what they are doing in the Pine Bush area of Albany. They say that the Karner Butterfly's habitat will be destroyed if construction is allowed. Do we really need more butterflies? We are talking about an insect that was once a caterpillar here! Don't we need more economic development and tax revenues instead of more insects? Our schools and streets need improvement. Let's use the tax money to improve minds and property. They're more important than butterflies.

_____

_____

_____

_____

2. There is a bias to outsource. Business unit managers usually seeks to reduce costs to become more competitive. Increasing revenues is also usually considered, but not as aggressively [as outsourcing] because this inevitably involves increased up-front expenditures (advertising, promotion, product development, etc.), given the financial problems of the business. "Why throw good money after bad?" was a comment often echoed by corporate-level executives and staff in our research.[4]

_____

_____

_____

_____

3. The critical errors in outsourcing are, in large measure, driven by a failure to view outsourcing strategically. Many managers view sourcing as a defensive, operational measure. The approach tends to be incremental and financial. Their mindset is often scorekeeping-oriented-reduce costs, improve returns, or increase brand share.[5]

_____

_____

_____

_____

Summary

IN THIS CHAPTER WE:

- Defined emotive force and explored its role in communication

- Discussed how persuasive language is used

- Demonstrated five persuasive techniques

Exercises

1. *Identify the emotive or loaded language in the following:*

   a) I suppose you've heard of Ms. Najar's run-in with the supervisor.

   b) We all thought that Ms. Berger graduated an Ivy League university. Didn't you?

   c) Everyone believes that Darwin was a godless, amoral, valueless cynic.

   d) Are you really going to leave the company without notice?

   e) These workstations are about as attractive as a cell at San Quentin.

2. *Locate your organization's public relations brochure or advertising pamphlet or some other document that is intended to promote the organization (such as an agency description or announcement). Identify any emotionally charged words or phrases. Specifically, pick out language that exaggerates, slants, stereotypes, or uses persuasive definitions or comparisons.*

TOPIC COVERED IN THIS CHAPTER

- Definition of an argument

- Arguments and explanations compared

- Recognizing arguments: Premise indicators and conclusion indicators

- Arguments without premises and conclusions

- The importance of recognizing arguments

Chapter

ARGUMENTS

KEY TERMS

argument

conclusions

explanation

premises

We must follow the argument wherever it leads.

–SOCRATES

"Watson, follow the money wherever it leads."

–ARTHUR CONAN DOYLE (SHERLOCK HOLMES)

Definition of an Argument

The Greek philosopher Socrates (470-399 B.C.E.) spent much of his life engaging people in discussions about topics in which they claimed expertise. In the course of these "discussions" (called Socratic Dialogues), Socrates would invariably reveal through unrelenting questioning that the expert's opinions were unfounded. Although this critical attitude did not endear him to the ruling class, which eventually led to his imprisonment and death, his method of arriving at the truth has survived throughout the ages. One of the most important lessons Socrates taught us is that we should never accept any statement without having good reasons to support it. The practice of establishing good reasons and the ability to distinguish them from bad reasons are essential to critical thinking. Whether you are trying to comprehend, analyze, or evaluate the communication of others, or trying to develop your own effective communication in constructing a convincing thesis to get your point across, the ability to distinguish good reasoning from bad reasoning is a necessary skill for critical thinking at work and in everyday experience. Reasoning that is presented to convince others of the truth of some statement is called an argument, the topic of this chapter.

As stated in Chapter 1, opinions become more secure when people give *good reasons* for accepting them as true. The process of trying to prove that your opinions are true requires that you *lend support* to them. This reasoning process is called an *inference* and identifies the statements that are being offered as evidence for some other statement, and then demonstrates that connection. The result of this reasoning process (called an inference) is an **argument**. An argument is a collection of written or oral statements where at least one of the statements is presented as grounds for (or reasons for) accepting that one of the other statements is true. You can call the statements you are trying to prove the **conclusions** and the statements you are presenting to prove the conclusions the **premises**.

Here is an example of an argument.

> This job description is inadequate because it is too vague. It doesn't even list the specific tasks that should be performed, and it doesn't say how my performance will be evaluated.

"This job description is inadequate" is the conclusion and is stated first in the argument. The reasons advanced to support this conclusion are: "It is too vague," "It doesn't list specific tasks," and "It doesn't state how performance will be evaluated." They are the premises. If you accept the premises as true, you have good grounds for accepting the conclusion as true.

This technical definition should be distinguished from more common definitions of an argument, which are characterized as quarrels or emotional debates or disagreements. Rather, the definition here is intended in the sense of developing an *informed, reasoned point of view*. To be informed by reasons is to be able to support a point of view. Whether you are taking a position in defense of your own ideas or critiquing the ideas of an opposing position, you will need to present an argument. In other words, if you want to convince others to accept, adopt, or at least consider your point of view, you need to construct an argument to *persuade* them of its truth. Just turn to any newspaper or journal editorial, a legal brief, or T.V. "opinion piece," to find good examples of arguments as attempts to persuade an audience. However, unlike Chapter 4, this chapter is concerned with the *formal* aspects of persuasion—their logical coherence, reasonableness, and support rather than their emotional elements.

It should also be noted that the definitions of "conclusion" and "premise" are stated in terms of each other. Although this makes the definition circular, it is intentional. The circularity is due to treating these concepts as purely *relational*; their meaning is derived only in relation to each other. Just as the concept of a parent is understood only in relation to offspring, a conclusion is understood only in relation to a premise, and vice versa. It follows from this definition that *any* statement can be a premise and *any* statement can be a conclusion, depending on its status as either providing proof or being proved. A premise in one argument can be a conclusion in a completely different argument, and a conclusion in one argument can be a premise in another. In the previous example, "It is too vague" is a conclusion for the subargument whose premises are "It doesn't list specific tasks" and "It doesn't state how performance will be evaluated." The latter two statements are reasons to accept the conclusion about vagueness, which in turn implies that the job description is inadequate.

Here is another example:

1. If we set aside at least an hour and a half for two days to set goals, we should be able to establish a strategic plan for our new focus teams. Once a plan is established, we can then develop another strategy for implementing the goals outlined.

2. If the new focus team concept is to be successful we should involve both management and staff at various levels in the initial discussions. Therefore, three hours on each of the next three days will be set aside for staff-management group "brainstorming."

3. If we decide to develop focus teams, we will need time to first sit down and establish a clear set of goals for these teams to accomplish. Therefore, we should designate the first hour and a half of the first two mornings to setting goals.

In paragraph 1 above, setting aside time for establishing a goal is a premise. Having a plan in place is an additional premise. The conclusion is that we can develop a strategy for implementing the plan. In 2 and 3, setting aside time is a conclusion.

Arguments and Explanations

EXPLANATIONS

When you give reasons for believing that a statement is true, you present an argument. However, when you give reasons or other information to try to explain why something is what it is, or explain how something came to be what it is, you are giving an **explanation**. A good deal of the process of defining what a concept means is by way of an explanation. For example, as we saw in Chapter 3, determining which sense of the ambiguous word "work" is intended required that you define or explicate (make clear by removing ambiguity and vagueness) the word in precise language. The definition functioned as an explanation of the concept.

But this is only one among many functions of explanations. An explanation can also make clear how something works by *elaborating* what it does. Explanations can describe what the object is good for, why it works the way it does, how it compares to something else, or why it was assembled the way it was. Explanations can provide reasons why it costs as much as it does, why we need it now, and why it will not work, and so on. As you can see, explanations are given in response to the questions *why* and *how?* Unlike arguments, their primary function is not to *persuade* or *convince* you that some statement is true, or *express a point of view* about the subject, nor is their function to show how some statements *follow logically* from some other statements. Rather, explanations tell you *what is* the case, whereas arguments *convince* you as to what *should be* the case. Arguments draw an inference to a conclusion based on the reasons offered in support of it. Explanations offer reasons that make clear why and how things were, are, or will be.

Unfortunately, there are many times when it is difficult to tell whether an argument or an explanation is being presented. For example, your coworker says,

> If you live at least 30 miles from work, you must use a lot of gas each week. With the price of gas so high and that 30-mile commute you have, it must cost you a small fortune.

The person is advancing an argument whose general structure goes like this:

> Since you travel 30 miles each day, and it takes a considerable amount of gas to travel 30 miles, and it is expensive; you should, therefore, spend a good deal of money each week.

If your coworker had said, "The reason you spend so much for gas is that gas prices have soared and you travel close to 30 miles each way," he or she is giving an explanation. The explanation tells you *why* the cost of commuting is so expensive. There is no inference to persuade you to accept the statements or a conclusion drawn from one statement to the other. The statements merely offer reasons why the events happen the way they do.

To determine if the passage is an argument, ask, "Am I being *persuaded* to accept the truth of something? Am I asked to accept a certain point of view? Is there some kind of *bottom line* (a conclusion) to this message?" As we shall see in the next chapter, identifying the conclusion as the "bottom line" is a helpful strategy in determining an argument's structure. Identifying the conclusion first allows you to trace the various threads that make up the evidence that supports the conclusion of the argument.

CONCLUSION AND PREMISE INDICATORS

Although it is difficult, if not impossible, in many cases to determine whether a passage is an explanation or an argument, there are some helpful hints. Following are words and phrases that indicate whether a conclusion or a premise is being inferred which are signs that an argument is being advanced.

Conclusion Indicators:

therefore, thus, hence, so,

we conclude that, for these reasons, consequently, it follows that, as a result of, we may infer that,

which demonstrates that, which shows that, which entails that, which implies that, which allows us to conclude that, which allows us to infer that, which allows us to imply that, which shows that

Premise Indicators:

for, since, because, due to, as demonstrated by, it follows from, inasmuch as, the reason is that, for the reason that, we may assume that, given that

it may be inferred from, may be derived from, may be deduced from, in view of the following, as indicated by

Unfortunately, there will be occasions when neither a premise indicator nor a conclusion indicator is present in an argument. And there will also be times when an *entire statement*, either a premise or a conclusion, will be missing

EXERCISES

I. Identify the premises and conclusions in the following arguments.

1. Since the government statistics show significant job growth in the technology area, I should plan to enroll in a training program soon in some technical field.

   _____

   _____

2. The new efficiency expert the company hired seems to be more sensitive to personal circumstances than the last one. The reason he's well liked is that he looks at your past performance history, considers your length of service, and considers a variety of options where you might fit elsewhere in the company if things aren't working out.

   _____

   _____

3. If I work 50–60 hours per week then I'm really tired when I get home evenings. And if I take two college courses per semester, then I have extra work to do when I get home. Hence, the reason I am always beat is that I'm either studying or working.

   _____

   _____

4. The projected job growth in technology, especially in medical related fields, is encouraging. The more health care turns to technology to help patients without adding costs, the more this area will grow. Thus, it is important to develop skills that will position you for a future in this industry.

   _____

   _____

5. The new efficiency expert is not liked very much. He's a bottom-liner. The only things important to him are quotas and production. He never takes into account personal circumstances or past performance.

   _____

   _____

(continued)

6. I'm just in a temporary slump right now, but I've done a good job for this company. I've been distracted by my wife's illness, that's the real reason.

    _____

    _____

7. If Anderson gets the promotion, then Diaz will have been passed over twice. If Diaz is passed over a second time, then there will be a grievance filed. Thus, if Anderson gets that promotion, you will see a grievance filed.

    _____

    _____

8. If you crack an off-color joke now and then it might be tolerated, depending on the circumstances. If you continue to tell off-color or sexually explicit comments and jokes, it can be rude, insensitive, and may offend others. But if you are warned and continue to tell these stories, and/or make unsolicited sexual advances, it's against the law.

    _____

    _____

9. If the quality control office sets minimum standards for exact measurement tolerances in measurement, then we must flag those items. It's my recollection that these standards do exist in the operating manual. It follows that we should flag those items anyway.

    _____

    _____

10. If the quality control office sets minimum standards for exact measurement tolerances, then we should flag those items. But I can't find those standards anywhere. So, we don't need to flag those items.

    _____

    _____

in an argument (Figure 5-1). In cases where there is doubt or confusion about premises and conclusions, ask, "Which statement is the speaker trying to *convince* me (an audience) should be true? Does the information attempt to *settle a question* about the truth of some statement(s)?" "Which statements am I being *persuaded* to accept as true? What point of view am I being asked to adopt or accept? What is the *bottom line* (a conclusion) to this message?"

On the other hand, if the speaker is trying to elaborate, define, or explicate what makes these statements true, you are presented with an explanation. Despite these helpful hints, however, the speaker himself might be confused as to whether he intends to advance an argument or an explanation. To make matters more complicated, an explanation may be contained within an argument and an argument may be contained as *part* of an explanation. In such cases, only the context will clarify whether an argument or an explanation is being offered. But as critical thinkers, you should be familiar by now with analyzing context. Rather than accepting the truth of the statements at face value, examining the context allows you to identify various parts of the communication, make connections among the parts, and clarify meanings, which will once again become important strategies as you analyze complex arguments.

FIGURE 5.1

EXERCISES

I. State whether the speaker is presenting an argument or an explanation in the following. If you believe that the exercise contains both, explain why you believe so. Then develop an argument to convince the reader of the truth of your belief that it is both.

1.   Tunwall is absent from work today because he has the flu.

2.   Tunwall must have the flu. He didn't show up for work.

3.   Tunwall must have the flu. He was coughing and wheezing yesterday. He also had a temperature of 101°.

4.   There must be a reason why Tunwall didn't show up for work today. I think the reason he's out is that he caught the flu from his children.

5. Whenever Tunwall misses work, you can bet that he is very ill with some kind of ailment. He almost never misses work.

_____

_____

6. It would be unfair to allow only married employees to come to work late on occasions. Just because they have childcare problems, it doesn't mean they get special treatment. I would like to be allowed to come in late now and then too.

_____

_____

_____

7. The reason DeSantis and Clough arrive 10 minutes late on Tuesdays and Wednesdays is that they have to drop off their daughters at the day care center.

_____

_____

_____

8. The reason I'm so confused about where I'm going in this company is that I never really figured out what my greatest skills are and what makes me feel satisfied the most.

_____

_____

_____

9. I've heard that these job fairs are very helpful in identifying your skills and interests. They have self-tests right there at the show. They have counselors who will talk with you. I think we should go the next time it's at the city center.

_____

_____

_____

Importance of Recognizing Arguments

This seemingly purely academic discussion about two closely related concepts has important implications for critical thinking. In order to analyze thoroughly *all facets* of an argument, including its subarguments, implications, connections, flaws, and assumptions, you must first identify its structure. But to identify its structure you must first be sure you are dealing with an argument. In the process of making this determination, you must identify which statements are premises and which are conclusions. You are then able to discern the connections among premises and conclusions and thereby capture the logical "flow" of the argument, an important skill in critically evaluating all aspects of persuasive communication. For example, when you carefully read an article, position paper, marketing report, or product analysis that is trying to convince you to adopt a certain marketing strategy, you need to know where the argument is headed. What is its conclusion? What are the reasons that support the conclusion? Are the reasons themselves established or well supported? Do they in fact support *this* conclusion? Only when you are satisfied with the answers to these questions can you accept the conclusion of the argument.

A little practice in recognizing arguments and explanations will help.

Consider the following:

1. a) The reason the stock market climbed today is that unemployment figures were up. It may seem ironic, but according to economic analysts, including Alan Greenspan, this indicates a loosening up of workforce availability. The potential high cost of labor in the recent economic boom could lessen profitability.

   b) The reason the stock market goes up in times of low unemployment is that low unemployment always means higher costs for labor. Higher labor costs lead to lower profits, which in turn will increase stock values. That's why they go up when unemployment goes down.

2. a) The wage increases for line supervisors were the result of added responsibility and added workload. Supervisors earn incremental increases with added responsibility, according to the number of people they supervise and their level of supervision.

b) Whenever a supervisor assumes added responsibility his or her earnings should increase correspondingly. After all, more responsibility means more stress, more work, and more influence in the company's direction. It is only fitting that he or she receives a raise.

In the two examples above, the first example (a) explains why some event or decision was made. The second example (b) tries to convince you that the decision was a good decision. The reasons are offered in supporting some position (the conclusion), which you are urged to accept. In both cases, if the author had added to the last sentence a phrase such as "thus, it is obvious that...", it would be clearer that you are dealing with an argument.

Summary

IN THIS CHAPTER WE:

- Defined arguments and how they compare with explanations

- Explored the terms "premises" and "conclusions"

- Discussed premise indicators and conclusion indicators

- Explained the importance of identifying the basic structure of arguments

- Demonstrated how to recognize arguments and explanations

Exercises

1. List three characteristics of arguments.

2. List three characteristics of explanations.

3. Explain why the distinction between an argument and an explanation is important.

4. Determine which of the following are arguments and which are explanations. Where there is doubt, explain your answer and then construct an argument to convince the reader of your position.

   a) Kahled has been working overtime a lot lately. He should be receiving a nice bonus in his next check.

   b) It is true that the new contract is popular among younger employees. But that should not encourage older members to disapprove it.

   c) The receptionist is rude and snappish on the phone. When you call asking for even the most basic information, she is gruff. However, when you ask why, you are always told that she is having a bad day.

   d) The management training program is open to all employees who hold at least an associate degree or have three years of continuous employment. So, if I finish this semester, I can apply for the program.

5. Setting aside for now the persuasive devices, do you believe the author in the following paragraphs is explaining why a problem occurs or arguing for a position (point of view) with regard to a problem?

   a) A brainstorming session is designed to produce as many ideas as possible to solve the problem at hand. The key ground rule is to delay criticism and evaluation of ideas until all ideas are on the table. The group simply invents ideas without considering their merits and without considering whether they are realistic or unrealistic. One idea should provoke another like a chain reaction.

   b) Since the divorce rate in the United States is over 50 percent and since women on average outlive men by more than seven years, it follows that many women will be either divorced or widowed at some time in their lives. Women's groups are urging women to plan ahead for the possibility of facing difficult financial times. They should develop a strong financial plan with a professional consultant or visit their human resources office now.

   c) When Anita Battershell, herself the mother of a 16-year-old and 10-year-old, opened her travel agency, the 16-year-old was just a baby. But she set aside a room for him to play in when he visited. "Then I realized that my employees might like to use this room for their kids too," she said. She's created an in-office kids' club, with beanbag chairs, bunkbeds, and a television. This turned out to be a creative solution to problems of employees leaving early, missing parts of the workday, or staying at home for childcare reasons.[1]

Writing from Experience

1. Locate a recent report, company newsletter, or work-related journal. Identify arguments and explanations contained in the report or in one of the articles, letters to the editor, or opinion pieces.

2. Locate a popular magazine and turn to the editorial pages and Letters to the Editor section. Describe at least two arguments and two explanations in these sections.

3. Construct a counterargument in response to two of the arguments discussed in Exercise 2 above.

TOPIC COVERED IN THIS CHAPTER

- Simple and complex arguments

- Diagramming the structure of arguments

- Arguments with dependent premises

- Arguments with independent premises

- Strategies for identifying arguments with independent or dependent premises

- Importance of the distinction for critical thinking

- Strategies for analyzing and diagramming arguments

- Arguments with unstated premises and conclusions

- Constructing your own arguments

- Relevance to critical thinking

THE LOGICAL FLOW OF IDEAS: ARGUMENTS AND THEIR STRUCTURE

KEY TERMS

dependent premises

hidden premises

independent premises

simple arguments

skeletal outline

structure (for an argument)

Logic alone rarely persuades people,
but it draws together facts, examples, and appeals to values.
Logic, then, is rarely perfect.

–M. GARRETT BAUMAN[1]

Think of the structure of an argument as you would an electrical appliance with all the inner parts connected so that when working properly, the current flows through each circuit until the device functions as intended. The various parts are connected to each other so that if one malfunctions, the device works either inefficiently, improperly, or breaks down altogether. Now think of the various parts as the premises that make up the circuits and the outcome (the device's functioning) as the conclusion. Tracing the flow of the electrical current is like tracing the flow of an argument. If one of its premises fails, the argument is weakened or fails to support the conclusion as well as it could, or fails altogether. However, identifying the parts is only a beginning in trying to understand how the appliance works. In order to understand it fully, we need to know *how* all the parts are connected and work together. Similarly, identifying the premises and conclusions is only the first step in analyzing an argument. To understand an argument fully, we need to know its **structure**, the connections among the various premises, the logical flow of facts, ideas, and concepts from the premises to the end point—the conclusion. That is, we need to know *how* the premises provide *support* for the conclusion.

Simple Arguments and Diagrams

For **simple arguments**, one-step arguments with only one premise and one conclusion, the connections are easy to analyze. Consider this argument: "All new executives are provided with reserved parking spaces. So Ms. Warren, the new sales CEO, will have a reserved parking space." With only one premise, it is easy to trace the reasoning process to the conclusion in just one step.

In a simple argument, the premise *directly* implies (provides adequate grounds for) the conclusion. To demonstrate the argument's structure, we will number the premise "1" and the conclusion "2." We can then diagram the argument by using an arrow to show that the conclusion follows the premise directly. The arrow reflects the "flow" of the inference from premise to conclusion. Here is the structure of argument, Figure 6-1.

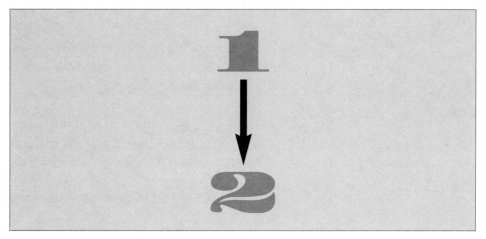

FIGURE 6.1

The diagram *represents* the inner structure of the argument. Here is another one-premise argument, Figure 6-2.

1) The new facilities quality control officer will be meeting with all staff to discuss specific changes to office workstations. 2) She reasons that a safe, comfortable, and pleasant work environment will decrease the number of employee sick days requested.

FIGURE 6.2

The conclusion is stated first in the argument, Figure 6-2 above, with the premise, sentence 2, providing support for it.

Arguments with More than One Conclusion

A single fact or generalization can serve as evidence for more than one conclusion. In other words, one premise can imply several conclusions. Consider this argument, for an example.

> 1) The economic principle of supply and demand implies that, in the short term, 2) the price for goods and services increases as supply decreases, and 3) the price for goods and services decreases as supply increases. Moreover, 4) long-term pricing strategy is determined by the fluctuations in both supply and demand.

The structure is represented in the following diagram, Figure 6-3.

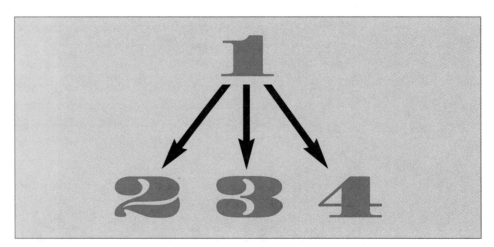

FIGURE 6.3

However, you rarely encounter such simple inferences, probably because they *are* so obviously logical and straightforward that they don't require detailed analysis. Their reasonableness is convincing at first glance.

Construct diagrams for the following arguments:

1. If the short circuit was caused by the extra printer hook-ups, then the lights on would have gone out.

2. All new employees must park in the green lot. Jillian is the newest employee.

3. If our department had contributed most to the United Way campaign, then we would have gotten the day off. The social services department gave more than us. Looks like we work this afternoon.

4. Since all new trainees must contribute to their health insurance until they receive permanent status, they will see a portion of their pay deducted for insurance premiums. That's why my check is less than yours.

Arguments with Dependent Premises

Consider this slightly more complex argument.

> 1) There are only four parking lots for the company's downtown branch office. 2) All executives park in lot A, and 3) all other employees park in lot B. So, 4) lots C and D must be reserved for visitors.

The structure of the argument may be captured by diagramming the relationship between premises and conclusion as we did in Figure 6-1. However, because it contains three premises, the conclusion does not follow from the premises in one simple step. The premises must first be *considered together, as one interrelated set*, to reach the conclusion. *Once connected*, the conclusion follows in one step. Thus, sentence 1 (There are four parking lots) does not *by itself* imply the conclusion, nor does sentence 2 (all executives park in lot A) or sentence 3 (all employees park in lot B). Each premise alone, or any two premises combined, do not imply 4, the conclusion. For these types of arguments we say that the premises *depend on each other* to reach the conclusion, thus called **dependent premises**. Figure 6-4 shows a diagram of the *dependent* argument about parking spaces.

For a complex argument, figuring out the relationships among the premises is a crucial first step in making the inference from the premises to the conclusion. Obviously, the more premises and conclusions involved in an argument, the more steps it will take to arrive at the conclusion (Figure 6-5).

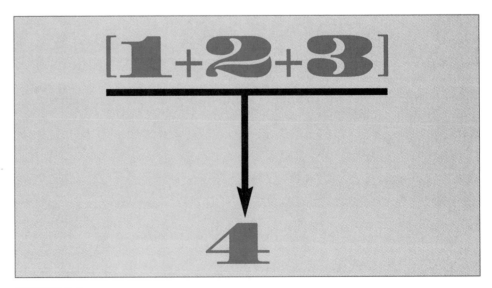

FIGURE 6.4

FIGURE 6.5 *A diagram of an argument is like a roadmap. It can render a confusing set of statements into a logical, ordered set of directions for reaching a conclusion.*

Arguments with Independent Premises

Many arguments establish their conclusion with the premises working *independently* of one another. For example, consider the following argument adapted from an article in *Working Mother* magazine. The article provides important suggestions to make the transition from home to work smoother after a period away from steady paid employment. But first, the article describes some of the issues and problems that must be addressed before making the leap from home or other nonpaid position to new, re-entry, or resumed employment.

1) Rejoining the workforce after a few or even several years off can be a frightening and daunting experience. 2) For one thing, you are probably not as confident as you would like to be that your technical skills are up to date. 3) Second, you are worried that a prospective employer might question the gap in your employment.[2]

The first sentence contains the conclusion. The next two sentences provide support for it by offering separate, **independent premises**. The second sentence expresses fear about the lack of up-to-date skills, the third expresses apprehension over a perceived weakness on a résumé. Each premise by itself *separately* provides grounds for the conclusion. In other words, they do not need to be taken together or combined in any way to make the inference from the premises to the conclusion.

Because each premise supports the conclusion independently of the other, the argument yields a different diagram from the preceding one. This argument can be diagrammed as follows (Figure 6–6):

FIGURE 6.6

If we add a third premise such as "another concern is that you might feel awkward as one of the 'older' employees hired for the job," the argument would still contain independent premises. The diagram would simply reflect '4' as an additional premise with a separate line to the conclusion. Because the third premise does not *depend* on the others to provide additional support for the truth of the conclusion, you would add it as follows in Figure 6-7.

FIGURE 6.7

Arguments with Both Dependent and Independent Premises

Here is another argument to consider.

1) Because many people believe that job stress affects overall health, 2) it is important that you try to identify those aspects of the job that are the most stressful. Thus, 3) we recommend that a daily log of activities would be helpful in monitoring which events cause the most stress. 4) Besides, illness or fatigue related to stress could affect job performance (Figure 6-8).

In this argument we have two separate reasons to keep a log or journal to help you monitor job stress. Reason 2 implies reason 3 in a straight line, a link in the chain of inferences. Unlike the premises in Figure 6-4, the premises shown in Figure 6-8 are not connected with plus marks (which function as conjunctions) and are dependent only in a direct inference from one to the other, as premises for new conclusions.

Now consider the argument below.

1) There is considerable research demonstrating that stress can affect the overall health of employees, no matter what the profession. 2) The research further shows that overall health directly

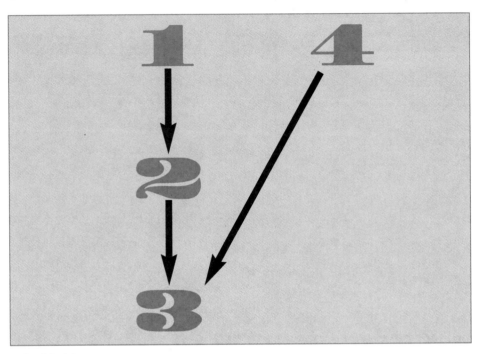

FIGURE 6.8

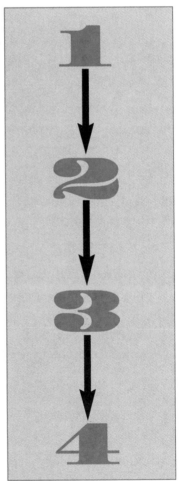

FIGURE 6.9

affects job performance. Thus, 3) monitoring your stress levels while on the job will help you identify which aspects of the job cause the most stress. 4) And this will lead to better understanding of the problems associated with health-related performance (Figure 6–9).

Note that one of the premises in argument 6-6 is now a conclusion in 6-9. Also, in 6-8 and 6-9 there is a series of inferences, an argument within an argument. Note also that the diagram method visually represents these connections clearly and succinctly.

Here is another fairly complex argument.

1) With good reason, single-story buildings are the most efficient and widely used types of new business construction. 2) They allow for easy movement of goods within the structure. 3) As single-level construction, they eliminate the need for elevators, multilevel conveyors, and escalators to move products. 4) The absence of elevators and escalators reduces the cost of building construction and maintenance, and 5) reduces the communication between separate locations on separate floors. 6) The one-floor construction also provides more opportunity for visual supervision of the product's movement from beginning to end (Figure 6–10).

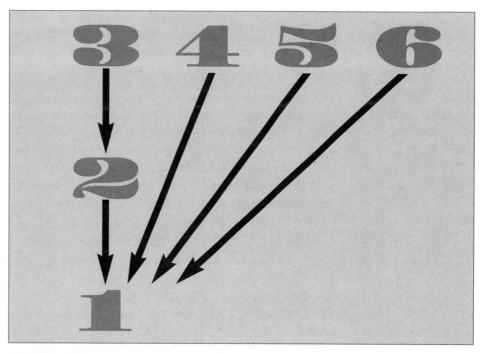

FIGURE 6.10

Strategies for Identifying Dependent and Independent Premises

To determine whether a certain premise is dependent or independent, you should first examine *what kind* of support it offers for the conclusion. An easy test to determine this is to ask what would happen if the other premises were eliminated, unknown, or false.[3] For example, if the impact of a premise is not diminished by eliminating one or more of the other premises, as if the others were not included at all or were untrue, then the premise functions independently of the others. In other words, if a premise still supports the conclusion, with or without the others, then the premise is independent. You should draw a separate line from the premise to the conclusion. Then apply this test to each premise you are unsure of.

For example, consider this argument.

1) Non-job-related activities can create as much stress as job-related activities, especially for adult students. 2) Balancing time demands

for work and family, for example, creates stress. 3) Balancing commitment to community activities and to friends also creates stress. 4) And, of course, pressure from taking college courses certainly adds another level of stress to the mix. 5) These factors feel as stressful as any stress factors at work.

The conclusion "non-job-related activities can create as much stress as job-related activities" is supported by three premises. Each one provides support for the conclusion separately, even though they are related to each other. Thus, if we eliminate the second premise, the first premise would still support the conclusion on its own. The same is true of premise 2 and premise 3. Even if we eliminate any one or two premises, the remaining premise(s) would still provide support for the conclusion independently. The last sentence premise merely repeats the conclusion and does not provide additional support (Figure 6–11).

FIGURE 6.11

The same test also applies when considering whether a premise is dependent. In the case of dependent premises, if you are *not* able to eliminate the other premises, then their inclusion is necessary to make the inference work; they are dependent on one another. In other words, if you cannot eliminate the premises because the inference would fail without taking them together, then the premises *mutually support* each other in providing grounds for the conclusion. You should connect them with plus signs and draw an arrow connecting them as a set (only those that rely on one another) to the conclusion.

Similarly, if a premise is offered as evidence for some other premise and the latter is then accepted as an established conclusion, one that is necessary for the inference to proceed further, then the premises are dependent on one another. If you cannot eliminate the intermediary premises, they are dependent. You should draw a line vertically with the arrow going from one premise to the premise it implies (now functioning as a subinference—a conclusion—in an intermediary step) and then proceed to the conclusion.

For example, consider these arguments.

> 1) Non-job-related activities can be just as stressful as job-related activities, especially for working adults. 2) Balancing work and family demands requires a creative way to manage time. 3) Managing time creates stress. 4) Balancing time for my college courses, plus time for family and friends is stressful, and 5) forget any free time for recreation or quiet time for myself.

The conclusion of the argument is once again stated first. Balancing time for work, family, and friends implies that nonrelated activities create time management problems. Time management problems create stress. So sentence 2 implies sentence 3. Premise 4, balancing time for college studies with time for friends also creates stress, is another independent reason why non-job-related activities create stress. A third, separate reason in support of the claim that nonrelated activities cause stress is the lack of time for recreation. You could treat the last factors—quiet time as separate from recreation time or as part of that same premise; either way it is an independent factor in support of the conclusion (Figure 6–12).

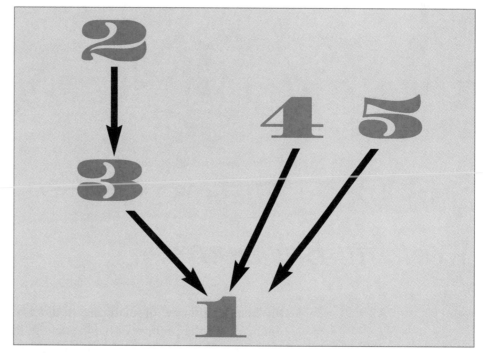

FIGURE 6.12

If my boss asks me to travel to a meeting on Wednesday, I will not be able to make it home for my daughter's school play. But if I work a few extra hours today and tomorrow, I can finish the project early. If I finish the project early, I can leave early on Wednesday and make it to the play. Therefore, I'd better get cracking on this project to make it to the play.

The conclusion (the last sentence) in this argument follows from two mutually supported premises and a third premise that is relevant but is not necessary for the conclusion to follow from the other two. If you eliminate premise 2, then premise 3 does not support the conclusion by itself. Finishing early does not imply that "I better get cracking to make it to the play." You need to add the premises together to make the inference to the conclusion reasonable (Figure 6–13).

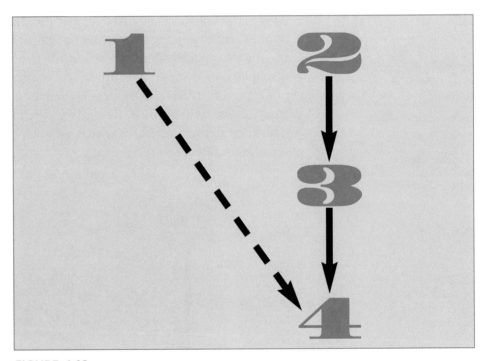

FIGURE 6.13

Working Backward

One helpful strategy for analyzing arguments is to work backward from the conclusion to the premises. That is, identify the conclusion *first* then trace it backward to see which premises dependently or independently support it (assuming, of course, that you first read the *entire argument* through before determining its conclusion). This is the "bottom line" strategy mentioned in Chapter 5. Posing the question "What statement am I asked to accept as true" is, in some ways, like asking, "What's the bottom line in this argument?" Once you identify the conclusion, search for the evidence that leads to it. A little logical detective work proceeding backward to sort out the evidence is usually a good strategy for analyzing all types of arguments and a good strategy for critical thinking in general.

Importance of Diagrams

As a detective uses a chalkboard to sort out and categorize the evidence in solving a crime, a critical thinker uses diagrams to help visualize the underlying structure of an argument. The arrows help sort out the steps (relationships) in tracing the flow of the argument from the premises to the conclusion. The resulting diagram is the **skeletal outline** of the argument's structure.

You can also think of a diagram as steel construction beams in a building providing structural support to the rest of the building. Some parts are connected so that their removal will weaken the structure but might not damage it severely, whereas other parts are integrally connected so that their removal will undermine whole portions of the structure, possibly contributing to its collapse.

> **Note:** We are assuming that language can be organized in this rigid mode of expression. This is open to debate. However, we are not assuming that this mode of expression is the most important, legitimate, or significant mode of expressing our thoughts and feelings. We are suggesting that that is a practical way to analyze communication appropriate to the working student.

Importance of the Distinction for Critical Thinking

As we shall see in subsequent chapters, the type of relationship between premises and conclusions is important to the strategies you will use in evaluating arguments for their strength or validity later on. For example, if you can disprove (i.e., show that it is false or unsupported) an independent premise in a series of premises, you would weaken the argument but not completely undermine it, depending on how many premises are shown false or unsupported. Because each premise supports the conclusion separately, the argument would still have *some* support. However, if you disprove dependent premises, *all* the premises that rely on that premise for support are also affected, perhaps fatally damaging the argument, depending on whether there is also *independent* support for the conclusion. Hence, one of your strategies for attacking a dependent argument is to look for the weakest link among the dependent premises. On the other hand, your strategy for attacking an independent argument is to assess each premise individually for its credibility. As you can see, evaluating and assessing arguments depends to a great extent on *which kind* of premises are offered to support the conclusion.

················ **EXERCISES** ················

I. Review Figure 6–10. Describe the strategies you would use to attack premises 3 and 2 compared to the strategies you would use in attacking premises 1, 4, and 5.

_____

_____

_____

_____

_____

_____

II. Construct diagrams for the following arguments. If you are unsure whether the premises are dependent or independent, state how the strategies discussed might help you decide which relationship is intended. Develop an argument defending your decision.

1. New job opportunities in high-tech fields are very attractive to those seeking new employment, looking to transfer skill for more career flexibility, or for re-entering the job market. However, some analysts say don't be so eager to quit your current job or jump blindly into the high-tech world. There are enormous risks involved. First, high-tech skills can be outdated within months. Be prepared to train continually in this field. Second, the high-tech industry is becoming extremely competitive and volatile in terms of long-range survival. The success rate of start-up companies is increasingly low.

2. Because technology, particularly computer-related technology, is one of the fastest growing career fields in recent years, it is advisable that anyone seeking a new career should consider computer-related education or training. However, technology is a very broad field, one that encompasses many subspecialties. Thus, one should explore a variety of fields, then narrow the scope of the area in which to conduct a more limited search. Because the subspecialties require specific training and education, anyone seeking computer training must first be sure that they have the aptitude, desire, and motivation to pursue those areas in detail. Thus, a career search in this field is much more complicated than it would seem on the surface.

3. The stock market responds negatively to increases in interest rates because higher interest rates lead to higher prices for goods and services. Most investors see this as an opportunity to advise their clients to seek investments in organizations that will benefit from higher interest rates, such as banks and bond markets. Thus, what is seen as a financial problem for one part of the investment market can be seen as a financial opportunity for another.

4. "Decision makers learn from experience what rule to use and simultaneously learn how to improve any rule that they use. The two forms of learning interact. The more a particular rule is used, the better becomes the performance using that rule, so the more likely it is that the rule will be reinforced by experience. The more a rule is reinforced, the more likely it is to be used."[4]

Hidden, or Assumed Premises and Conclusions

In ordinary language, we rarely state explicitly *all* the words and phrases relevant to or necessary to express our ideas and experiences. Likewise, in presenting arguments, we rarely state explicitly all the premises and conclusions relevant to or needed to convince an audience. This means that some premises and conclusions are *assumed*; they are not stated explicitly in the argument. Because it would be tedious in many cases to state every single idea, premise, fact, or concept that is possibly relevant to the argument, particularly when many of them are obvious, we usually leave out those that everyone already knows or does not absolutely need to know. However, in critical thinking this is a dangerous practice. For it is extremely important, sometimes essential for a *full* understanding of an argument, to know all (or as many as is practical) the underlying messages contained in it, including the implicit premises.

Whether the assumptions are deliberately implicit to mask certain facts or to imply certain ideas without actually stating them, as in the cases of innuendo and loaded questions, or whether they are too obvious to state overtly, is not

FIGURE 6.14 *Should we conclude that the management team meeting didn't go well?*

important to the *structure* of the argument. Examining *why* there are hidden statements involves understanding the intention of the arguer and critically analyzing the language used, as you did in Chapter 3, which is not the focus of this chapter. However, once you recognize that some premises and/or conclusions are implicit, it is important, if not crucial, to critical thinking to *make them explicit* for a full analysis of the argument. Hence, some additional detective work is required to ferret out the **hidden premises** and conclusions. Moreover, it is necessary to identify explicitly *all parts* of the argument in order to construct a complete diagram of the argument. Here are some examples for practice.

I. Hidden Premises

1. Learning how to get along with coworkers is essential to team building. Thus, it's obvious Ms. Lobello is not a good team player.

Hidden premise: Ms. Lobello does not get along with coworkers.

2. Saving for retirement now, while you are young, via the supplemental retirement plan, is a wise decision. For those of us who missed the opportunity, it's probably too late.

Hidden premises: There are some of us who are not young, or those of us who did not begin saving, are not wise, or both.

3. If you car pool three days a week instead of taking the bus, it will save at least nine dollars a week on bus fare. Hence, now you can see why you are spending at least fifteen dollars every week on buses.

Hidden premise: You spend three dollars a day taking the bus.

II. Hidden Conclusions

1. Freida dislikes the new spreadsheet program the manager wants her to use. You know Frieda, if she doesn't like it she won't use it. Guess what will happen when that new data report is due next week?

Hidden conclusion: Frieda will not have used the new spreadsheet program for the new data report.

2. All management level 2 positions require a bachelor's degree. All management level 1 positions require only an associate's degree. Rolanda is a level 2.

Hidden conclusion: Rolanda has a bachelor's degree.

3. If an automobile company takes extra steps to ensure that their product is completely safe, it will ensure confidence in the consuming public. The public has become much more safety conscious in recent years. And we all know that high confidence leads to better sales.

Hidden conclusion: The automobile companies will increase sales with extra safety measures.

EXERCISES

I. Identify any hidden premises and/or conclusions in the following.

1. Someday I plan to send children to college. I guess that supplemental retirement plan is right for me.

   _____

   _____

   _____

   _____

2. The Individuals with Disabilities Act requires that public buildings and buildings constructed with public funds must provide access to persons with disabilities. Besides, providing access to all persons in this day and age is simply expected and is good business. Those staircases in the old wing need attending to when we begin renovating this fall. Other projects will need attending to as well.

   _____

   _____

   _____

   _____

   _____

3. The security company we just hired last year seems to be working out. Workplace violence is down 3 percent and vandalism down 4 percent.

   _____

   _____

   _____

   _____

   _____

Constructing Your Own Arguments

Although an entire subsequent chapter is devoted specifically to the practical application of critical thinking skills in solving problems at home and at work, and another one is devoted specifically to problem solving using principles of scientific reasoning, you should now begin to think about general strategies to develop your own arguments for solving problems and for constructing your own persuasive positions. Until now you have been examining arguments provided by others and have not addressed situations that confront you on the job or at home.

The reasoning strategies you have acquired in analyzing arguments can help resolve problems that require gathering information and drawing inferences from those data. Analyzing others' arguments is one thing; constructing your own is another. Nonetheless, both require practice.

Also, diagramming helps you to determine which facts (premises) are absolutely required (dependent) and which contribute separately (independent) to supporting your case. This strategy helps further in determining the relevance and importance of your evidence. If the premises can be eliminated without weakening the argument, then *perhaps* they are not relevant to *this* conclusion, or constitute mere "fluff" in the argument. For example, in constructing your own outline for a paper or report, which is like constructing a diagram, you should ask, "What are the consequences if I eliminate this information?" If it is significant, then retain it and show how it supports your case. If not, consider eliminating it or saving it for some other argument you will be developing later on.

Summary

IN THIS CHAPTER WE:

- Discussed simple and complex arguments

- Explored the role of dependent and independent premises in argument structure

- Demonstrated how diagrams illustrate the underlying structure of arguments

Writing from Experience

1. Construct an argument (and then diagram it) for which you have had to gather information, then organize and sort it into sets of related and interrelated segments (premises). Now arrange those pieces of information into a coherent outline. Fill in the outline by adding ordinary language that transforms it into an argument where you have had to convince a boss, coworker, or subordinate to take some course of action.

2. Construct a similar argument where you have had to convince a family member or friend to take some course of action, then diagram the argument.

3. Imagine that a minor fire occurred in your home (where there was minimal damage). An insurance adjuster comes to your home and you are asked to justify your claim that the fire was caused by faulty wiring and not carelessness. Construct an argument to convince the adjuster.

4. If you have ever served as a member of a jury, you have observed how sorting out evidence and constructing an argument to convince a jury is at the core of the legal process. If not, you can imagine (there are enough television shows about courts of law) what it would be like. Assume you are a prosecutor attempting to convince a jury that the fire was the result of negligence.

TOPIC COVERED IN THIS CHAPTER

• Fallacies defined: Formal and informal

• Types of informal fallacies

• Fallacies of ambiguity

    • Semantic

    • Grouping

    • Syntactic

• Fallacies of bias

    • Subjectivist

    • Common belief

    • Ad hominem: personal attack and circumstantial

    • Appeal to authority

    • Appeal to force

• Fallacies of relevance

    • Burden of proof (fallacy of ignorance)

    • False dilemma

    • Circular argument (begging the question)

    • Fallacy of relevance (non sequitur)

Chapter 7

INFORMAL FALLACIES

...[Y]et this is what I call rhetoric, a branch of a thing which has nothing 'fine' about it at all.

– SOCRATES

In Chapter 6 we analyzed the structure of arguments whose premises provided support for the truth of their conclusions. In this chapter, we will examine the structure of arguments whose premises do not provide such support. In these arguments, the premises only *appear or purport* to provide support for their conclusions but on close analysis fail to do so, even when the premises are true.

The reasons the premises fail are many and varied but fall into two general categories. The first involves the truth or falsity of the premises themselves. Common sense tells us that if the premises of an argument are false, it is impossible for them to establish grounds for the truth of the conclusion. Hence, arguments based on false premises are always unsound or weak at best. However, the methods for determining the truth or falsity of the premises is the subject matter of subsequent chapters, which we explore in great detail later on.

The second way in which premises fail to support their conclusions is due to an error in the reasoning process that connects the premises to conclusions. Commonly called *fallacies*, these errors are the subject matter of this chapter. We will focus on the *linguistic* reasons why the premises, *even when true*, only appear to support the conclusion. We will call them **informal fallacies**. The formal, *structural* reasons why the premises fail to support the conclusions are called **formal fallacies**. First we will consider formal fallacies.

Formal Fallacies and Deductive Arguments

Formal fallacies occur in the context of deductive arguments, wherein the language is *presumed* clear and relevent. This presumption allows us to focus on the formal, logical structure of the argument—the precise relationship between premises and conclusions devoid of extraneous and confusing language. In fact, if the language is not clear or contains any of the ambiguities and vagaries discussed thus far, we must translate it into a form suitable for logical analysis before analyzing its structure. However, once you distill the language into its bare essentials and convert it into a suitable form, you must then apply a set of agreed upon strategic rules for evaluating it.

TECHNICAL DEFINITION OF A DEDUCTIVE ARGUMENT

In the context of formal logic, a **deductive argument** is defined as any argument whose premises provide conclusive grounds for its conclusion. That is, the premises not only support the conclusion, they support it with absolute certainty. Deductive arguments are categorized as either valid or invalid. Validity is defined as the impossibility of the premises being true and the conclusion false. Thus, in a valid deductive argument, no matter what the premises actually say, *if* the premises were true, the conclusion must also be true. Another way of stating this is to say that the truth of the conclusion of a valid deductive argument follows absolutely from the truth of the premises.

One classical example of a deductive argument is:

> All humans are mortal.
> Socrates is a human.
> Therefore, Socrates is mortal.

According to this interpretation, the conclusion follows with absolute certainty given the meaning of certain connecting words, that is, the linking verb "*is*" and the meaning of class relationships. The reasoning is as follows: Humans *belong to* (they are a member of) the class of all mortal things, the larger class. Since Socrates is a member of the class of human things, he must also belong to the class of mortal things.

This argument can be adapted to the workplace as in the following argument.

> All employees are paid staff members.
> Ms. Kravec is an employee.
> Therefore, Ms. Kravec is a paid staff member.

In both examples, the truth of the conclusion follows validly not as a matter of opinion or belief, but as a matter of certainty based on the definition of validity and class relations.

Here is an example of another type of deductive argument.

> If tuition reimbursement were available to all emplyees, then the corporation would gain better trained and educated workers.
>
> If workers were better trained and educated, then the corporations would have an edge on its competitors.
>
> Therefore, if tuition reimbursement were available to all employees, then the corporation would have an edge on its competitors.

The example has the following form:

> If A implies B and B implies C,
> Then A implies C.

The conclusion of this argument follows from the premises based on the meaning of the connectors "*if*" and "*then*" and the structure of the argument. If the premises are true, the conclusion must be true.

There is an important clarification that needs to be made at this point. If an argument is valid, it does not mean that the premises are true. Here is an example of a valid argument with one *false* premise.

> All humans are angry people.
> The president of the United States is a human.
> Therefore, the president is an angry person.

The conclusion follows validly from the premises even though one of them is false. This potentially confusing aspect of validity arises because it is possible for a valid argument to rely on a falsehood. Intuitively, this seems odd and an unfortunate outcome of our definition. But keep in mind that according to the technical definition of a valid argument, validity is tied to the structure of the argument, the meaning of connecting words, and class relations—*not the actual truth of the premises*. (The methods for establishing the credibility and truth of the premises are examined in Chapters 9 and 10.) Here we are concerned only with the relationship among the parts of an argument, not the truth of the statements or the language in which they are expressed.

A valid argument that does have all true premises is called a *sound argument*. A valid argument that has at least one false premise is called an *unsound argument*, such as the argument regarding the president.

A formal fallacy occurs when all the premises are demonstrated or given as true and the conclusion is shown to be false. Thus, all invalid arguments contain a fallacy. The fallacy identifies the specific reasons why the argument is invalid.

Types of Informal Fallacies

Fallacious reasoning has been around probably as long as humans have been advancing arguments, and it is certainly not new or limited to situations at work or at home. Recall that the ancient Greek philosopher Socrates spent a good deal of his life pointing out errors (fallacies) in the arguments of his contemporaries (even though he himself was not immune to errors in logic). However, it was another ancient Greek philosopher, Aristotle, a student of Plato, who categorized fallacies into various types. Although Aristotle's categories are still used today, there are no generally accepted fast and easy ways to group them. In the following sections, the fallacies are grouped around common causes of the errors, although all share the problem that their premises do not clearly support the conclusions. However, the groupings are for convenience and have no other underlying or substantive bases for the distinctions.

Informal fallacies have their roots in the nuances, misapplications, misunderstandings, grammatical mistakes, and other malapropisms in language, usually ordinary language. We will examine three types of informal fallacies—fallacies of ambiguity, bias, and relevance.

As you will soon see, most of the fallacies discussed in this chapter contain examples of ambiguous language discussed in Chapter 2 and loaded language discussed in Chapter 4. You will quickly recognize the rhetorical devices, emotional appeals, ambiguities, vagaries, loaded questions, stereotypes, exaggerations, and other persuasive techniques that mislead and confuse an audience. However, you will now examine how this language leads to fallacies in reasoning. The important difference in this chapter is that the ambiguities and loaded language are used as *evidence* (i.e., as premises) in advancing an *argument*. As critical thinkers, your task is to scrutinize the content of what is actually being conveyed to determine whether the premises do in fact directly support the conclusions they are intended to support.

Informal Fallacies of Ambiguity

Since you are already familiar with problems of ambiguity, let's begin with arguments that rely (intentionally or unintentionally) on this characteristic to persuade an audience. Remember, an ambiguity occurs when a sentence contains at least one word or phrase that has more than one established meaning, and the audience does not know which meaning is intended. A fallacy occurs when the ambiguous word or phrase is used in a premise with one meaning and then used again in another premise or in the conclusion with a different meaning. Because it is unclear which meaning is intended, it cannot be clear that the premises provide support for the conclusion or even if they are relevant to them at all. We will examine three types of fallacies of ambiguity—semantic, grouping, and grammatical. (A review of Chapter 2 would help.)

FALLACIES OF SEMANTIC AMBIGUITY

This fallacy occurs when two different *senses* of a word or phrase are confused, the meanings shift in the course of the argument, and a conclusion is drawn without clarifying which sense is intended. Sometimes called the **fallacy of equivocation**, these errors can be very difficult to detect because different senses of a word can shift subtly within an argument and slip by without our noticing. Usually, the premises are plausible, even obviously true, yet the argument containing them is seriously flawed. Moreover, all the nuances and subtleties of *relative* terms apply to this type of fallacy of ambiguity. Consider the following argument:

> Everyone said the supervisor liked Josh's work and thought he was doing fine. He is a quick learner and makes few mistakes. However, when the computer counted the number of pieces Josh had produced, it showed that his work was not up to what others in the department produced. So Josh must not be doing well in the job.

The ambiguous word "work" has come back to haunt us once again, along with a few familiar but troublesome relative terms. You can see the shift in meaning from one premise to the next, which leads to confusion and, thus, a fallacy. The first premise talks about the *quality* of Josh's work, probably its carefulness, or exactness, or some other qualitative measure. The next premise talks about the *quantity* of work Josh produced. The first premise is not directly relevant to the conclusion, which also appears to be about the quantity of work. Another way to state this is to say that the author *equivocated* on the word "work." You can also argue that the phrases "doing fine" and "doing well on the job" are equivocated, each expressing a different meaning related to different contexts. It is not clear which sense is intended. The following example also contains a shift in meaning:

> The manager of the maintenance staff is being considered for an achievement award. He is being cited for his skills in promoting quality work among his staff, high standards for achievement, and effectiveness in getting the job done in a timely way. This is the second award he's received, each accompanied by a sizable raise. I'd say he's managing quite well at this point. Wouldn't you?

FALLACIES OF GROUPING AMBIGUITY

Sometimes called **fallacies of composition and division**, each of these fallacies involves two types of confusion. The first type involves ambiguity as to whether a group or individual members of a group are intended as referents. The second involves ambiguity about whether the parts of a complex entity should be taken individually or whether the complex entity should be taken as a whole. Let's examine fallacies of composition first. This is best explained by way of example.

> I've examined this large piece of machinery and believe it is made of a light alloy, probably aluminum alloy. All the parts I've picked up so far are rather light in weight. Therefore, this machine must be light.

Arguing that the property of the parts (the small pieces of machinery) extends to the property of the whole object (the machine itself) commits the fallacy of composition. Based on observation of the parts alone, without comparing the weight of the entire machine to other machines, leads to the unwarranted conclusion. Thus, the old adage, "the whole is not identical with the sum of its parts" is relevant here (Figure 7-1).

FIGURE 7.1 *Now how much does a pound of feathers weigh?*

Here is an example of the second type of composition fallacy based on membership in a group.

> The company pays each clerical staff member slightly more than the minimum wage, which is not much money. Thus, the company's payroll for clerical staff must be small.

In this case, the premises assert that a property of individual members holds true as a whole property of the entire group (the entire clerical staff). Because the conclusion is stated in relative terms, additional information about the size of the payroll as it compares to other payrolls is required before we can draw this inference. Note that in both examples, the premises are presumed true but lead to unwarranted conclusions.

Arguing in the opposite direction from the properties of the whole entity (or group) to properties of each individual part or member of the group commits the *fallacy of division*. Here is an example of a division fallacy involving a group.

Supporters of the National Rifle Association advocate the repeal of all gun control laws. Therefore, George W. Bush, a supporter of the NRA, will work to repeal all gun control laws if elected president.

Here we are reasoning from a characteristic of the group (those advocating the repeal of gun control laws) to stating that each and every individual member of the group must have that characteristic. This inference commits the fallacy of division. As in the other examples, additional information, in this case about George Bush's actual intentions, is required to reach the intended conclusion. Here is another example.

Technology stocks have skyrocketed in price for the past four years and are predicted to climb even higher. Therefore, the stock value of Hoolahoop Technology Incorporated will skyrocket this year.

Once again, we see that arguing from a characteristic of the whole group (technology stocks as a group) to characteristics of each of its members can lead to fallacious reasoning.

To see an example of a division fallacy involving the parts-to-whole relationship, simply reverse the composition fallacy involving the aluminum machine as follows:

This Boeing 747 aircraft is constructed of aluminum alloys and weighs several hundred tons. It's a wonder it can get off the ground at all. Thus, each part, the wings, fuselage, tail, even the nuts and bolts, must be really heavy for it to weigh that much.

FALLACIES OF GRAMMAR AND SYNTAX AMBIGUITIES

Fallacies of ambiguity in this category are caused by improper, ungrammatical, or confusing sentence structure and/or by unclear referents. Sometimes called **amphibolies**, they are often committed inadvertently. The obvious confusion created by the following example is probably unintentional.

My son plays more with his toys than his sisters. Therefore, we should remove them from his room.

Intentional or not, diligence is required in attending to precise wording to avoid the ambiguities involved in the fallacious argument above. However, more serious consequences could result from the ensuing confusion in the following example:

> It is not clear what happened between the supervisor, Ms. Calderi, and her administrative assistant, Ms. Higgins. Ms. Higgins claimed she was harassed by her supervisor while on the phone. Thus, Ms. Higgins should tape her phone conversations from now on. It should be clear that verbal or any other type of harassment will not be tolerated by this company.

The ambiguity in this example seems inconsequential on the surface. But it may become important if Ms. Higgins pursues legal or disciplinary action against her supervisor. Did the harassment take place while Ms. Higgins was talking on the phone with someone else, or did it take place during a phone conversation with her supervisor? The former is not related to the conclusion about taping phone conversations, but the latter is.

EXERCISES

I. Identify the fallacies in the following arguments:

1. Because we cannot explain all the workings of the whole human body, neither can we explain the workings of each of its parts.

    _____

    _____

2. The workings of the minute parts of the human body are fascinating. Just think of all those organs, systems, and tissues working in harmony. It's so complex it's beyond comprehension. If we can't even understand the workings of the smallest parts, how can we understand the workings of the entire body?

    _____

    _____

3. Ethan is such a good manager! He is sensitive in his management style. He is a good person because he is a good manager.

    _____

    _____

4.　Juan saw the thief pilfering the supply room with his video camera. We should be able to catch him now.

_____

_____

5.　We need extra copies of this document. Please go to my office and retrieve the binder with the original. It's to the left of my stationery. So you should find it easily.

_____

_____

6.　The sales and marketing departments of all computer software companies set prices for their new products. They should all get together as a group and compare pricing. Then they should jointly set prices so that each of the members of the group maximizes profits.

_____

_____

7.　Women are the best managers. There's no doubt that if they can manage a family, they can manage a department.

_____

_____

8.　American children consume millions of gallons of soft drinks each day. It's a wonder they don't have higher incidents of tooth decay with all that sugar.

_____

_____

9.　Working all day, studying at night, and finding time for my family is hard. Everyone I know certainly is. Working students are the most conscientious people in the world!

_____

_____

10.　Maintenance people work some of the most erratic hours of all frontline employees. Julian, the custodian for the second floor, must be tired all the time.

_____

_____

(continued)

II. Rewrite exercises 4, 5, 8, and 10 in unambiguous language.

_____

_____

_____

_____

_____

_____

_____

1. Construct a brief argumentative essay in which you commit the following fallacies. Then explain how you would "fix" the error.

    a) Fallacy of semantic ambiguity that involves a miscommunication between you and a coworker.

    _____

    _____

    _____

    b) Fallacy of composition that involves members of a social or community group you belong to.

    _____

    _____

    _____

    c) Fallacy of a syntactic ambiguity where you provide specific but confusing instructions to a coworker. The instructions direct him or her to a new diner for lunch.

    _____

    _____

    _____

2. Locate a letter to the editor, report, advertisement, inter-office memorandum, or other document that contains an ambiguity that led to confusion. Rewrite the document in clear, unambiguous language.

Fallacies Involving Bias

The next set of fallacies is loosely grouped together because in one way or another they contain a bias. The bias may be due to an individual's personal perspective or due to an affiliation with a group, profession, cause, or some other circumstance. Or, the bias could be due to an unquestioned common practice, characteristic, or generally accepted set of principles. In each case, there are questions regarding the objectivity or credibility of the arguer due to a potential or existing bias, prejudice, or preconception. In many cases, the bias is due to stereotyping, innuendo, or exaggeration.

SUBJECTIVIST FALLACIES

Wishful thinking can lead to some of the greatest accomplishments of humankind. Without wishful thoughts about what is possible, dreams could not come true. But in simpler, ordinary contexts, wishful thinking—asserting that something should be true merely because we believe or wish it to be true—often leads to fallacious reasoning. An argument that is based on wishful thinking or is based on one's personal beliefs is called a **subjectivist fallacy**. It runs as follows:

I believe (wish) that x is true; therefore, my belief (wish) is evidence for x being true.

Adding that you *strongly* or *sincerely* believe a statement is true does not increase the *evidential support* for its truth. These qualifiers rarely contribute to the evidential support of the premises and should be avoided unless you can demonstrate *how* they contribute to the credibility of the premises. (Would you *insincerely* believe something is true?)

The fallacy is called subjectivist because the inference is based on the author's personal, subjective beliefs or wishes. It arises because "thinking that it is true does not make it true"—only sufficient evidence can accomplish that role. Consider this argument.

I know you think entry-level employees like us are taken advantage of. But that's your opinion and is true for you. But I'm an optimist, and I think the company will take care of us. Thus, we are earning what we deserve at this level.

The author is expressing his optimism and an opinion about how he is treated by the company. In and of itself, this assertion does not create a problem. However, when offered as evidence in an argument, it leads to a subjectivist fallacy. An analysis of pay scales in the context of working conditions and expectations would be required to develop a convincing argument.

Subjectivist fallacies often use phrases like, "that is true for you, but I've got my beliefs and they are true for me." Or, "I was brought up to believe...and that's what I will believe"; "It works for me, even if you do have proof otherwise." The problem with these phrases is that they block further communication and analysis of the merits of each case. If the parties are interested in arriving at a mutually agreeable resolution to a conflict, these phrases prohibit that from occurring. Further discussion is cut short and resolution is impossible.

Nonetheless, we don't want to overstate the severity or frequency of this fallacy by casting doubt on *all* assertions of subjective opinion or personal statements of principle. Just because some people state that they "feel," "think," "wish," or "believe" something is true does not necessarily mean that they are committing a subjectivist fallacy. They may be merely stating an opinion as their own opinion, or expressing their feelings or point of view about the subject. Or, they may not want or care to question their beliefs on these subjects. Nor are we suggesting that you will actually hear or see the fallacy stated in such obvious terms as in the characterizations above. Most cases of subjectivist reasoning are subtler than the above examples. Critical thinking is required to determine which cases involve premises with beliefs offered as evidence, which could lead to fallacies, and which involve mere expressions of emotions, personal opinions, and unquestioned beliefs (such as religious dogma), as beliefs not offered as evidence.

Here is an example of an argument about which there is room for debate as to whether a fallacy is committed.

You can try to convince me, but I am firm in my beliefs. I was taught that we should teach our children that abortion is wrong under all circumstances. We may have the illusion that we have a choice over our decision, but that is not true for me. Therefore, all situations where abortion is taught as an acceptable or viable option are unquestionably wrong. It is not an option for me and not for anyone else either.

Without engaging in the controversial debate itself (for the object here is not to convince the reader one way or the other on the abortion issue), closely examine the *content* of the argument. Even if the premises were true, does the last sentence in the conclusion follow from the premises *without further explanation or argument?*

APPEAL TO MAJORITY OR COMMON BELIEF

When you accept statements just because most people believe they are true, without seeking additional concrete evidence or critical analysis, you commit the fallacy of **appeal to common belief**. Like the subjectivist fallacy, the argument relies on evidence that has not been objectively established or closely scrutinized by the arguer. But unlike the preceding case, the evidence consists of *group or majority* opinion rather than a single person's personal belief. The author is biased by group thought because he has not conducted an investigation or critical assessment on his own.

Obviously, not all appeals to popular belief lead to fallacious reasoning. Citing an established popular belief is appropriate when you have no other information to go on or you know that the commonly held belief is well established by standard means. But accepting the truth of a statement merely because "they say" it is true or "everybody knows" it is true, can lead to a fallacy. "Everybody knows it's true" does not make it true. Critical assessment, diligence in questioning, and close scrutiny of popularly accepted norms and beliefs in seeking out the truth through the best means available to you are key elements in avoiding fallacies. Consider this example.

> Opinion polls show that the most popular way to raise revenue is to increase corporate taxes. Plus everybody knows that this type of tax places the brunt of the burden on those who can afford it most. Therefore, the proposed tax on corporate earnings is the easiest and best way to raise government revenue.

Opinion polls serve an important and legitimate function. Ask any marketing researcher, behavioral researcher, or politician just how important they are. However, as in the above case, they can also lead to fallacies. The fact that the polls show that a popular way to raise revenue is through a tax on corporate earnings does not imply that the tax is the most effective way to accomplish the intended goal. Also, the phrase "everybody knows" does little to add credible support to the conclusion, but it does contribute to the fallacy of appeal to common belief. Here is another example.

> You should oppose the governor's proposed increase in inheritance taxes because it goes against a basic, long-standing tradition in America that allows us to keep what we earn. And when we pass on, the rewards of that labor should be passed on to our children. Therefore, due to the violation of this deeply held tradition, this tax is ill conceived.

To base the argument on a long-standing tradition is to base it essentially on beliefs that are widely accepted. Traditions are commonly held beliefs by a group of people that have persisted over time, usually without being questioned. But the fact that traditions have been accepted over time, even by a large majority of people, does not make them true. This amounts to another version of appeal to common belief. (Note that there is an equivocation on the euphemistic phrase "pass on" in the premises as well.)

We can also include in the appeal to common belief appeals, common practices, practices that are accepted by the majority or some other large group. Just as appeals to tradition lead to fallacies, so do appeals to common practice as shown in the following example:

> The direction of the European Union, which is a common-market strategy, is the direction of the future. Every economist has argued that a unified market has enormous buying potential that can command discounted prices on goods and services by purchasing through a common system. Thus, the proposal to establish an American Union with Canada and Mexico is the way to go for the future.

Once again we see that the appeal to a common set of beliefs—"every economist"—and an appeal to a common practice—consolidated purchasing power—are the bases for the argument. In this case, the beliefs are directed toward future actions but still rely on a commonly accepted practice. The practice itself may in fact be a good strategy (e.g., consolidating purchasing power and eliminating competitions, etc.) but the premises regarding the merits of the practice do not establish the conclusion about a possible Pan-American union.

A related version of a common practice fallacy occurs with the phrase, "but we've always done it this way." This phrase, like the earlier phrases, closes off serious discussion and prohibits further analysis as well as overlooking the potential for *improved* practices.

For example, suppose a supervisor selects four or five employees to participate in a cross-training program. He argues that cross-training would avoid some delays in output when employees are absent. The employees argue in response that their output has been above average for years, the system is working fine, they all know each other well, and they don't want to change their current working relationships. They conclude that the situation shouldn't be changed. Even though the responses in fact may be true and relevant to existing working conditions, they are irrelevant to the conclusion that cross-training would avoid delays in production. The attitude expressing, "We've always done it this way. Therefore, don't change it" diverts discussion away from the real issue and resists a solution that could be mutually satisfactory regarding the problem of delays.

AD HOMINEM ARGUMENTS: PERSONAL ATTACKS AND FALLACIES OF CIRCUMSTANCE

Ad hominem ("*to the person*") arguments occur when the arguer directs the premises toward a person's character or circumstance rather than what the person says. All versions of ad hominem arguments avoid direct analysis of the statements (i.e., their content) and misdirect the discussion toward personal characteristics. There are two popular types of ad hominem argument: abusive (personal attack) and circumstantial.

Ad Hominem Abusive (Personal Attack)

In its crudest form, this argument consists primarily of slurs, insults, name-calling, and other types of abusive language. It attempts to disparage the character of an opponent, question his integrity or intelligence, and then infer that the person's reasoning must be faulty. The error arises because the premises devoted to character assassinations are *irrelevant* to the actual content of the positions advanced by the argument. In its more subtle forms, it directs attention to an opponent's character flaws by means of stereotype, innuendo, composition fallacies, and exaggerations that *appear* related to the conclusion. The following is a blatant version of the fallacy:

> That HRM department supervisor's stress management program can't possibly be worth the time. It's run by a bunch of "touchy-feely" types who don't know stress management from stress fracture.

The personal attack on the character of the stress management team is not only inappropriate, but it could influence some employees who could benefit from the program if they dismiss it without any thought (unless they are critical thinkers, of course).

These types of personal attacks occur fairly frequently in political arenas. Although unfortunate for the voting public, campaign rhetoric can cloud serious debate on national issues when the focus is on (unrelated) personal attacks (Figure 7-2).

FIGURE 7.2 *Stereotyping can damage not only reputations, they damage our own image.*

Senator Goldgift, or "Senator moneybags" as I call him, has been known to spend money lavishly. Look at the yacht he owns and the mansion he lives in. That carefree, spend-at-all-cost attitude will be reflected in his voting on budget matters. You can count on that.

The obvious flaws in this extreme example need no explanation.

Ad Hominem Circumstantial (Poisoning the Well)

A subtler version of an ad hominem argument that is not as insulting as personal attacks is an argument directed at a person's position in life (e.g., job title, career, role in community, political affiliation, etc.) or his personal circumstances that just happen to be true of that person. Consider this argument involving social groups.

> I urge you not to vote for the new school budget. The majority of the school board is comprised of rich people who can afford higher school taxes and seniors who don't have kids in our school and vote down all increases in the budget. There's no way the board can come up with a fair budget.

The statements about the personal characteristics of school board members may be true and might even be related to the prediction of how they will vote. However, they are *not* relevant to the conclusion about the fairness of the budget. Additional evidence is required to draw that conclusion.

Here is an argument based on a person's position in a company.

> Because Mr. Cutler is lead negotiator for management's bargaining team and is a long-standing member of the CEO's advisory council, he will have management's main interests in mind. Therefore, the agreements and conditions of the employment contract he is proposing will be opposed to everything the union contract is proposing.

Let's assume that the first sentence is true. Even if it is, the conclusion does not follow from this one premise alone. That is, the premise describing the negotiator's role in the company does not imply that the *content* of his proposal is in opposition to the content of the union's proposal. The argument, which contains exaggeration and stereotype, is fallacious because the premise is directed at the person's position in the company, which is irrelevant to what is actually stated in the contract proposal. The premises about character or position alone cannot establish the truth of the conclusion. In other words, the argument is built on circumstantial evidence, evidence that is irrelevant to the content of the proposal. To make the inference work, if possible, requires additional information provided in the proposal itself. Its content must be evaluated on its own merits.

Conversely, the argument would be just as flawed if the conclusion stated that the proposal must be antimanagement simply because it was proposed by a union representative. Because the premise about the employee's position is irrelevant to the content of the proposal, it cannot establish the truth of the conclusion, which is about the content of the proposal.

This version of the fallacy is also called "poisoning the well." It directs attention to personal circumstances and characteristics by questioning the person's objectivity, claiming he is *predetermined* to hold some particular stance toward the conclusion. The implicit message is that the person has a vested interest or *bias* that prejudices the case before anyone has actually analyzed it. It assumes that the person *can't possibly* be objective, given who they are or what they do. The earlier example about Mr. Cutler can be construed as an example of poisoning the well because it assumed that Mr. Cutler cannot be objective because he represents management. The attitude toward management is tainted (poisoned) before you draw the conclusion (and vice versa).

APPEAL TO AUTHORITY

When you appeal to an expert's authority in your field to validate or lend credence to your argument, you are following generally accepted procedures to support your position. For example, if you argue that an experimental approach to management supervision is credible by citing recent scholars and noted practitioners in management who have tested the approach, you are advancing a well-supported argument with appropriate appeals to authorities in the field. Not only is this an appropriate practice in work situations, particularly for written and oral reports, but it is a good practice for developing any convincing argument at home, school, or social situation. Like using expert witnesses in a court of law to establish your case, such appeals add credibility to your argument. However, when you cite an authority who has no legitimate claim to expertise in the matter under consideration, you commit a fallacy of **appeal to authority**.

For example, Albert Einstein was a brilliant scientist and an expert on various matters concerning physics, rocket science, mathematics, and even cosmology. However, to appeal to Einstein about matters of economic theory as it applies to current global issues would be to extend his area of expertise beyond reasonable boundaries. He was indeed a genius about many things but not economic theory—at least not in published writings. However, you might, for example, appeal to his theories with regard to certain mathematical formulas of probability and relativity that could be applied to certain economic calculations and forecasting. But this would be relying on his *mathematical* expertise about *mathematical* issues in economics, which is perfectly appropriate. On the other hand, you would not want to rely on his mathematical theories as *authoritative* in ethical or religious matters.

It is difficult to know where to draw the line in deciding when it is reasonable to appeal to one authority over another and in what areas, especially because we may not know all the areas in which a person is an expert. A helpful hint is to question whether this person is widely known in the public arena for his or her expert views on this subject. If not, it is up to the arguer to establish the person's credibility to support appeals to his or her authority.

The most common occurrences of this fallacy probably arise in advertising, particularly where *testimonial* evidence is offered. For example, basketball great Michael Jordan might be an expert on athletic shoes owing to his experience as an athlete, but probably is not an expert on the nutritional value of cereal products or telephone company service, no matter how many times he expresses his views on television or billboards about these subjects. When he provides a testimonial about how good a particular company's phone service is, he has probably exceeded his range of expertise.

The following argument stretches the limits of authority in supporting the conclusion.

> I have relied repeatedly on Dr. Spillman's book on raising difficult adolescents. Dr. Spillman, a professor of literature at Harvard University, tells the most humorous and interesting stories about bringing up his own children. He gives such expert advice. This should be required reading for any adolescent psychology course.

Dr. Spillman's ability as a writer is probably unquestioned. However, his expertise in adolescent psychology *is* questionable, unless we have independent reasons to accept his expertise in this area. If the arguer is trying to convince us that Dr. Spillman's well-told stories show insight into raising children, and that he allows readers to learn important information about the subject, then the claims about his expertise as a writer *are* relevant for including his book in a psychology course. But his experience in the literary field alone does not establish his expertise in the field of adolescent psychology. The inference regarding his expertise in psychology commits an appeal to authority fallacy.

APPEAL TO FORCE

An appeal to force as a method for convincing an audience to accept a conclusion seems like a topic that belongs in a speech on discipline rather than a topic for a college textbook on critical thinking. After all, bullying techniques are hardly subjects for a rational discourse on developing convincing, credible arguments. However, there are subtle ways to coerce people to accept the truth of a statement, especially when the threat is veiled, implicit, or disguised in "sweetened" terms so that the listener does not detect its subtle intimidation. Consider the following argument:

> We all remember the days when everyone looked out for employees' long-range welfare in terms of job security. The recent decision to outsource the company's mailroom operation shows us what has happened to that old outlook. If you support the outsourcing of the accounts receivable department, you support the loss of jobs. Your job could be next. I suggest you rethink your position.

The implicit threat in the last sentence would make most people think twice about supporting the outsourcing project, especially if the threat is intended to convey that there could be retaliation (subtle or overt) from coworkers if you openly support the decision. However, even though the general issue of outsourcing is a relevant consideration to job security, the decision regarding the accounts receivable department must be judged on its own merits. The intimidation does nothing to provide additional relevant information on which to base your judgments. Moreover, the decision could result in considerable cost savings, which might be used to hire more people in your department, thus increasing your job security.

Consider this memorandum.

> To: Mr. Joseph Kahled, Department Manager
> From: The Employees of Phone Sales Department Two
> Re: Vacancy for Office Supervisor
> Date: February 3, 2001
>
> Because you asked for written input from the office staff, we have taken this opportunity to express our collective ideas about hiring a new office supervisor. First, we need a family-friendly boss in this department, one who will support liberal leave time, flextime, extended maternity and paternity leave, on-site day care, and ability to cross-train for higher level positions. If we don't get one soon,

management will feel the pressure of employees who miss work periodically, arrive late, and leave altogether for childcare reasons. Then you will know what it's like to hire new staff every few months. We ask that you take these suggestions seriously. Thank you.

Again we see a not-so-veiled threat to management rather than objective analysis of the situation that might meet the needs of both parties. Although many of the statements are relevant and have merit, the intimidation does not contribute to establishing the conclusion, therefore creating a fallacy.

···················· EXERCISES ·····················

I. In a brief essay, discuss more effective ways to write the preceeding memo so that you convey the essential message but the intimidation is omitted.

_____

_____

_____

_____

_____

_____

_____

_____

_____

_____

_____

_____

_____

(continued)

II. Write a brief essay in which you intimidate a colleague or family member into accepting a position they might oppose.

_____

_____

_____

_____

_____

_____

_____

III. Discuss the following arguments:

1. Secretary of State Madeleine Albright is such an accomplished woman. She has dealt diplomatically with representatives from the Middle East, Africa, and the Far West with dignity and forcefulness. I hear she also exhibits impeccable manners and demeanor at high-level state dinners. I'll bet she knows exactly what to do in bringing up her children to be dignified and respected.

    _____

    _____

    _____

    _____

2. Have you seen the commercials featuring Mia Hamm, the great soccer player for the U.S. World Cup team that won the world championship? She is some kind of great athlete. Just look at the physical shape she is in. I'll bet she actually does eat Wheaties® for breakfast.

    _____

    _____

    _____

    _____

    _____

········WRITING FROM EXPERIENCE········

Develop a brief argument in which you appeal to an authority at your place of work or in your local community. Then develop an argument in which you appeal to that authority in an area outside his or her area of expertise.

_____

_____

_____

_____

_____

_____

_____

_____

_____

_____

_____

_____

_____

_____

_____

_____

_____

_____

_____

_____

_____

_____

Fallacies of Relevance

In one important sense, all the fallacies considered so far involve errors of relevancy. However, we have been focusing only on the specific linguistic causes for why the premises are irrelevant and thus fail to support their conclusion. We traced the errors to specific types of problems in ordinary language and then categorized them according to the cause of the problem. But the main point of this chapter is not how the fallacies are categorized but how they fail as arguments. The categories were constructed as a convenient way to organize and study them. The most important outcome is that you are able to recognize the fallacies and can trace the source of the error.

This next set of fallacies is loosely grouped together because their only error is that the premises are irrelevant to the conclusions. The language is generally clear, unambiguous, and lacks emotional appeals and stereotypes. The premises just don't support the conclusion.

BURDEN OF PROOF (APPEAL TO IGNORANCE)

Those of us who have watched hours of courtroom dramas on television are familiar with the phrase "the burden of proof is on the prosecution to establish its case." This rule of law follows from the principle that a person is innocent until proved guilty. It means that the legal system *requires* that the prosecution establish its case in the *affirmative* before it can even consider arguments in the negative. However, in ordinary, nonlegal contexts we do not place the strict requirement that we prove the positive side first (even though it is still a good strategy in critical thinking). That is, it would be more effective if you were able to present the *positive* reasons for your case rather than the negative reasons against your opponent's case first, but you are not restricted from establishing both sides and from presenting them in any order of sequence. In ordinary circumstances the burden of proof can be shared by both sides of the debate. The **burden of proof** asks only that you demonstrate how your side of the debate establishes the truth of its conclusions. By showing that the other side is false or lacks supporting evidence does not establish the truth of your position in the affirmative.

In other words, showing that the opposing premises lack merit does not prove that your position *does* have merit. Sometimes called the appeal to ignorance, it can be summarized as follows:

> Let 'c' be the conclusion and 'p' the premise.
> The premise 'p' has not been proved true.
> Therefore 'c', its opposite, is true.

For example, the fact that you are unable to prove that a merger at company x is being seriously considered because you cannot find any evidence for it does not prove (i.e., provide evidence) that it is not being considered. Nor does it prove that one is being considered. The absence of evidence means only that you simply don't know enough to make a judgment. The burden of proof, however, is on the arguer to provide the evidence for the impending merger.

Consider this frequently heard attack on television programming.

> There's no doubt that television violence is responsible for most crimes, especially juvenile crimes. Nothing else has changed in the last twenty years except that children watch too much TV, which is filled with violent actions. Otherwise, children are the same and there's no other explanation except for all that violence on TV.

To establish that television violence is a cause of juvenile crime requires *evidence in support* of the hypothesis. Stating that there is no other explanation to the contrary does not provide the evidence. The burden of proof is on the arguer to supply the research data connecting the two activities. The lack of contrary evidence commits the fallacy of appeal to ignorance (i.e., basing the argument on ignorance of opposing evidence). However, recent mounting evidence is beginning to establish this connection.

FALSE DILEMMA

Most decision making occurs in the context of choosing among alternative courses of action. A dilemma, by its very definition, presents us with a choice of action among at least two possible paths, sometimes involving difficult choices wherein both alternatives are bad. The fallacy of false dilemma arises when *all* relevant possibilities are not considered. In essence, there are more choices available to you than presented by the premises.

One version of the fallacy occurs when you are asked to consider only the extreme ends on both sides of an issue. For example, suppose you are discussing intelligence requirements for hiring qualified people for a specific entry level management position. Your colleague says, "We want only those people who score in the high nineties on the company's exam before we will hire them for the job; otherwise we will end up with a bunch of dummies." Obviously, there is quite a bit of ground between the extremes of top scorers and dummies. There must be other options that will satisfy the company's needs.

A slight variation of this "extreme ends" version of false dilemma arises when you are asked to accept polarizing positions. For example, the statements, "This is a great company. Love it or leave it," do not contribute to constructive discussions about your company's policies and actions. Once again, there is a great deal of middle ground between these extreme alternatives. However, in some cases you might agree with one of the extremes but disagree with the second extreme in seeking an alternative. Here is another example of the polarizing version.

> You don't support alternative schooling for your children? I didn't realize that you were such a conservative toward education.

The way this (loaded) question is posed forces you into a false dilemma. Either you are for alternative schooling or you are a conservative toward education, which are only a few among many perspectives toward education. In fact, you might agree with and accept the label "conservative" and still not support alternative schooling.

An example of a more sophisticated version occurs when faced with limited choices on a multiple choice survey. There may be other reasonable choices omitted from the possibilities offered, leaving only what appears to be weak or unacceptable choices. The most sophisticated cases occur when all alternatives appear to be reasonably true and the limitation on choices is not overtly expressed. Yet, on close examination it is revealed that more options are in fact available. Consider this fairly reasonable argument.

> I've heard that the treatment of part-time workers is becoming a real problem. I can't decide what to do about re-entering the workforce.

Consider the options when you apply for a job in this competitive job market. You can apply for a full-time job, with full benefits, full compensation, retirement packages, clear advancement opportunities, and other social niceties that go with full-time employment. On the other hand, you can choose part-time employment with limited health benefits, partial retirement benefits, few advancement opportunities, and fewer other perks granted to full-time employees. But part-time employment option allows me to choose if I want to stay home with my family or do more work in the community.

Now consider the alternatives at the end of the last sentence in the following direct quotation from *HR Magazine*.

The number and types of employer-provided benefits have increased steadily for the past few years as companies experiment with alternative ways to reward and retain workers.... Employers are having to rely more on people who work part-time or have non-traditional working arrangements. [1]

There may be more alternatives between nontraditional working arrangements and part-time employment, which are not enumerated in the passage in this example or in the preceding example. However, the article does go on to describe many of the creative ways companies are dealing with this issue and provides several other alternatives.

CIRCULAR ARGUMENTS (BEGGING THE QUESTION)

Technically, this fallacy does not fit neatly into any of our categories. The problem is that in circular arguments, the premises and the conclusion say essentially the same thing but in slightly different words. Because the premises and conclusions restate each other, the distinction between premises and conclusions is blurred. Hence, it is not entirely correct to say that the premises are irrelevant to the conclusion because they *are* the conclusion. So why are we calling it a fallacy at all?

A circular argument (**begging the question**) is a fallacy because, according to our definition of the term, it presents an argument in which the premises do not provide *grounds* for the truth of the conclusion—the primary purpose of arguments. The premises cannot provide such grounds because they are iterations of the conclusions.

The following examples of gender stereotyping form the foundation for two circular arguments.

> Women make the best secretaries because a female is better at clerical skills.

> Men rarely make good nurses because they are so unemotional.
> Thus, a male cannot empathize well with the emotions of patients.

In the first example, the premise states essentially the same thing as the conclusion. The words "women" and "females" and "secretarial" and "clerical" are nearly interchangeable. The premise conveys no *new* information in support of the conclusion. The same reasoning holds true of the second example.

Here is another explanation of the underlying problem with circular arguments. As in all arguments, the arguer tries to convince us that a conclusion is true because the premises provide grounds for it. However, if we accept the premises of a circular argument, we must also accept the conclusion because it states the same thing. Hence, we are back where we started with respect to establishing the truth of the conclusion. The very thing we are trying to prove is now offered as its own evidence.

Suppose you are trying to convince someone that the tax codes are unfair. You then cite passages of the code to support your conclusion, but the tax code is what is at issue in the first place. Its unfairness is established by different evidence, perhaps a different kind of evidence. You might use different passages in the code to show that the code is inconsistent or unclear, but fairness is not discussed in the document. That's a separate issue. It's like citing passages of the Bible (or other sacred text) to support your view that the Bible is correct about a moral issue. If the listener rejects the Bible as true in the first place, then further support from it probably will not convince him or her about its truth on moral issues. On the other hand, if the listener already accepts the Bible as true, then he or she does not need to be convinced of its veracity on moral issues. However, reference to excerpts from a sacred text could serve to *remind* the audience of what it actually says on that issue, that is, to bring it to our attention—but not as additional *proof* of its truth. If it is accepted at the outset, it is already proved true and accepted as given.

Here is another argument that begs the question.

> I don't think I manage my time well. Every year time seems to fly by faster and faster, and I get farther and farther behind. The faster time flies, the more it convinces me that I don't manage it well.

The conclusion of the argument states that the speaker does not manage time well. The reason for this conclusion is that the speaker is not managing his or her time.

EXERCISES

How would your revise the above argument so that it avoids circularity? Hint: the author is probably saying he or she needs advice *on time management.*

_____

_____

_____

_____

_____

_____

_____

_____

_____

_____

_____

_____

_____

_____

IRRELEVANT CONCLUSION (NON SEQUITUR ARGUMENTS)

This fallacy, like begging the question, is difficult to place in any one category. It may be seen as a "catchall" for fallacies because it contains any fallacy that doesn't clearly fit into one of the other categories. Because the other fallacies involve problems with relevance (but in one clearly identifiable way or another), they, too, are fallacies of relevance. But this category contains arguments that contain only one identifiable flaw—the premises are not relevant to the conclusion. Often called a "non sequitur" (nonsequence of ideas), this fallacy occurs because there is no direct link between the premises and the conclusion without supplying missing steps or demonstrating a direct connection. As the name implies, there is a "leap in judgment" or "gap in logic" between the premises and the conclusion. Most often, the premises are true and do support *some* conclusion, possibly a related one, but not this conclusion. When used as a diversionary tactic, irrelevant conclusions can be very convincing because the premises are true and the author confuses the reader by providing a scenario that loses him or her along the way. The tactic of misdirecting the discussion with reasonable but unrelated premises makes this fallacy difficult to detect.

Here is a non sequitur that is easily detected.

> The car pool isn't working out as well as I had hoped it would. Thus, the trains are the fastest method of transportation.

Obviously, the conclusion does not follow from the premises without a leap or gap in logic. You need to fill in the gap with relevant information to be able to draw this particular inference. Here's another argument requiring a leap from premise to conclusion.

> Look, I am all for environmental quality. But there ought to be a law that prevents Greenpeace from disrupting legitimate commerce.

The fact that the speaker is for environmental quality does very little to establish the conclusion about Greenpeace's methods.

Summary

IN THIS CHAPTER WE:

- Defined informal and formal fallacies

- Explored how fallacies are arranged in three categories associated with the cause of the error in reasoning: ambiguity, grouping, and relevance

Exercises

1. Critically assess both examples on pages 152–153 dealing with part-time employment issues. List other alternatives for resolving this issue.

2. Discuss a false dilemma you have faced recently at work or at home.

3. Create your own false dilemma in an effort to convince a coworker to accept your position.

4. Evaluate this bumper sticker.

   If gun laws were enforced, more criminals would be in jail.

TOPIC COVERED IN THIS CHAPTER

- Inductive reasoning contrasted with deductive reasoning

- Arguments by analogy

- Principles for evaluating analogical arguments

- Refutation by analogy

- Inductive generalizations

- Inductive arguments

- Problems in inductive reasoning

Chapter

8

INDUCTIVE ARGUMENTS

Scientific method is similar to the procedures of everyday life.
Given a problem, we search for data to help us solve it;
if a belief is questioned, we look for data to confirm or refute it.
In everyday life, however,
we rarely sift or scrutinize the data on which our
beliefs are based; we rarely make further conscious, explicit tests
to see if our beliefs are actually confirmed.
In science no theory is acceptable unless these conditions
have been satisfied."

– Maurice Mandelbaum, *Problems in Philosophy*[1]

Inductive Reasoning

Most of us accept unquestioningly statements such as "The crime rate in our city decreased by 10 percent," "Regular chiropractic care improves your immune system by 60 percent," "It must be the flu that's causing the dizziness," or "Big business is insensitive to the average consumer" (Figure 8-1). In everyday experience we encounter these assertions, and the arguments built on them, without much reflection. In this chapter we will take a closer look at these types of statements and develop a set of tools for evaluating them. In Chapter 9 we will establish strategies for constructing convincing inductive arguments based on credible evidence.

Inductive Arguments

In Chapter 7 we stated that the conclusion of deductive arguments follow from their premises with certainty. The premises provide evidence for the truth of their conclusions because the premises are assumed true. However,

FIGURE 8.1 *So much for percentages.*

we often accept many reasonably good and important arguments whose premises provide only *adequate* or *strong* evidence for their conclusion. In these cases, the conclusion is only *likely* or *probably* true. Even when the premises of inductive arguments are *obviously* true, the conclusions do not follow *necessarily* from the premises, unlike the conclusions in deductive arguments. Inductive arguments are assessed on the basis of their *strength or weakness, which varies in degrees*, rather than on their validity or invalidity, which does not vary in degrees.

Although we can assert with a *high level of confidence*, for example, that smoking causes cancer, we cannot claim that it does so with the same confidence we can of a valid, deductive argument, wherein the premises *entail* the conclusion. For example, we've all heard of the exception to the rule—the 90-year-old man who smoked like a chimney for fifty years and never contracted cancer. Based on the evidence we have, we may conclude that cancer and smoking are *causally linked*, but we cannot, as yet, conclude with the kind of certainty of deductive arguments that smoking causes cancer. Yet few of us would doubt the overwhelming evidence that smoking does cause cancer. One might say that the problem with deductive arguments is that they set a standard for certainty that cannot be met by many obviously well-supported and convincing inductive arguments. (In the next section we explain how an inductive argument can be transformed into a deductive argument.)

ARGUMENTS BY ANALOGY

Arguments by analogy are among the most common types of inductive arguments. Let's say, for example, that you want to convince someone that the skills learned for coaching a soccer team are similar to those for managing a small office. You need to learn and practice those skills before you can become proficient in them. You argue that a manager must teach cooperation among workers so they interact like a smooth running unit, you have to instill motivation and winning spirit, you have to provide leadership, and, like a coach, you have to determine who will merely participate and who will lead. In essence, you are arguing that the contexts for each are similar in relevant ways. The reasoning used in one case is appropriate and analogous for the other. In other words, you have provided an **argument by analogy**.

Another example of an argument by analogy is as follows. Suppose you are trying to convince someone that managing a household budget is basically no different from managing a department budget. Achieving the bottom line is accomplished in similar ways according to standard accounting practices and methods, except that the complexity and size of the budgets differ. Your argument establishes that because the methods and principles in each case are similar in relevant ways, balancing the family budget should accomplish similar results as balancing a department budget. Moreover, the analogy can be extended further by arguing that similar principles and methods can be used in balancing a corporate budget. Thus, you should expect similar results in that case as well. Of course, you must be careful not to "stretch" the analogy too much so that you would overlook important relevant differences that would override the similarities. The key is to focus on the analogies between relevant characteristics leading to the specific conclusion you are seeking.

Here is one more version of an inductive analogical argument. Your computer at work was connected recently to a new internal electronic mail system. Your office coworkers are equipped with similar computers and were connected to the system at the same time. The icons on their monitors become fuzzy whenever they log on to the system. You reason that because your computer is like your coworkers' computers, you will, therefore, experience the same problem.

> Premises: Your neighbors' images turn fuzzy when they log on. Your computer is like their computer.

> Conclusion: The images on your monitor screen will turn fuzzy when you log on.

You should distinguish an *argument by analogy* from a simple *comparison* or *simple statement asserting an analogy*. Analogical arguments go beyond a comparison by making an *inference* based on the similarity of the objects compared. Arguments by analogy also differ from explanations by analogy. Explanations by analogy take unfamiliar concepts or language and compare them to familiar concepts or language, making the original concept clearer to the reader. In these cases, you are not trying to *convince* the reader of some conclusion, only to make the ideas clearer. There is no further inference. To determine which are arguments and which are explanations, you use the same techniques learned in Chapter 5 for identifying all arguments—look for premise indicators like "since," "assume," and conclusion indicators like "therefore" and "thus." However, the methods for evaluating arguments by analogy (and all inductive arguments) are significantly different from evaluating other arguments you've examined so far.

The basic structure of an argument by analogy is as follows:

> A and B are similar.

> A has some property P.

> Therefore, B has that same property P.

A and B are two things being compared—similar computers in the same office, for example. The conclusion states that B has a certain property—fuzzy images on the monitor. The argument is that B has this property because it is similar to A. But notice that the conclusion does not follow in the same way a conclusion follows logically in other deductive arguments. The argument asserts only that A and B are *similar*, a crucial difference. Similarity is not enough, by itself, for us to infer with certainty that the conclusion will follow. Hence, there may be similarities that are irrelevant to the argument.

For example, it would be quite easy to find *some* similarity between two things, and infer any number of conclusions. You could try to prove that two cars should handle curves in the road in the same way simply because they are both white, an unconvincing argument at best. Or, your neighbor's computer images should turn fuzzy in the same way as yours simply because you both have blue mouse pads.

Note: An inductive argument can be converted to a deductive argument by claiming, for example, that all Brand x computer monitors turn fuzzy when connected to an e-mail system. This computer is a Brand x computer. Therefore, this computer's monitor will turn fuzzy when connected to the e-mail system. This version is a valid deductive argument.

Relevant Properties

As in a court of law, *relevance* is the all-important factor in establishing a conclusion in an analogical argument. In the road handling example above, the key element should be the *relevant ways* in which the two cars are alike. The more relevant ways in which the items compared are similar, the more confident you are in the conclusions drawn from the comparison. Color is simply not relevant to the ability to maneuver turns in a road. Nor is the color of a mouse pad relevant to the performance of the computer monitor. We'll discuss strategies for determining relevancy in more detail later in this section, but as you analyze an argument, make sure to ask, *in what ways* are the analogous items in the compared situations connected? Are the connections relevant so that the conclusion can be *inferred* from them?

EXERCISES

I. Identify which of the following are arguments by analogy, which are mere comparisons, and which are explanation by analogy.

1. "Kissing a smoker is like licking an ashtray" (billboard—U.S. Ad Council).

   _____

2. The office manager is like an angry hornet in the morning if he does not have his coffee.

   _____

3. Being a researcher is like being a miner—if you know where to dig and use the right tools, you'll strike gold.

   _____

4. "A good intuitive decision maker is like someone with a photographic memory. He has a gift."[2]

   _____

II. Analyze the following analogies by identifying the properties being compared. Then summarize the main point by identifying the premises and conclusion. Lastly, discuss whether this analogy is effective in establishing its conclusion.

1. Over the past year there have been a number of thefts of personal items locked in secure file cabinets. Eventually, police are called to assist in solving the crimes. They note that there have been thefts in another company in the same building and more thefts in an adjacent building. They further discover that the M.O. (method of operation)—the use of a specialized tool among other things—has been the same in all the cases. They search their records of other crimes to see if other criminals have used this method.

   _____

   _____

   _____

   _____

   _____

   _____

(continued)

2. There have been several cases of computer "hacking" in your company's e-mail system. The computer experts suggest that the cases are similar to the problems the large Internet companies have been experiencing with hackers. They reason that the solutions to the problems would be along similar lines as in the Internet cases.

_____

_____

_____

_____

_____

III. Construct your own argument by analogy from a situation at work. Identify clearly which characteristics are similar. Then describe how they are relevant to establishing its conclusion. List three factors that are irrelevant to the conclusion.

_____

_____

_____

_____

_____

_____

_____

_____

_____

_____

_____

Creating Analogies

There are times when analogical reasoning is an effective tool even when you are presented with contexts that are very *dissimilar*. In the preceding examples you were given contexts where the items compared were already related in various ways. However, analogies can be used in problem solving for many different situations and different contexts. For example, how many times have you said about an event that's happened at home, "I think that's just like the situation we have at work"(and vice versa)? Likewise, you would use an argument by analogy when you compare figuring out a schedule for car pooling children to school, after school events, to sporting events, or to friends' homes, with apparently dissimilar situations in scheduling training meetings or scheduling shipping routes for distribution of products at work. You *create* analogies in dissimilar events by showing that they do have at least *some* relevant properties in common. In doing so, you approach the problem from a familiar knowledge base and reason to a less familiar one, strengthening the analogy even more. Being creative in constructing analogies involves discovering or inventing similarities where there appears to be none. It may take some ingenuity to discern the analogy, but practicing these skills can help prepare you when such situations arise.

•••••••••••••••••••• EXERCISES ••••••••••••••••••••

1. Explain how developing a college curriculum is like creating your own road map. You know where you want to go, but you need to develop a strategy for getting there. Provide specific examples that draw on the similarities.

   _____

   _____

   _____

   _____

   _____

(continued)

2. Find two similarities where you used an analogy from work to solve a problem at home, with friends, or at some civic or recreational organization.

_____

_____

_____

_____

_____

3. Create an argument by analogy comparing the administration of a volunteer organization with ten support staff with managing the secretarial pool in a company office with ten support staff.

_____

_____

_____

_____

_____

Some Principles in Evaluating Analogical Arguments

THE LARGER THE NUMBER OF ENTITIES BEING COMPARED, THE STRONGER THE ARGUMENT

In other words, the larger the sample size, the stronger the argument, provided all the members of the sample group have the property in question. This follows common sense reasoning. The more items and times you compare objects that are alike with respect to some property, the more confident you will be that the next item similar to it will have that property in question.

For example, suppose you are interested in purchasing a new style of keyboard for your computer. If your experience is with just two keyboards, you might be disappointed in the next one you try that is like it. It may have a different touch, a different arrangement of special functions, and so on. However, if you have tried several dozen similar keyboards from the same manufacturer, and they all responded in the same way, you will be more confident that the next one like it will perform in the same way. Put simply, as in comparison shopping, the more items you try on, the better the results.

THE GREATER THE NUMBER OF SIMILARITIES AMONG THE ENTITIES COMPARED, THE STRONGER THE ARGUMENT

In other words, the more *ways* in which the items are alike, the more confidence you will have in the conclusions drawn from the comparisons, and the stronger the argument. If the entities have many other similarities among the objects compared in addition to the ones you are interested in, the more likely they will be similar in the property you are testing for.

For example, you are going to purchase a new packaging and labeling machine for a new plant. Speed and the ability to print labels of various sizes are extremely important to you. You examine several machines from various companies and discover one with similar size, weight, and overall construction. It has the capacity to package the same number of items with the same speed, accepts the same size packages, and uses the same type of inks. You reason that if the salesperson says it is also capable of printing the same variety or more varieties of labels, you are likely to believe her based on all the other similarities. Given the number of ways they are similar, it is likely the new machine will be similar in the specific characteristic you want it to be.

THE GREATER THE DIVERSITY IN YOUR SAMPLE, THE STRONGER THE ARGUMENT

Here we are concerned with studying a class of entities where the entities compared are *dissimilar* in many ways yet share the property in question. You could argue that even though they are dissimilar, they still are analogous with respect to *this* property. You will then have greater confidence in the property they do share.

For example, let's suppose that two political parties disagree significantly on nearly every major ideological issue except one. They agree on the need for a restrictive clean air policy. The fact that they disagree on so many important issues (i.e., their policies are dissimilar) and agree on this one, is a good reason to believe that this point is extremely important to both parties. You can have a great deal of confidence that the policy will receive strong support based on their differences as well as their agreement in this case.

THE NARROWER YOUR CONCLUSION, THE EASIER IT IS TO ESTABLISH ITS TRUTH

This, too, follows from common sense and from what was discussed in Chapter 4 with respect to "hedging your bets." It is easier to conclude to a smaller number of properties than to a multitude of properties. There are many more valid argument forms with particular conclusions than with universal ones. In inductive reasoning, it is easier to establish that *some* objects have the property in question than it is to argue that *all* or *most* objects have the property in question. Conversely, it is more difficult to *disprove* an argument with the narrower conclusion because the narrower conclusion asserts less than a general conclusion asserts.

For example, suppose that you have been working as a member of a management quality team in a company location for the past several months. The team has worked extremely well in assuring quality control. The company then decided to expand this approach throughout all its domestic locations, which has also resulted in increased productivity and worker satisfaction. The company expects to continue expanding this approach for its overseas locations next year. You reason that if these locations are similar to yours, the program probably will work successfully. However, if you reason that *all* locations will work equally well based only on your experience, the argument will be more difficult to establish. It is easier to say that it will work in some or many locations than saying it will work in all locations. The latter requires a stronger argument, which would establish a *causal link* between the two events. A causal statement asserts more than an inductive connection and requires additional support for its verification. Causal arguments are the subject matter of Chapter 9.

Refutation by Analogy

An additional tool in your collection of critical thinking strategies is the refutation by analogy. Suppose you are presented with a fairly convincing inductive argument but you have serious doubts about the truth of its conclusion. One strategy for confirming your doubts is to construct a counterargument with essentially the same overall design as the argument you want to refute. You know that your counterargument is seriously flawed; you already know the conclusion is false or highly improbable. Your strategy is to argue that the argument you want to attack is similarly flawed, thus casting doubt on your opponent's argument. It is like saying, "your argument is like this one, which is undoubtedly flawed. Thus, there must be something wrong with *your* argument." In politics, economics, science, and everyday experience, we often use refutation by analogy when the premises of an argument appear convincing but the conclusion appears false.

Here is an example of a refutation by analogy.

> Your friend says that the company is inconsiderate to its employees because it does not allow her to smoke anywhere in the building. She believes that she has a basic right to do what she wants with her body even if it is harmful to herself as long as it is not harmful to anyone else. The company should provide at least one location where she can smoke and does not bother others.

You can respond as follows.

> Asking the company to provide a location so you can engage in harmful activity to yourself is like asking the company to provide a location for anyone who believes they have a right to drink alcohol on the premises. As long as I am of legal age and it is done in moderation so that it does not harm anyone else or my performance, the company should provide me with space to drink legally.

EXERCISES

Construct a refutation by analogy of the following argument.

Professor Mach of Harvard University argues that the stories of alien abductions in the United States are so frequent there must be some truth to them. He claims that the number of reports that are so similar in content far exceed normal statistical acceptability of accidental or coincidental reporting. He states that the people reporting the abductions can't all be having such similar delusions; it's not statistically valid.

_____

_____

_____

_____

_____

Concluding Remark on the Importance of Analogies

To appreciate the importance of analogical reasoning, just consider the study of history. We often reason that because the events of the past are *similar* to current events, we should be able to better explain what is happening now and better predict what is going to happen in the future. And if we can change certain features of our present condition (make them dissimilar) we should be able to avoid past mistakes in the future. Here, too, we must be careful to relate the *relevant* aspects of history to the point we want to make about present and future events.

For example, we learned from past experience that taking for granted a competitor in the world economy can lead to disastrous results. This happened with the so-called Japanese total quality management model, which had been discussed in America before the Japanese adopted it. The model led to great successes in the global marketplace for the Japanese. Learning from this experience, American companies now take seriously potential competitor management and marketing models before dismissing them because of their source.

Inductive Generalizations

Inductive generalizations may be divided into two types: generalizations about entire groups and generalizations about partial groups. Let's consider universal generalizations (statements about entire groups) first.

GENERALIZATIONS: ENTIRE GROUPS

It is an easy step from making analogical inferences based on similarities to make general statements about members of a whole class, even if you have not actually observed every member of the class. For example, you can claim that all workers employed by the government earn at least the federal minimum wage without meeting every federal employee. Statements that refer to all members of a group or class are **generalizations**; the reasoning based on these generalizations are **inductive generalizations**. In essence, we are saying that if part of a class has a certain property, the employees we observe for example, then the entire class (probably) has that property.

Here is a sample inductive argument based on inductive generalizations:

> Premise: Every line employee I have met so far in an auto assembly plant belongs to the United Auto Workers union.

> Conclusion: Therefore, all line employees of the assembly plant are members of the union. Furthermore, the next line employee of the assembly plant I will meet will most certainly be a member of the U.A.W.

This claim can be transformed into a definition if we restrict all employees who can work in the plant to union members only. Known as a "closed shop," no nonunion employees can work in the plant. Thus, the inductive generalization becomes a statement true by definition.

GENERALIZATIONS: PARTIAL GROUPS

Not every inductive generalization will result in concluding that *all* members of a group share a property in common. You could reason that based on the samples you have observed, most, many, or a certain percentage will have that property. Let's say, for example, that you survey several employees about their choice for purchasing a new copying machine. The people you spoke to said they preferred one type over another, but you did not get a chance to ask all the employees in your department. You conclude that most will prefer this copier. The generalization allows you to go beyond particular experiences to make inferences about groups, parts of groups, and future events. You can state with confidence that most people prefer this machine and, therefore, you should purchase it.

When you use inductive reasoning to reach a general conclusion about a portion of a group, one that is stated as a percentage, the term *statistical generalization* applies. This type of generalization is common not only in scientific reasoning but in popular presses, advertising, opinion polls, and other areas, particularly where it is impossible or impractical to study the entire group.

FIGURE 8.2 *"Fudging" the data is a practice occurring all too often in scientific investigations, including political investigations. (Cartoon from B.C. By permission of Johnny Hart and Creators Syndicate, Inc.)*

EXERCISES

Evaluate the following statistical generalizations:

1. Studies show that the immune system improves by 60 percent with regular chiropractic care.

_____

_____

2. New Spray 409® now has 50 percent more free in each family size bottle.

_____

_____

3. Nearly 80 percent of all of the U.S. economy is controlled by 5 percent of the people.

_____

_____

4. Seventy percent of all men prefer blondes.

_____

_____

5. Ninety percent of all women prefer sensitive men.

_____

_____

6. Three out of four mechanics who use commercial oils prefer Pennzoil®.

_____

_____

7. An accident involving a car equipped with side airbags is 30 percent less likely to result in a fatality.

_____

_____

GENERALIZATIONS AS PREMISES

Although inductive arguments do not guarantee certainty, inductive *generalizations* often form the premises on which many deductive arguments are based. In deductive arguments the truth or falsity of the premises was already given; you did not need to conduct an investigation in order to establish or confirm their truth-values. However, establishing the truth-values of premises is the focus of this chapter and Chapter 9. The reliability of inductive statements is a matter of empirical investigation, the foundation of inductive reasoning. Empirical investigations rely on observation, experimentation, and testing. The primary purpose of inductive arguments is to verify the truth of the conclusion to the highest degree of reliability possible. Those conclusions, once taken as true, can also become premises in deductive arguments. Without extending our knowledge by inductive reasoning, you would not be able to make the inferences about people, events, and values, or the ideas that result from generalizations. Nor would you be able to ensure that your deductive arguments rest on true premises. The following are helpful strategies for developing credible inductive arguments.

SELECTING THE SAMPLE: DEFINING THE PROBLEM

One of the first steps in problem solving using inductive reasoning is to *define* the problem clearly. As we discussed in Chapter 3, a good definition will limit the scope of the subject matter about which you will generalize. Defining the problem involves making precise decisions on the population, the target, and the means by which you want to study them. Here you are concerned primarily with *how* you characterize the group or items you want to examine.

By limiting the group you want to study, excluding the members who are irrelevant and including all the members you want to study, it will be easier to formulate a strategy for gathering the relevant evidence. Unfortunately, there is no hard and fixed rule or percentage for deciding relevancy, which will allow you to limit the study. However, one way to test for relevancy is to be sure that the relationships you do establish between entities are *connected to the conclusion* in a way that they *directly support it*. You should ask, "does this evidence and these connections lend further support to the conclusion?" As discussed in Chapter 7, Fallacies of Relevance, the important question is whether *these data* provide evidence for *this* conclusion? Can you *infer* each piece of evidence from the evidence available? Can you *infer* the conclusion from the data presented?

Some might argue that the quote at the beginning of this chapter by Maurice Mandelbaum, particularly the statement about scrutinizing the evidence, may have summarized a great deal of the field of critical thinking. You might say that critical thinking amounts to little more than being careful in analyzing the data on which your arguments rest and then determining if the conclusions follow logically from these data. This may be an oversimplification, but it is an important point to remember for all aspects of critical thinking.

BIASED GENERALIZATIONS: CONSIDERING OTHER POINTS OF VIEW

One way to avoid bias in inductive reasoning is to look for counterexamples or disconfirming instances. If we base our conclusions on our own experience and only search for positive cases, those will probably be the only ones we find. To avoid this kind of bias, look for cases that might *disprove* your conclusion as well.

As with the importance of considering disanalogies, considering other points of view and other disconfirming evidence strengthens the argument. If you can show that you have considered other options and apparently contradictory evidence, your argument will be more convincing.

Using these strategies should also enable you to recognize bias in other arguers' positions. Have they thoroughly considered other views, *including yours*? Have they taken into account possible contradictory views? Do they have a vested interest in establishing the conclusion? (See also "objectivity" in Chapter 1.)

HASTY GENERALIZATION

Hasty generalization leads to fallacious reasoning by treating a single instance or few instances as a general rule. When you conclude that all assembly line workers are paid hourly salaries based on your experience with one or very few assembly line workers, you would be committing the fallacy of hasty generalization. All you need to do to disprove this claim is to provide one counterexample of an assembly line worker who is paid by the number of products he or she assembles.

ANECDOTAL EVIDENCE

An *anecdote* is defined as a short personal story or reference to a personal experience, often given as an example of something interesting that's happened to you or someone you know. In the context of inductive reasoning, you should be cautious of anecdotes given as *evidence* to support an inductive generalization. **Anecdotal evidence** in the form of personal "testimonials" based only on personal observations can lead to both biased and hasty generalizations.

An example of its negative use is as follows.

> "I don't care what the American Management Association says about the level of education needed for success in the business world. I hear Bill Gates of Microsoft doesn't even have a college degree. Who needs an education? They can't prove it to him or to me that you need an education."

An example of its use to develop a positive generalization is, "I hear that packaging color dramatically affects consumer choices. Boys prefer certain colors, and girls prefer others. This must be true because my niece and her sister always pick lavender for their toys."

Figure 8-3 shows a schematic representation of inductive reasoning process.

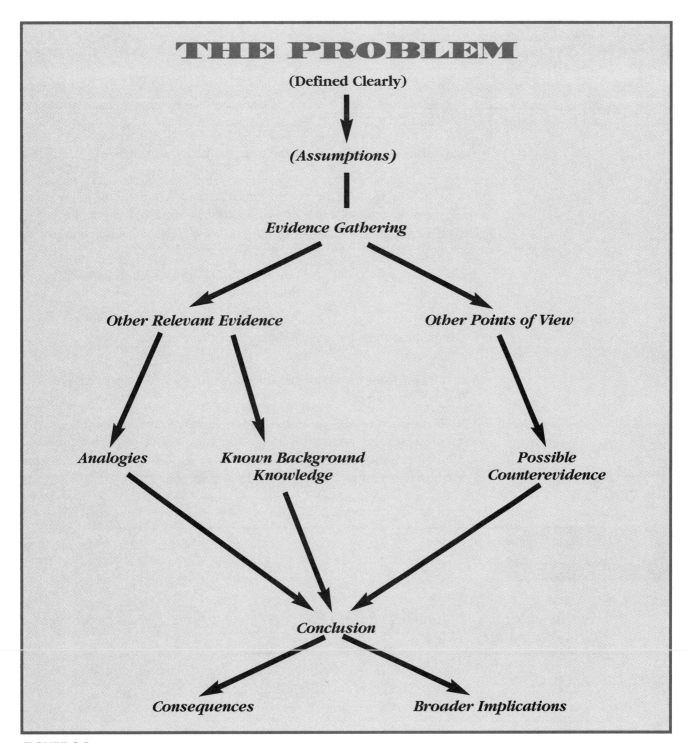

FIGURE 8.3

Summary

IN THIS CHAPTER WE:

- Distinguished inductive reasoning from deductive reasoning

- Stated that the truth of the conclusions of inductive arguments follow from their premises with a degree of probability. The truth of the conclusions of deductive arguments follows from the premises with absolute certainty.

- Examined a variety of applications for arguments by analogy and refutations by analogy

- Described methods for evaluating analogical arguments

- Transitioned from analogical arguments to inductive generalizations and inductive arguments

- Presented several strategies for evaluating inductive arguments and described three common flaws in inductive reasoning: biased generalizations, hasty generalizations, and anecdotal evidence

Exercises

I. Identify which of the following contain hasty generalizations, biased generalizations, or anecdotal evidence.

1. Let's buy our software off the Internet. We bought it at Software.com before and it was cheaper than the department stores. Come to think of it, we should buy all our equipment off the Internet because it will be cheaper.

2. You know, we should really jump in on the NASDAQ market. It's been up several hundred points over the last few years. You can't miss with that track record. Let's invest now.

3. If you think Californians are laid back, just try getting directions in a hurry from someone from Iowa. Most people we know from Iowa have that slow country drawl. I'll bet this couple from Des Moines will take at least ten minutes to give us directions.

4. We've traveled to Europe a lot. Our group always meets up with some Australians. You can always count on seeing some Aussies on any trip. They travel more than any other group of people.

5. I think Darlene is one of the best supervisors in the company. I know a few of them, and I think she's great. She's got to be better than the others, take my word.

6. Scientists have shown that women are better listeners than men. So if you want to see a counselor, see a woman counselor.

7. A 56 gigabyte drive is the fastest we have here. However, it is also the largest machine we have. Thus, all fast machines must be quite large.

8. We surveyed nearly 200 managers in the central offices in the suburban New York City area and most of them were Republicans. I guess that most people in this company are voting Republican this fall.

9. I have personally witnessed at least three minor accidents with this shredding equipment. You can't tell me most of them aren't defective.

10. The report on the "Today Show" said a lot of people who live in California are health fanatics. They surveyed over 800 people on the beaches of Malibu and nearly 60 percent said they rarely eat meat due to health reasons. I always thought Californians liked to live the healthy lifestyle.

11. I know at least ten people who are health enthusiasts myself. I think that most people in this country are leaning toward healthy lifestyles.

12. It seems that women who work and take care of young children are more likely to be stressed out. They seem more stressed out than women who work and go to school. You can just ask the two women in this office. One goes to school and one has three kids at home.

13. I am not particularly crazy about our new boss. Every time he arrives early in the morning he waits until someone else makes coffee. He won't make a move himself. I think he tends to be a bit on the lazy side.

14. Homeowners take better care of their homes than do people who rent.

15. In countries with a democracy, people are allowed to earn more money than in countries with dictatorships.

16. Women are always looking for a new place to shop.

17. Men are always looking for one thing.

18. Foreign cars are really very good on gas. Just look at some of those new Japanese and Korean models. I'll bet that next foreign car you buy will be good on gas.

19. Accidents are usually preventable.

20. The new secretary makes sure she takes every minute of her break time. She never comes back a second early. I guess most secretaries do that nowadays.

21. During the summer it is really hard to find more than a few bosses in their offices. Most are out on the golf course supposedly conducting business. I guess that most "big wigs" do that nowadays.

Writing from Experience

1. Locate a written report you submitted for a college class or a written report for a project at work.

a) Identify at least three generalizations you advance as conclusions in your report.

b) Reread your report carefully to look for hasty generalizations, biased generalizations, or anecdotal evidence. Rewrite those sections so that they avoid these errors.

c) Identify any analogies used as premises in arguments and then summarize any analogical arguments you advanced in the report. How could you improve those arguments? If there are no arguments by analogy, then show how you would improve the main argument.

d) In general, how would you strengthen your report by using the techniques discussed in this chapter?

TOPIC COVERED IN THIS CHAPTER

• The importance of understanding causal relationships

• Necessary and sufficient conditions

• The difference factor

• The common factor

• Levels of analysis

• Combined common and difference factors

• Factors among groups

• Scientific reasoning

• Some common fallacies

• Causal Laws

• Criteria for evaluating scientific reasoning

Chapter

9

CAUSAL REASONING

*Facts are stupid things, until brought into connection
with some general law.*

– LOUIS AGASSIZ, AS QUOTED BY NORMAN COUSINS

Suppose you notice that you've been feeling unusually tired lately and the feeling occurs only when a full moon appears in the evening sky. You wonder if this is just a coincidence. Could the moon really cause you to feel tired? You ask, "Do other people feel this way when a full moon appears?" "Do scientists have any evidence about the moon's gravitational pull on the earth, and is its relation to changes in the electrochemical activity in the human body causing these feelings?" "Is there really a pattern here or am I imagining a connection?" Or, "is all this schoolwork combined with working at home and at my job finally getting to me?" In seeking answers, you are looking for a **causal relationship** that would explain your periodic tiredness (Figure 9-1).

Questions such as: How did I catch this nasty cold? Why is my coworker so testy lately? How can I create an atmosphere at work that will cause people to be more motivated? Why is the department down the hall less (or more) productive than the other departments? What is causing that annoying sound when my car exceeds 50 miles per hour? All attempt to establish a connection that would explain how one set of events brings about (i.e., causes) some other set of events. Understanding causal relationships is central to our daily lives.

However, causality can be a difficult concept to define. Just what do we mean when we say that two events or objects are causally connected? What does it mean to say that the properties of an object are related to properties of another such that one set should *always* follow the other? In trying to understand our physical and social environment, the behavior of people, and the processes that occur within it, we are looking for knowledge of underlying causal connections. These connections yield a fuller understanding of the world around us and allow for reliable predictability of how events should occur in the future.

In Chapter 8, we were concerned with identifying connections, patterns, and analogies among characteristics, which allowed us to form generalizations about current and future events. But the kinds of questions above seek stronger connections that go beyond mere inductive generalizations. In this chapter, we will examine the specific requirements for causal statements and assess the arguments that are offered in support of them.

FIGURE 9.1 *If the moon can have such a huge affect on an entire ocean, I wonder what affect it can have on humans?*

Causal Relationships: Necessary and Sufficient Conditions

We will begin with the definition of two concepts that will help explain the relation between cause and effect: necessary and sufficient conditions.

When an event must be present before another event can occur, the first event is called a **necessary condition** of the second event. In other words, its absence would prevent another event from occurring. For example, you will probably remember from your old science classes that the presence of oxygen is a necessary condition for combustion to occur. If oxygen were absent, there would be no combustion. However, the presence of oxygen is not the *only* condition that must be met. Oxygen alone is not sufficient for combustion. You also need to reach a specific temperature relevant to other conditions (e.g., a temperature high enough to create a spark) and, of course, combustible materials. Each of these necessary conditions must be met before you can say that you have **sufficient conditions** for the occurrence of the desired event, combustion.

Compare this example with another case of conditional reasoning. Let's say that promotion to a management position within a department depends on meeting specific conditions. Some of these conditions are required (i.e., they are necessary) before you can enter the applicant pool of candidates for the job. When enough necessary conditions are met, you are *eligible* to receive the promotion and be placed in the candidate pool. Hence, you have sufficiently met all the basic (i.e., necessary) criteria for promotion. That is, you've met the sufficient conditions.

The following could be considered necessary conditions:

- A minimum of five years in your current position

- A rating of "very good" or higher on each of your performance evaluations

- Satisfactory completion of three out of four management training seminars

- A recommendation from your immediate supervisor supporting your application with a rating of "highly recommend" or higher

- Ability and willingness to travel to other sites as needed

If all the necessary conditions are met, then you are sufficiently qualified to apply for promotion to manager. Now suppose also that there is a set of conditions that are considered "desirable" for promotion. These conditions are neither necessary (you *can* be promoted without them) nor sufficient (it is possible that you will *not* be promoted even if you did have all of them). For example, it might be desirable for candidates to be willing to work some weekends and some evenings. It might also be desirable for candidates to be familiar with a certain software program for spreadsheets, even though the skill can be learned on the job. However, the promotion will not *depend* on these factors. Willingness to work weekends and evenings, and familiarity with certain software programs, are *optional* conditions, that is, additional considerations once the other conditions are met. But if you did not receive a "very good" performance rating, a necessary condition, then you cannot be considered for promotion. And if you do not meet all of the necessary conditions together, you cannot receive the promotion.

The concept of causality is sometimes used in the sense of necessary conditions, sometimes in the sense of sufficient conditions. When used in these ways, the conditions are said to bring about (cause) the subsequent events. For example, suppose you are investigating the cause of low production output in a manufacturing department that occurs only during certain time frames during the year. If you find the cause, you believe you can eliminate the problem. You reason that you need to first determine the most obvious factors that are directly and necessarily connected to production in that department. Through the process of elimination, you determine that each of the following necessary conditions is being satisfactorily met: the staffing is at maximum levels, vacation schedules don't conflict with production deadlines, the equipment is working properly, the employees are carrying out their responsibilities efficiently, and so forth. However, you later discover that during peak periods for one of your suppliers of raw materials, important items are delivered later than scheduled. The delay occurs concurrently with high demand times for the department in question. The total amount of material delivered over the course of routine quarterly inventories remains the same, but there are lags in delivery during certain production periods. You reason that the low level of raw materials during peak demand is the cause of the problem. The smooth flow of raw materials is a *necessary* condition for satisfactory production levels; its absence would cause the problem of low production to occur. Now you have a strategy to address the problem. You might alter your production schedule to better suit the supplier or ask the supplier to deliver the product in larger quantities at non-peak times or other possible tactics. The main point is that your reasoning is an example of causal analysis based on necessary conditions.

Now suppose you are *not* trying to determine a cause by identifying necessary conditions and eliminating undesirable ones, but attempting to determine factors that would *improve* production beyond its current satisfactory levels. You could use causal analysis of *sufficient* conditions. In this case, all the necessary conditions are met, but there are other sufficient conditions that you believe could improve the situation even though they are not optional for doing so. (This type of analysis involves future-oriented reasoning instead of past-oriented reasoning.) That is, you want to *create* something desirable rather than *eliminate* something undesirable.

Let's say, for example, that you want to develop a more efficient communication system between the main office and outlying satellite offices even though no one has complained about the system so far and no glitches have been reported. You assume that the necessary conditions have been met for normal communications. However, your telecommunications expert informs you that increased bandwidth and improved hardware used in communication lines result in faster communication of electronic data. In terms of necessary and sufficient conditions, the increased bandwidth is a cause of faster communication. It is a sufficient condition that is added to or is replacing existing conditions in the form of new equipment that *suffices* for the production of faster communication.

Having defined causality in terms of necessary and sufficient conditions, we can now infer a cause from an effect in the sense of necessary conditions and infer an effect from a cause in the sense of sufficient conditions. When we make inferences in both directions, we should understand "cause" in the sense of both necessary and sufficient conditions.

You will note that in the examples above, the conclusions, like most statements expressing causal relations, are expressed in terms of *degrees of probability*, either explicitly or implicitly. You conclude that, "A is the probable cause of B," even if you are nearly certain of the relationship. In this sense, causal reasoning is a form of inductive reasoning. In fact, it is an extension and specific application of inductive reasoning. Thus, causal inferences will always contain an essential element of *generality and probability*. The evidence you gather constitutes the premises of a causal argument, and the causal relationships you infer based on that evidence constitute the conclusions. The important point is that causal relationships are discovered through experience, one event at a time, through inductive methods.

One reason that the statements are expressed as probabilities is that there may be necessary or sufficient conditions that we simply do not know about or are not clever or creative enough to identify. Or, the conditions may be so remote that they would not occur to anyone as causally related to some specific effect. Because the premises are expressed in terms of empirical statements and the causal arguments built on them are inductive, the conclusions do not follow from the premises with the same degree of certainty as they did in deductive arguments.

The Difference Factor

A third sense of causality is used when discovering the precise action, event, or incident that was the **prevailing factor** among the necessary and sufficient conditions that made the difference between the occurrence or nonoccurrence of an event. This is called the **difference factor**. Suppose that you

EXERCISES

Identify the necessary and sufficient conditions in a causal analysis of the following example:

1. In the past three months there has been a slowdown in production due to a significant number of breakdowns in the printing machines that produce packaging labels. The machines are fairly new and maintained by the night maintenance staff. The day shift workers are experienced employees who are very familiar with operating the machines properly.

   _____

   _____

   _____

   _____

   _____

2. Reconsider the example of low production in the department experiencing periodic delays in delivery of materials. Can you think of at least two other possible factors that could have led to low production? Which, if any, of these factors are necessary and which are sufficient?

   _____

   _____

   _____

   _____

   _____

3. The most recent Congress is debating what is causing the increase in the federal deficit. Some argue it is the high spending practices of liberals, whereas others argue it is the overzealous tax cutting of conservatives. The bottom line is that spending exceeds revenues—both are conditions that contribute to the deficit. If tax revenues increase, the deficit is reduced if spending stays the same. If spending decreases, the deficit is reduced if tax revenue stays the same.

(continued)

Analyze how this debate can be made clearer by explaining the problem in terms of necessary and sufficient causes.

_____

_____

_____

_____

_____

4. Analyze the following quote from Bruce Kimbal[1]: "The pursuit of truth is a necessary educational ideal; but not a sufficient one."

_____

_____

_____

_____

_____

are again investigating the cause of an undesirable event. Let's say, for example, that you are trying to determine why your VCR suddenly started buzzing each time a videotape is inserted in the machine. You remember that you used it last weekend, and it worked fine. Since then, your children were the only ones who used it to tape a favorite television show. Shortly after they used it the buzzing noise started. You reason that something they did while taping the show must have caused the buzzing. Your preliminary analysis assumes that the only relevant *difference* between the occurrence and nonoccurrence of the buzzing is the children's taping.

In summary, your reasoning is as follows:

Event B occurred (the buzzing), which is the effect of some unknown cause, A. You know that there were other occasions when B was absent (i.e., when the buzzing was absent). The only difference between the two occasions is A. In comparing the two situations, you reason that A caused B.

Reasoning by the difference factor is a common and effective method used not only in scientific analysis but in ordinary forms of reasoning as well. But there are always cautions in any kind of inductive reasoning. The old adage, "don't jump to conclusions" is an appropriate caution. In this example, the preliminary investigation could miss other factors that could cause the buzzing. We can get quite imaginative here, but it is fairly safe to say that the children are the most probable cause. The key to this type of analysis is to try to gain assurance within reasonable certainty that you have identified the *only* relevant difference. Remember, although this type of reasoning is practical, it is not a fail safe. It is possible to think of other possible causes, no matter how remote they might be, that could have caused the effect. Depending on how in-depth you want the analysis to go, critically assessing other factors before accepting this one is the only safeguard against superficial or incomplete analyses. After all, before blaming the kids, you could try to determine whether a malfunction within the machine itself caused by normal wear could have caused the problem. It is *possible* that the malfunction just happened to occur when you used it.

The Common Factor

As with the difference factor, isolating a **common causal factor** among many other possible causal factors takes a bit of detective work and critical thinking. In these cases, you are looking for the *one* factor or circumstance that is *constantly associated* with the effect under investigation. In your search for a cause you pursue some special event or set of events that is always present when the effect occurs. The shared characteristics or instances are called the common factor. You should ask, "What events are present that invariably result in the effect under investigation?" "What factor remained constant throughout the event among several possible factors?"

This type of reasoning is often the first line of attack in scientific reasoning. To take a relatively simple example, suppose one of your coworkers became ill after returning from the company cafeteria. Your immediate reaction is to inquire whether she or he ate lunch there. Second, you might ask if other people who also ate lunch in the cafeteria suddenly became ill. If the answer is "yes" to both questions, you begin to form a *causal generalization* (a causal *hypothesis*), which relates eating lunch in the cafeteria with the illness. Eating lunch in the cafeteria is isolated as a common factor. The more people you find who ate there and became ill, the more *confirming instances* you have that eating in the cafeteria is the common factor possibly causing the problem. Once this is determined, you should investigate further to ascertain what specific item in the cafeteria caused the illness. You would inquire as to what specific items *all* of them ate. If it turns out that each person who became ill ate something different, then there is no one thing in common, and you begin to look elsewhere for the cause besides the food. Perhaps the drinking fountain in the cafeteria, the utensils, plates, or glasses, are the source of the problem. On the other hand, if all of them ate *one common item* (the seafood salad, for example), you begin to establish a more specific causal connection.

Of course, it may turn out later that the seafood salad was served with a garnish that had not been properly washed and it was the common causal factor. Or more specifically, it turns out that the mayonnaise used in the seafood salad was contaminated with bacteria. Nonetheless, the line of reasoning is the same; you are looking for a common cause. The detective work involves making sure that the common factor is the *only* common factor before you blame the seafood distributor or cafeteria staff. And, you need to be careful not to assume a common factor is involved when none actually exists. Once again, critical thinking involves digging deeper, going beyond first conclusions, and questioning assumptions. Most important, it involves looking at the problem from several angles and perspectives to include all the possibilities.

Levels of Analysis

Just how far you carry out the causal analysis depends on several factors, including the kind of information available to you, the tools available for gathering information, background knowledge, and, of course, the amount of time available and needed to conduct the investigation. But the most important factor is your *purpose or goal* in carrying out the investigation. For example, you can probe more deeply into the investigation about your coworkers' illness by identifying the precise properties of the mayonnaise that caused the exact reaction in each individual. Let's say you identify various strains of bacteria, isolate which ones caused the specific type of reaction in the employees in question, and then investigate the specific biochemical changes in the body. The level of analysis is determined by the goals of your inquiry. If you don't need to know more about the tainted mayonnaise, such as which bacterium caused the illness and how it reacts with certain antibodies, then your investigation may be complete. However, it is possible but unlikely that all people who ate seafood are allergic to shellfish, which was used in the seafood salad, and no bacteria were present in the mayonnaise.

Combined Difference and Common Factors

Because each of the methods discussed so far yields some degree of probability, *combining* them in one investigation should yield an even higher degree of probability, leading to more accurate results and reliability. Let's suppose, for example, that when you return home from vacation you find that one of your ceiling fans is not working. You set out to investigate the cause of the problem. Your first line of inquiry is to determine if any other electrical appliances in the home are not working properly, beginning with the room in which the fan is located. You notice that two other electrical appliances in the room failed, but the remaining electrical outlets and appliances work properly in this room and in the rest of the house. Further investigation shows that all three appliances use the same electrical circuit. The commonality of all three malfunctioning in the same room on the same circuit, however, does hold some promise for suggesting a probable cause. The first logical candidate, the circuit breakers, turns out to be a dead end. Close inspection shows that all of the circuit breakers feeding those lines are functioning properly. You then remember that the appliances in question were installed by your brother-in-law. All the other appliances were installed by a licensed electrician. The only difference between the working units and the three units in question is the installer. You have isolated a possible common cause and identified differences. By using both methods in conjunction, the reliability of your analysis is enhanced, even if you know very little about electricity.

However, to achieve the kind of thoroughness required of critical thinkers, particularly in more complex cases, you may also need to repeat the testing procedures several times until you are satisfied that you have properly identified the causes. You might use one of the methods or both over and again until you locate the most probable factors. For example, in the early seventies several people became ill while attending a conference for the American Legion in Philadelphia. Later called Legionnaire's disease, the cause of the illness was elusive. Several tentative causes were identified but were dismissed as contributing factors. After numerous *repetitions* of the methods discussed above, and more detective work, testing, imaginative reasoning, and hypothesizing, it was determined that a microbe, rickettsia, had been airborne in the ventilation system in the conference center where the Legionnaires held their meetings. It took dozens of scientists and several months of investigation to reach the conclusion that the microbe was the cause. The point is that, depending on the level of analysis required, a single application of these methods may be inadequate for identifying a cause and effect relationship.

EXERCISES

1. Let's say, for example, that you are investigating a potential leak in confidential information in your twelve-person office. Detailed personnel data were discussed at a recent staff meeting, which should have remained confidential. However, everyone at the meeting believed that because the information was available, the information was no longer private.

    a) Identify the probable cause of the leak by using a common factor analysis.

    _____

    _____

    b) Identify the probable cause of the leak by using the difference factor analysis.

    _____

    _____

    c) Identify the probable cause of the leak by using the combined method.

    _____

    _____

    d) Which factors in your deliberation were necessary conditions for a successful analysis?

    _____

    _____

2. Suppose you own a distribution company and you want to improve the effectiveness of your operations by decreasing the costs in three areas: highway use tolls, time on the road for drivers, and secretarial support needed to track deliveries. List five factors that you would consider necessary and sufficient to improve your operations.

    _____

    _____

    _____

    _____

    _____

3. Sharon came down with a cold on Friday. On Monday, Alison showed up at work with a cold. On Tuesday, Maria had a cold. By Thursday, four out of five coworkers had colds. Sharon concludes that she caught her cold at work.

   a) Describe Sharon's reasoning according to the causal analyses in the text.

   _____

   _____

   b) Is this a reasonable argument?

   _____

   c) What other factors should she consider?

   _____

   _____

4. Sharon is one of five employees who use the coffee room for regularly scheduled breaks. On the last three occasions she noticed that her clothes were damp after returning from the coffee room. The first time she noticed this she had sat at the end of the table near the exit door to the outside, which is also next to the radiator. The second time she had sat away from the exit door but still near the radiator. The third time she had sat near the window, which is also near the radiator. She concludes that the radiator must leak or emit steam, which is causing the dampness in her clothes.

   a) What causal relationship does Sharon conclude from her experience?

   _____

   _____

   b) Describe the type of reasoning she used to reach this conclusion.

   _____

   _____

   c) Can you think of other conclusions Sharon might draw from the information presented in the example?

   _____

5. In the summer of 1999, several people became violently ill, some fatally, after attending a county fair in upstate New York. All the fairgoers had eaten and drunk a variety of foods and beverages at various concession stands at the fair. All had used the restrooms, water fountains, amusement rides, and amusement galleries. Pathologists determined that the bacterium *Escherichia coli* was

(continued)

the culprit. *E. coli* is found in fecal matter and on any object or person who comes in contact with animal waste, including human waste.

After exhaustive investigation, the food concession stands were cleared of being contaminated. The restrooms, amusement rides, and galleries were cleared, and contact among the victims was eliminated. After further investigation, the source of the contamination was found. It turned out that after an extended period of drought, a severe rainstorm caused local wells, drainage ditches, and barn drains to overflow. Farm drainage equipment was overworked and runoff of cow waste from the dairy farm seeped into the overtaxed drainage systems. The water eventually made it into one of the wells that had been below its normal levels because of the drought. The low level of the well allowed the surface water to seep in, contaminating a water supply that made its way to the fairgrounds. *E. coli* was found in the water.

a) Using the methods you have studied in the text, describe how you would have investigated this incident. Begin by succinctly stating the causal relations established by the investigators.

_____

_____

b) Describe the difference and common factors used in the analysis.

_____

_____

c) How did the investigators use the combined difference/common factor approach?

_____

_____

d) Can you think of other factors that might have contributed to the contamination?

_____

_____

6. Sharon and her four coworkers observed a new maintenance worker hanging around the boss's office just before closing for the last four nights. They have never seen him before, but he was wearing the proper uniform and identification. Sharon heard Roberto, the office manager, say that some personal items have been missing in at least three of the offices on this floor. She and her coworkers wonder if the maintenance worker has anything to do with the missing items.

a) Describe the reasoning Sharon and the others might have used in reaching their speculative conclusion.

_____

_____

b) List other factors that may be related to the missing items.

_____

_____

c) Evaluate the argument. Is this a reasonable argument?

_____

_____

7. Describe an incident where you used causal analysis to solve a problem at work or at home. Be specific in describing the possible factors you considered and either rejected or accepted as contributing to the results you were investigating.

_____

_____

_____

_____

Causal Factors Among Groups

The three methods discussed focus on individual, single causes or a set of causes and individual, single effects. In each case, we were looking for the cause of stomach illness, the cause of the electrical malfunction, and the cause of improved communication. The methods were essentially eliminative in nature. We arrived at conclusions by eliminating possibilities that might have the caused the effect under investigation. We eliminated common factors by determining, for example, who ate in the cafeteria but did not fall ill. The healthy employees who did not eat seafood salad were not our primary concern in the investigation except to exclude them from further consideration. We then eliminated other possible factors that might have caused the illness, such as the plates, utensils, and so forth, and then isolated items that were different for each person. By repeating this eliminative process, we identified the probable causes.

But there are situations in which these methods are impractical, if not impossible, to apply. For example, if you wanted to know the precise relationship between aspirin and its impact on heart attacks, the above methods would be inadequate for arriving at a definitive answer. Similarly, a simple cause and effect analysis of individual causes would be ineffective in an investigation into the various effects of certain packaging colors on purchasing habits of selected consumer groups. In both cases, we are concerned with causal relationships among *populations*. We are looking for certain factors that affect whole groups of people and large numbers of objects or events. For example, you would not be able to say with certainty that *each person* who consumes an aspirin a day will *never* suffer heart attacks, or that each *individual* who chooses one packaging color over another color will do so each time she or he chooses. A thorough analysis of several possible factors affecting the reactions among thousands of subjects is required before anyone can say with any degree of certainty that one event or condition causes the effect in question. Statements asserting causal relations among populations establish only that there would be *fewer instances* of heart attacks among a group of people than there would be if no one consumed aspirin. Likewise, statements asserting a causal relationship between packaging color and product choices establish only that among large groups, *more* (expressed as a percentage) people would choose one color over another in more instances. Causal generalizations concerning populations establish *trends*, which are expressed in the form of statistical probabilities among possible causes and effects.

One type of causal analysis used in analyzing factors among groups is called **concomitant variation**. In these analyses, we are seeking a correlation between the *frequency* in the number of times we observe the effect as it relates to the *frequency* in the number of times we observe possible causal factors. We then correlate the two concomitant occurrences. For example, recent scientific studies show that there is indeed a *correlation* between taking just one aspirin per day and the occurrence of heart attacks in humans. Thus, scientists are interested in the *percentage of people* who experience heart attacks who take an aspirin in relation to the *percentage* who experience heart attacks who do not take aspirin. Changes in the behavior of individuals in one group, for example, those taking an aspirin a day, are correlated to changes in *future* behavior among that group, for example, less frequent instances of heart attacks. The changes are then correlated with another group who did not take aspirin and did not suffer heart attacks. The same type of reasoning applies to packaging colors and consumer choices. When one factor varies directly in relation to some other, we may establish a causal connection between them based on concomitant variation. The correlation directs investigators to focus on more specific causal relationships such as the particular properties of aspirin as they relate to particular aspects of the human body associated with heart disease.

However, we only begin to establish a causal relationship by means of concomitant variation. The relationship must first be expressed in the form of a *tentative* causal hypothesis, which explains the connection between the causal factors in the populations under investigation. The hypothesis must be tested by means of a thorough scientific investigation before we can say with any degree of certainty that one factor causes the effect in the populations studied. There may be several other factors to explore such as heredity, age, gender, ethnicity, race, health habits of the subjects, physiology of the subjects, and dosage, among many others. Without extensive research to explain the connection, it is possible that a lower frequency of heart attacks is due to any one or more of the other factors. Or, the concurrent variation may be just an unexplainable coincidence. Significant research conducted over several years of experimental study in the context of a theoretical foundation explaining the connection is essential for solving such complex problems. For example, just think of the years of research involved before scientists could say with "scientific certainty" that smoking *causes* cancer.

The method of concomitant variation represents an ideal. There are several ways in which a correlation can be established between two events without establishing a causal relationship underlying the correlation. Moreover, concomitant variation does not always tell us which is the cause and which is the effect. It only shows that one factor varies in connection with another factor.

EXERCISES

I. Analyze each of the arguments below.

1. Scientists have shown that the death rate for those who smoke a pack of cigarettes a day is six times greater than those who do not smoke. For those who smoke more than a pack a day, the death rate is twelve times higher than for those who do not smoke. It should be clear: smoking causes cancer.

_____

_____

_____

_____

_____

(continued)

2. Marketing data collected on over 600 consumers show that women are 2.5 times more likely to choose a pack of cigarettes that has more red in its packaging over a pack with more green or blue packaging. The more red on the package, the more likely women were to choose it over others. Men also choose cigarettes in a similar pattern. They chose a pack with primarily red packaging but their frequency in choosing was only 1.3 times more likely than for other colors.

_____

_____

_____

_____

_____

3. Managers who were visible but not intrusive in interacting with their employees in manufacturing plants were two times more likely to receive a "highly rated" performance rating from their employees than those managers who were less visible. The more "supportive" visibility received from the manager, the higher the rating. In conjunction with the higher rating, the shifts these managers worked also demonstrated either equal or greater productivity than other shifts. Thus, a "hands-on" manager does not get in the way of productivity—he or she actually enhances it.

a) Identify the causal relationship expressed in the conclusion.

_____

_____

b) Describe how the argument makes use of the method of concomitant variation.

_____

_____

c) Evaluate the argument in terms of its strength.

_____

_____

4. In addition to correlating aspirin with the reduction in the number of heart attacks, scientists have also investigated the relationship between "good" (high density lipoproteins [HDL]), "bad"(low density lipoproteins [LDL]) cholesterol levels, and heart disease. In studies of 300 male patients over 10 years, doctors were able to correlate cholesterol levels according to type and heart disease. The HDLs are believed to protect against clogging of the vessels that supply the heart. LDLs are thought

to increase fatty tissues, clogging the vessels that supply the heart. The frequency of arteriosclerosis (hardening of the arteries) in men increases with higher LDL levels and decreases with lower HDL levels by nearly 30 percent. However, if the HDL levels are high but LDL levels are normal, the percentage of men who experience heart disease still increases but at a rate of 25 percent. Low LDL and low HDL yielded only a marginal increase in incidents of heart disease over normal counts by 10 percent.

_____

_____

_____

_____

5. Research data have shown that drinking red wine in moderation decreases the frequency of heart disease in both men and women. Scientists believe that a particular element in red wine, possibly tannin, contributes to the decrease in plaque buildup in arteries supplying the heart.

_____

_____

_____

_____

In terms of the concepts discussed in this chapter, describe how would you analyze this above case? How, if at all, does it differ from the aspirin a day case and the HDL/LDL cases?

_____

_____

_____

_____

POST HOC FALLACY

Alluded to above, a *post hoc* **fallacy** occurs when we conclude that one event or condition causes another event simply on the grounds that the two events are associated either sequentially or contemporaneously in our experience. Often called *post hoc, ergo propter hoc* (after this, therefore because of this), the fallacy assumes a causal relationship based on association where there is little or no evidence that one actually exists. For example, the moon's appearance may be associated with your tiredness, but it is probably not the cause of it. The inference that the moon caused your tiredness is an example of post hoc reasoning.

These kinds of fallacies often occur in social scientific reasoning as well as in everyday experience. For example, suppose that when you arrive home after a hard day at work your nerves are bit on edge, leaving you irritable and short tempered. As you arrive home, your daughter (or other loved one) seeks comfort and attention. You react to the attention-seeking behavior as if it were an annoyance and respond with a scolding. This incident is repeated four days in a row. The child begins to conclude that attention seeking is the cause of your harsh treatment toward her. If the child then seeks attention elsewhere (at school, for example), and is again treated harshly, she may perceive the treatment as confirming her negative perceptions regarding attention seeking. This kind of fallacious reasoning is common in all aspects of human interactions at work and at home. It is an example of post hoc reasoning.

•••••••••••••••••••• EXERCISES ••••••••••••••••••••

1.   Analyze the following arguments. Identify any fallacies you detect in them. Describe how you might strengthen the argument.

a) Each time I see a person arrested on a television news show, the perpetrator is on public assistance. This just shows you that poverty causes crime.

_____

_____

b) The gossip mill is in full gear again this week. I hear the boss resigned because she was tired of rumors about her and her secretary. It seems that personal relationships are the biggest cause of resignations in this company.

c) It seems that students who attend private and parochial schools fare much better on the SATs. One reason is that private schools have smaller class sizes. I would bet that the small classes is the reason those students do better on the SATs.

d) Every time I see people on their breaks, they light up their cigarettes. If we had fewer breaks, there would be less smoking. The breaks just cause smoking habits to get worse.

Scientific Reasoning

Many of the examples and questions discussed so far involve gathering evidence, asking questions, eliminating possibilities, finding commonalities, examining concomitant variations, and proposing hypotheses, all in an effort to explain something we don't quite understand. Often in every day experience the unknown, unusual, unfamiliar, and unexplained appeal to us simply out of a sense of curiosity. Other times we seek a better understanding to improve our lives and the lives of those around us. The kind of knowledge sought through such explanations usually involves *scientific reasoning*. Understanding causal relations is at the heart of scientific reasoning. Explaining why and how things come about, how one thing causes another to happen, is essential to the success of scientific investigations.

Webster's New World Dictionary[2] defines scientific reasoning as systematized knowledge derived from observation, especially facts, principles, and techniques that may be verified through experience. However, according to our criteria for good definitions, this definition is too broad because it includes almost any kind of knowledge. For example, the definition may include extrasensory perception, hallucinations, folklore, and other types of knowledge that are normally considered outside the boundaries of science. Knowledge in these other areas is also derived from facts (according to the person who experiences them) and observations. And the knowledge is verified through the experiences of the perceiver. So how do we distinguish scientific reasoning from other forms of reasoning? The key word is "verifiable." Although its meaning is controversial in some circles, verifiability and the concept of a causal law (see below) are at the core of scientific reasoning, which helps to distinguish it from other types of reasoning. We will discuss both in more detail in the section "Criteria for Evaluating Scientific Reasoning." However, a review of the concept of objectivity in Chapter 1 will help set the stage.

A **scientific explanation** is defined as a tentative or provisional proposal in the form of a *hypothesis* explicating why certain events occur the way they do. The central piece of the explanation is the hypothesis, an inductive statement that accounts for the relevant facts and evidence in the context of background knowledge and available theoretical frameworks. Central to theoretical frameworks is the concept of a causal law or principle.

CAUSAL LAWS

A statement establishing a causal relationship goes beyond simple enumeration of events in succession by implying that there is an underlying *causal law* in operation that *extends* beyond the occurrence of individual events. For example, if the successful experiments were repeated in the aspirin case, you would expect the results in the current investigation to be similar to the results in future investigations. That is, similar causes consistently produce similar effects. This relationship is more than just a sequence of events where one event *happens* to follow another or a sequence of events where one event is merely concurrently *associated* with another. (Post hoc reasoning is based on this unwarranted assumption.) A **causal law** asserts that event A will *always be followed by* event B (to the best of our knowledge). The causal law itself is confirmed within a *system* of theories, frameworks, and explanatory hypotheses. This system has been tested and confirmed through experience and accepted as the "best" explanation of the facts available.

For example, in the science of economics the law of supply and demand is used to explain certain behaviors affecting the flow of goods and services in the context of the availability and need for such goods and services. It is more than a generalization about behaviors; it is a well-proven theory of why events should occur the way they do. If an event does not fit the theory, we would question the validity of your data rather than dismiss the theory. As in the case of the Newtonian law of gravity, if an object does not fall to the earth, we would be confused and demand an explanation. We would look for some kind of trick or unusual set of circumstances before we attempt to question the law. These kinds of laws distinguish scientific reasoning from other types of reasoning.

CRITERIA FOR EVALUATING SCIENTIFIC REASONING

There are absolutely no foolproof methods for assessing the reliability of causal generalizations. Your investigation may be influenced by your personal point of view, frame of reference, and cultural context, among other things. Insufficient or false information can affect the outcome of the investigation, no matter how careful you are in trying to be objective. The *interpretations* of evidence and limitations of the study could lead to overlooking relevant possibilities. As one philosopher contends, "Evidential reasoning—both every-day and scientific is context dependent...Science is social knowledge."[3] In other words, the obstacles to critical thinking and objectivity described throughout the text, especially those in Chapter 8, apply equally to scientific reasoning. The cautions against biased generalizations, hasty generalizations, and anecdotal evidence should be adhered to in scientific reasoning as well.

For example, we stated in Chapter 8 that citing personal testimonials or one or two counterexamples should not undermine the credibility of an inductive generalization. Similarly, citing one or two examples in which the causal connection did not hold does not destroy the credibility of the causal hypothesis (although this can lead to undermining a causal law). The case of the elderly woman who shows no signs of cancer but sneaks outside the nursing home to smoke a cigarette, does not disprove the causal generalization asserting that smoking causes cancer. Nor does the fact that some people die of lung cancer who never smoked a day in their lives disprove the statement that smoking causes cancer. These examples of anecdotal evidence lack the credibility, evidential support, and theoretical grounding to pose a serious threat to the causal statement.

Nonetheless, scientists have developed a set of criteria that will increase objectivity and skill in scientific investigations. The usefulness of the criteria listed here, however, is not limited to scientific investigations and can be applied to all types of situations where critical thinking is required.

RELIABILITY OF DIRECT OBSERVATIONS

A causal generalization is only as reliable as the observations on which it is based. As already noted, recognizing the biases, perspectives, loaded language, fallacies, and superficial analyses are just as important in causal reasoning as they are in all the other types of reasoning. Identifying potential problems and taking into consideration that your observation is influenced by both psychological and physical factors are the first steps in establishing the credibility of your own observations and observations of others.

DEGREE OF CORRELATION AND REPRESENTATIVE SAMPLES

A small degree of correlation between the samples under investigation yields a weak causal argument. Just as in analogical reasoning, a small number of items sampled and a low degree of correlation (the ways in which they are similar) could lead to conclusions in which the variables are accidentally rather than causally related. This criterion parallels the guidelines described for all types of inductive reasoning. However, in causal reasoning this criterion is crucial because causal statements imply a closer relationship between events than do mere generalizations.

RELEVANCE

Always a difficult criterion to articulate precisely, the criterion of relevancy is one of the most important aspects of critical thinking, one we have discussed throughout the text. It is particularly important in scientific reasoning. The difficulty lies in determining where to draw the line for including or excluding pieces of information as relevant or irrelevant. For example, we mentioned earlier that a critical thinker tries to consider a broad range of information "no matter how remote it might be" as a potential contributing factor in a causal analysis. But how do we know when a piece of evidence is too remote to consider? How do we know when we have exceeded the boundaries of remoteness in trying to determine which facts are relevant to the hypothesis under investigation and which are completely outside the realm of possibility? Although no hard and fast answer is readily available, one effective strategy is to trace the evidence along each path from a known point of fact or accepted knowledge base to connect it with the evidence you want to establish. You should examine how this piece of potential evidence fits with what you already know and how it fits with other pieces of evidence under consideration. The final crucial question is: Can the evidence be *inferred* from information you have already?

Once you identify the evidence as possibly relevant, it is like fitting pieces into a puzzle; you need to see if and where each piece interlocks with the others and in the whole picture. Once again some creative and critical thinking is required so that you remain open to all options, perspectives, and possibilities.

COMPATIBILITY WITH KNOWN SCIENTIFIC LAWS

This criterion follows from the previous one in requiring consistency with background knowledge. Your explanation must be also consistent with accepted scientific laws and theories in addition to what you yourself have already established as true. If the data make sense to you initially, you may propose them as a preliminary explanatory hypothesis. But you must also check whether they contradict an established scientific principle or causal law. Only then can you reject or accept the data. If insufficient evidence is available, you should withhold judgment with respect to its credibility until further information is available.

VERIFIABILITY

We mentioned earlier that this criterion is one of the defining features of scientific reasoning. In effect, it requires that in any scientific inquiry it must be *possible* to gather relevant evidence through either direct or indirect observations. In other words, a scientific explanation must be *testable*. The methods and procedures for testability must conform to an accepted standard as described in Chapter 1. However, testability need not be based on first-hand, direct observations. Indirect or *inferred* observational evidence is acceptable in confirming a scientific explanation. For example, prior to lunar space exploration, scientists believed that the surface of the moon on its dark side was similar to the surface on its bright side (the side visible to earth receiving the sun's rays). Once lunar exploration made it possible to test the hypothesis through direct observation, it was confirmed that both sides were similar in terrain. Today, the hypothesis is accepted as scientific truth. The point is that there was considerable prior *indirect* scientific evidence and well-established theories that supported the hypothesis without directly observing the surface itself. Scientists had solid evidence allowing them to *infer* the existence of certain features they could not see directly. Thus, the hypothesis was testable *in principle*. The inferred evidence was *connected* to other evidence that was observable through direct experience.

SIMPLICITY AND UNNECESSARY ASSUMPTIONS

Most of us like to keep things simple. "The simpler, the better," the saying goes. This recommendation is as true in scientific reasoning as it is in ordinary experience. Thus, if two rival scientific explanations of the same facts meet the criteria already set forth, the simpler explanation is the one adopted.

Although some philosophers have argued that this criterion amounts to no more than an aesthetic or intuitive preference with little or no grounding in scientific proof itself, it is a commonly accepted practice. Setting aside the philosophical debate, let's agree that a simpler explanation is preferable to a more complex one.

Although not an easy criterion to measure, much less apply, the simplicity criterion does have an interpretation that has practical consequences and is based on sound reasoning. This interpretation relies on the concepts of necessary and unnecessary assumptions—the simpler explanation requires fewer assumptions than the complex one. For example, if one theory assumes the existence of unusual, dubious, or unexplained entities and the other theory assumes fewer such entities, the latter explanation is most often accepted, depending on how unusual or dubious the assumptions are considered. The more an explanation relies on natural, familiar phenomena, the more likely it will be accepted.

For example, suppose you have been experiencing bouts of depression on the occasions of massive solar flare-ups. You could explain these bouts by appealing to the existence of magnetic waves caused by ancient solar explosions, which reached earth eons ago. You assume that the magnetic waves remained on earth and are now activated by the current storms, affecting human emotions, which cause depression. The assumption is that past magnetic solar activity affects current human emotions. On the other hand, you could explain the depression by appealing to the positions of the stars and moons appearing in certain configurations in the zodiac, which depict mythological creatures. Both appeal to unproven, untestable events. But the concepts in the first explanation are more natural to us than the dubious concepts of configurations of celestial bodies in the zodiac. Of course, there may be other less esoteric and more reasonable explanations that do not appeal to either of these hypotheses (Figure 9–2).

On a grander scale, think of the Darwinian explanation of the evolution of new species. According to Darwin, new species evolve over millions of years through natural selection. Only successful entities adapt to changes in their environment and survive to procreate. The successors produce offspring, which perpetuate the successful survival traits. Prior to Darwin, many scientists believed that new species were not evolved from other species through natural selection but were special, unique creations of God. Still other scientists believed that species evolved as the result of a "striving for life" by means of a "life force" (an entelechy) that exists within the living entity. This life force preexisted in living matter and is responsible for the evolution of species

FIGURE 9.2 *An ad hoc explanation or lucky guess, a more plausible explanation could be that OPEC increased production.*

through its striving for perfection toward a higher form of existence. Although neither Darwin nor others could scientifically prove their theories at the time (they either had not read or not understood the importance of genetic theory, nor could they observe evolution of over hundreds of thousands of years), one theory was simpler than the other. Darwin's theory was eventually accepted over its competitors' because it did not require the assumption of entelechies, a dubious and unexplained force. Rather it relied on natural phenomena, such as geological evidence, and observations of natural phenomena, such as competition for food and mating behaviors, from which entities would ensure survival traits.

EXERCISES

Define the criteria of relevance, simplicity, and verifiability in the context of a work or home-related investigation. Provide specific examples of how you would use the criteria in developing a sound, testable, and simple explanation.

_____

_____

_____

_____

_____

_____

_____

_____

_____

AD HOC HYPOTHESES

A hypothesis developed solely for the purposes of "rescuing" a theory or explanation is considered an *ad hoc* ("for this" in Latin) **premise** (hypothesis). Ad hoc hypotheses account for some of the facts under investigation but their inclusion involves *adjusting* the other hypotheses you have already accepted to make them fit the facts. The specially created hypothesis has little or no explanatory power of its own and is created only in an effort to make sense of the facts under investigation when all else fails. It is offered without testing its credibility in the context of this investigation. For example, if you try to explain a glitch in your computer software by appealing to evil gremlins in the machine, you are *inventing* a causal hypothesis just for the purpose of explaining this particular problem. (Of course, reference to the word "glitch" in this case can also be considered as an ad hoc hypothesis if not fully explained. In recent years, the word has taken on a special meaning with a factual basis assumed in its use. It is no longer an ad hoc hypothesis.) However, appeal to evil gremlins does make use of an ad hoc hypothesis.

Not all examples of ad hoc hypotheses are this ridiculous. Entelechies were seriously considered as viable explanatory entities in light of the available evidence and theories of the time. The explanation was not unreasonable in that context, but given current knowledge about genetics, carbon dating, and other scientific discoveries, the assumption of entelechies was seen as an example of an ad hoc hypothesis and was later abandoned.

EXERCISES

I. Develop an argument supporting the testability of Darwin's theory of evolution.

_____

_____

_____

_____

_____

_____

II. Develop an argument explaining why you believe evolution is not a testable theory.

_____

_____

_____

_____

_____

_____

EXPLANATORY AND PREDICTIVE POWER

The more facts a hypothesis can explain or predict, the stronger the hypothesis, assuming that the other criteria are met. If two competing hypotheses explain a set of observable facts, but one also allows us to deduce additional facts and allows us to predict more potential consequences, it is the accepted hypothesis.

For example, let's say that the director of human resources is having difficulty recruiting mechanical engineering graduates for its manufacturing plants. She considers two explanations. The first relies on the fact that beginning salaries for graduating engineers is $5,000 more than it was four years ago due to a recent shortage of mechanical engineers. She also knows that the manufacturing plants are located in congested areas without convenient access to a commuter train or bus line, making it difficult for some employees to get to work. She proposes two hypotheses: Potential recruits do not want to drive in traffic, and potential recruits want higher wages than the company is advertising for starting salaries. She then checks with several other human resource professionals. They also report difficulty in recruiting new engineers in all their plants. The first hypothesis is supported by the theory of supply and demand and explains why *all* companies would have trouble hiring new recruits *regardless of location*. The second hypothesis explains only why this company is having trouble in these circumstances. We can infer a much broader set of consequences from the supply and demand theory than we can from the commuter preference hypothesis.

Summary

IN THIS CHAPTER WE:

• Examined the role of causality as central to scientific reasoning

• Discussed various strategies for examining causal arguments and described some of the obstacles to credible inductive reasoning

• Examined criteria for evaluating scientific reasoning and provided examples for its use

Exercises

I. Evaluate the following arguments according to the criteria provided in this section.

1. Describe the extent to which the argument meets or fails to meet each of the criteria listed.

2. State why you believe the argument is strong or weak.

3. Identify any fallacies you see.

4. Provide an alternative explanation for the events.

   a) Helene must have some special powers. She always knows when Jessica is going to arrive late for work. She doesn't even know where Jessica lives or anything else about her personal life. She must have ESP.

   b) It's really terrible that the supervisor's husband passed away over the weekend. He was such a nice man. I hear he was considerably older than she. The obituary said he died of natural causes. I bet at his old age his spirit just left him. That was the real cause of death.

   c) You know, they finally determined why that department down the hall had such low productivity in June. The supplier gets extra busy in the summer months and couldn't deliver the supplies in time. But I hear the real reason is that the manager over there is moody as can be. He has bad months every summer and everyone else suffers. He was probably just in a bad mood from the heat anyway. That's why the materials arrive late.

II. Evaluate the following:

For several years scientists have been wondering why people in certain countries experience a relatively low rate of heart disease in view of their apparently unhealthy dietary and smoking habits. For example, French citizens consume per capita more heavy desserts with cream and rich toppings, smoke more cigarettes, and eat as much meat and milk products as Americans, yet the rate of arteriosclerosis in France is lower than it is in many parts of the United States.

Scientists began looking at other aspects of the French diet. They focused on the consumption of wine, particularly red wine. Over a period of years they studied several hundred adult men who drank at least one glass of red wine per day. They correlated wine consumption with the frequency of men who experienced heart attacks and with men who did not drink wine and the frequency of heart attacks. They were than able to identify qualities in the wine that contributed to plaque reduction in arteries. The results, they contended, were that clear, red wine prevents heart attacks.

It didn't take long before some groups began touting the merits of drinking wine, even recommending it for the prevention of heart attacks. However, we in the mental health field, and members of Alcoholics Anonymous, as well as Mothers Against Drunk Driving call for a moratorium on such claims. We believe that until all the evidence is in, scientists should refrain from such dangerous claims. First, just as we predicted, producers of all kinds of alcohol products jumped on the bandwagon. Now a few glasses of white wine are also good for you. Just recently, a scientist proclaimed that the merits of beer and wine coolers in moderate consumption is a healthy practice. What next? Are they going to rationalize drinking to excess as a step toward a healthy heart? To say that men who drink a glass of wine a day will reduce their risk of heart failure is bad science. The causal links between health and wine consumption is far from being established as scientific fact. A correlation by itself does not prove that one factor is causally related to the other. After all, there could be other reasons why the rate of heart disease is lower among such groups.

The social implications of such claims are scary. We don't want our children to see billboards and magazine ads with adults having a grand old time toasting the benefits of drinking alcoholic beverages.

1. Describe the main argument and subarguments presented in this letter to the editor.

2. Identify any loaded language contained in the letter.

3. Identify any formal or informal fallacies contained in the letter.

4. Evaluate the argument according to the criteria presented in the text.

5. Do you believe that the supporters of wine consumption present a good argument given the definition of science presented in the text? Explain your remarks.

6. Do you believe that the coalition of organizations critical of wine consumption and of advertisements promoting drinking present a good argument? Explain your answer.

7. Critically assess the merits and weaknesses of each argument.

8. Diagram the main argument.

Writing From Experience

1. In a brief essay of 300 words, describe a situation at work or at home in which information that you thought was confidential was "leaked" to other people. Then describe, in terms of causal analyses explained in this chapter, how you discovered the cause of the leak. Specifically, list necessary and sufficient conditions to identify the source and then provide a rationale in terms of causal analyses on how you discovered the leak.

2. Describe a situation at work or at home in which you mistakenly concluded that two events were causally related when in fact they were merely coincidentally related. In your essay, explain the basis for establishing a causal connection. Then explain how your reasoning committed the fallacy of "post hoc."

TOPIC COVERED IN THIS CHAPTER

• Information literacy research skills:

    • Recognizing the need for usable information

    • Developing strategies for locating information

    • Accessing information

    • Evaluating information and sources

    • Organizing and applying information

    • Using information legally and ethically

CRITICAL THINKING: INFORMATION LITERACY AND RESEARCH

KEY TERMS

access tool

background knowledge

Boolean searching

information literacy

intellectual property

on-line catalog

plagiarism

research question

search strategy

thesis

truncation

For today's and tomorrow's workers,
the workplace is going through cataclysmic changes that
very few will be prepared to participate in successfully and
productively unless they are information literate.

–AMERICAN LIBRARY ASSOCIATION INFORMATION LITERACY REPORT

The Information Age...The Information superhighway... Information technology...Infomercials...Information overload. We hear these terms every day. Information has become big business. In light of its importance, a new expression has recently surfaced: information literacy. This seems to be the current catchphrase both in today's educational circles and in the business world. But what is information literacy? How does it relate to critical thinking? And why is it so important in today's world?

Information literacy is the ability to identify, locate, evaluate, and effectively use information. In its Information Literacy Report (Figure 10-1), the American Library Association (ALA) outlines its importance.[1] Thinking critically about information has always been a vital part of our ability to be productive and successful. However, the increase in the amount and sources of information made available to us by today's technology makes the critical thinking skills inherent in information literacy essential in all aspects of our lives—in the home, in the classroom, and in the workplace. In all these situations, we must gather information, analyze it, and use it effectively.

The Importance of Information Literacy

Why is information literacy important to you at home? Think of the amount of information that comes into your home every day through newspapers, magazines, radio, television, and now the Internet. Advertisers are trying to sell you something. How do you know which products to buy, which ads to believe? Political candidates are trying to convince you to vote for them. How

INFORMATION LITERACY SKILLS

The abilities to know when there is a need for information, to identify information for that need, and to be able to locate, evaluate, and effectively use that information are not new abilities that have emerged as a result of the Information Age. In fact, these abilities have always been important to success and quality of life. The only thing that has changed is the amount and variety of information that is now available. Fifty years ago, people had limited sources from which to obtain needed information: books, newspapers, radio, journals, community experts, and government offices.

Today, however, information is not only available from those sources but also from television, CD-ROM, online databases, the Internet, multimedia packages, and digitized government documents; and the amount of information from all of those sources is staggering. Although there has always been a need to find, evaluate, and effectively use information, the abilities needed to do so have just grown larger, more complex, and more important as the volume of available information has mushroomed beyond everyone's wildest imagination.

FIGURE 10.1   *(ALA Information Literacy Report)*

do you know if they are telling you the truth? Newscasts are telling you what happened in the world. How do you know if they are accurate and unbiased? Deceptive techniques discussed in Chapters 5 and 6 illustrate how to use critical thinking skills to detect the truth underlying fallacies and persuasive language. You will learn in this chapter how information literacy skills can help you apply critical thinking to what you see and hear at home.

Why is information literacy important to you in the classroom? When you are actively seeking information for a research project, you will be inundated with information from all kinds of sources. In an academic setting, it is important that you be able to locate, evaluate, and use information accurately. The success of your scholarly pursuit depends on these skills. You will learn in this chapter how information literacy skills can help you apply critical thinking to what you read as you do your research.

Why is information literacy important to you in today's and tomorrow's workplace? According to the ALA's Information Literacy Report (Figure 10–2), technology has brought about a change not only in the *quantity* of information now available but also in the *quality* of information with which we are bombarded.[2] The worker of the present and future must critically review, evaluate, and apply this information in order to be successful and efficient in the "global marketplace." Analyzing information in a discriminatory way will guide you in making decisions that can increase your success and productivity. You will learn in this chapter how information literacy skills will help you apply critical thinking to what you read and hear in relation to your job.

INFORMATION LITERACY AND TODAY'S BUSINESSES

The workplace of the present and future demands a new kind of worker. In a global marketplace, data is dispatched in picoseconds and gigabits, and this deluge of information must be sorted, evaluated, and applied. When confronted by such an overload of information, most workers today tend to take the first or most easily accessed information—without any concern for the quality of that information. As a result, such poorly trained workers are costing businesses billions of dollars annually in low productivity, accidents, absenteeism, and poor product quality. There is no question about it: for today's and tomorrow's workers, the workplace is going through cataclysmic changes that very few will be prepared to participate in successfully and productively unless they are information literate.

FIGURE 10.2 *(ALA Information Literacy Report)*

Although information literacy skills are important to you in all situations, as outlined above, we will focus on these skills in this chapter as they relate to researching information for a paper, presentation, or problem-solving project at work. Once you have acquired critical thinking skills in these areas, you can easily apply them in other settings and situations.

1. Provide a semantic and denotative definition of "information literacy."

   _____

   _____

2. List five reasons why information literacy skills are especially important in today's society.

   _____

   _____

   _____

   _____

3. Give an example from your own experience where the lack of information impeded a project at work. How did you solve this problem?

   _____

   _____

   _____

   _____

Information Literacy Skills

The abilities possessed by an information literate individual have been summarized in various ways by many educational and business-related groups and organizations, but presented here is a logical set of information skills a critical thinking individual must have in order to meet personal, academic, and work-related goals.

A critical thinker must be able to:

1. Recognize the need for relevant and usable information.

2. Develop strategies for locating information.

3. Access information effectively.

4. Critically evaluate information and sources.

5. Organize and apply information effectively to answer questions or solve real-life problems.

6. Access and use information legally and ethically.

SKILL #1: RECOGNIZING THE NEED FOR RELEVANT AND USABLE INFORMATION

A person must be able to identify and refine the question or problem, relate this to what is already known, and identify what further information is needed. In order to do this, and to complete the other steps in finding information, the critical thinker should formulate a **search strategy** (Figure 10-3).

The first part of this strategy involves topic selection and refinement. This may sound easy, but it is what holds most of us back from beginning our research. Even if we have a concept or an idea for a topic, we still don't know where to start. Here's where critical thinking comes in. In choosing a topic, there are certain guidelines that make sense. Because most of you are (or will be) taking college courses, the following are criteria for choosing and narrowing a research paper topic for a class assignment. Naturally, if you are working on a predetermined project or presentation assigned to you, consider only those guidelines that apply to your work situation. We will discuss selecting a topic for research at home later in this chapter.

Selecting a Topic

• It should be something that interests you. This will help motivate you when the research gets difficult, and it will keep you from being bored while you are reading lots of material on the subject (Figure 10-4).

• It should be something that you know a little about, but not everything. If you don't know much about the topic, you will be starting from scratch on

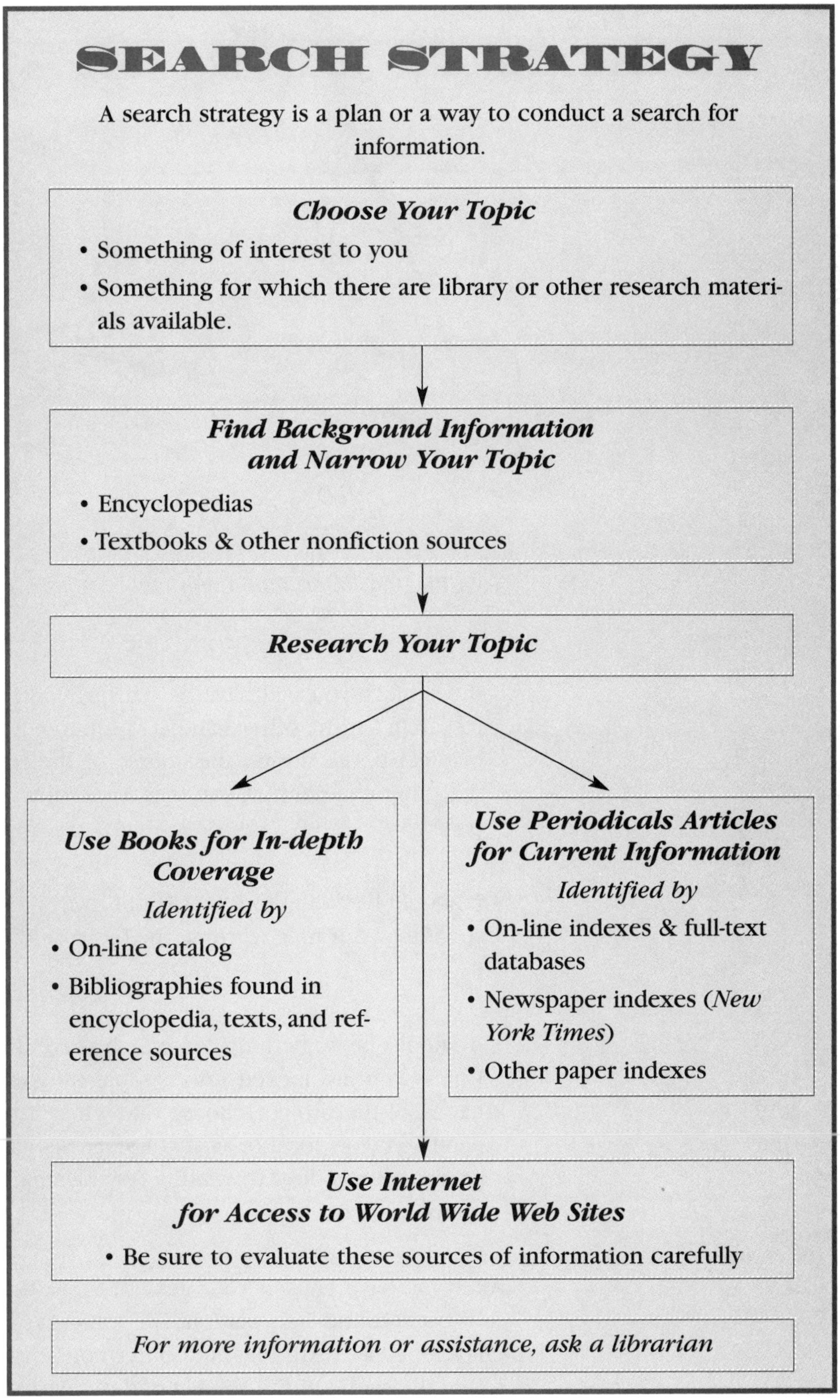

SEARCH STRATEGY

A search strategy is a plan or a way to conduct a search for information.

Choose Your Topic

- Something of interest to you
- Something for which there are library or other research materials available.

Find Background Information and Narrow Your Topic

- Encyclopedias
- Textbooks & other nonfiction sources

Research Your Topic

Use Books for In-depth Coverage
Identified by

- On-line catalog
- Bibliographies found in encyclopedia, texts, and reference sources

Use Periodicals Articles for Current Information
Identified by

- On-line indexes & full-text databases
- Newspaper indexes (*New York Times*)
- Other paper indexes

Use Internet for Access to World Wide Web Sites

- Be sure to evaluate these sources of information carefully

For more information or assistance, ask a librarian

FIGURE 10.3

FIGURE 10.4 *Information overload.*

the subject; you will have no background material on which to base your research. On the other hand, if you know a great deal about the topic, you may get bored during the course of the research and may be so familiar with the material that you may forget that it must be cited. (See skill #6, page 250).

• It should be something that is not overly technical. Otherwise, you will be spending your time learning the basics and the jargon that goes along with it.

• It should be something for which there are research materials available. Unless you are locked into a topic by your instructor, supervisor, or the nature of the project, choose one where the materials you need will be at hand—in your local or virtual library. Specialty topics that require unusual or rare sources lead to waiting (or traveling) for materials and a lot of frustration.

After you have chosen your general topic, the next thing you need to do is find background information. Do some exploratory reading: Look through encyclopedias, textbooks, and other nonfiction books and reference sources to see the scope of the subject and the narrower subtopics. Formulate a few questions that seem worth researching, or put the purpose for researching your project in the form of a **research question**.

For example, if you are interested in finding information on management, you may begin with the question, "What does a manager do?" or "How can I become a good manager?" Once you begin researching your topic, you should further refine your research question based on what you discover in your resources. Begin making a list of subjects and other related terms you can use in searching for information. For example, in the course of your searching under the general term "management," you might also find information on the duties of a manager—supervising people, time management, delegating responsibilities, etc. Perhaps your research question will then become "How can a manager make a team work?" or "What is the best way to delegate responsibilities?" and your list of subjects and related terms might include leadership, managing people, personnel management, personnel administration, manpower management, human resources management, and supervision of employees as well as other keywords such as teamwork, time management, business meetings, delegation of duties, etc.

Summary of information literacy skill #1: To establish the need for and scope of information required, a critical thinker must create a search strategy and:

• Choose an appropriate, narrowed topic based on the nature of the assignment or project.

• Put this topic in the form of a research question.

• Scan encyclopedias and other books to locate background information.

• Record subjects and related terms to use for further searches.

EXERCISES

1. Assume you are enrolled in a class or training seminar in the psychology of motivation. The instructor has asked you to research a topic of your choice. Describe how you would use the strategies discussed in this section to carry out research for the specific topic you selected. Give specific examples.

_____

_____

_____

_____

(continued)

_____

_____

_____

_____

2.   Choose a topic from a previous class in which you conducted research on a broad topic. Discuss the strategies you used to narrow the topic. Then describe how you would improve your efforts by citing the strategies discussed above.

_____

_____

_____

_____

_____

_____

_____

_____

SKILL #2: DEVELOPING STRATEGIES FOR LOCATING THE INFORMATION

The next search strategy step is to identify the types of sources that will provide the needed information and determine where these sources can be found.

Identifying Types of Sources

To identify the most productive sources for your needed information, think critically about your research assignment or project and consider the following:

- *Type of assignment:* An oral presentation? A research paper? A project at work? The type of research assignment will determine the types of information and sources you look for, whether you need in-depth analysis or simply some statistics.

- *Quantity of information:* Enough for a 3-minute presentation? A ten-page paper? A problem-solving project? You must have a good idea about how much information you need so you know how many sources to investigate and when you can stop collecting information. If you are doing research for a class, a presentation, or a project, be sure to ask the instructor or supervisor how long the final product should be. (This will also help you narrow your topic.)

- *Currency:* Do you need current information? Do you need historical or background information? This is one of the most crucial decisions you must make, because it is the criteria for selecting the types of sources and publications you will need to use (see below).

- *Type of publication(s) or sources needed:* Professional journals? Trade magazines? Newspapers? General interest magazines? Government publications? Books? Reference books? Internet? Personal interviews? There are plenty of resources at your disposal. In general, for research assignments that require an historical perspective or detailed background information, use books. For assignments that need current or narrow information, including statistics, use periodicals or the Internet. (See "Sources of Information".) In all cases, it is important that you take into account the date of publication for any source you are considering.

- *Point of view:* Your own opinion? Opposing viewpoints? A variety of viewpoints? For argumentative papers, oral presentations, or debate topics, for example, you may need to find information that presents a particular point of view or a range of viewpoints.

Use critical thinking to view your project or assignment. Approach it from various perspectives to identify the types of sources you will need.

Sources of Information

Books are a valuable resource because they can give you historical background, general information, and/or a detailed exposition of all aspects of the issue at hand. The table of contents of a book is very helpful in giving you an overview of the subject; also, because it breaks down your topic into subtopics, it can even give you some ideas on how to narrow your topic. Reference books, which include encyclopedias, handbooks, and the like, contain concise, factual overviews on a great number of subjects. These entries will help to familiarize you with your topic by introducing you to the vocabulary, main points, and people related to your subject. They often contain short bibliographies of other books you might want to consult. Many reference sources, such as encyclopedias, are now offered in easy-to-search computerized formats. *Encyclopedia Britannica* at http://www.britannica.com and *Encarta* at http://www.encarta.msn.com are two examples.

A *periodical* is published on a regular basis (daily, weekly, monthly, etc.). It designates several related types of materials: professional journals (scholarly publications with articles written by experts in the field), trade magazines (published by those involved in a particular trade or business), magazines (usually of general interest), and newspapers. Some reference books, especially those published by the government (see below), are revised periodically (often yearly) with up-to-date statistics and other information. For information on very current or very narrow subjects, periodical publications may be your most reliable source.

Government publications are another excellent source of information. Federal, state, and local governments are constantly publishing information, especially statistical data, on every topic imaginable, from census and insurance data to information about economic, political, and social conditions in all parts of the world. You can also find data on market trends, income trends, inflation, crop production, manufacturing output, and international trade. You can generally find these in the reference section of your library, in pamphlets put out by the government, and on the Internet.

The *Internet* is a global network of computers that links users and allows them to communicate and share information. The Internet can give you information on just about everything, and its resources are increasing every day. The Internet can provide you with historical as well as very current information on many topics. The two main problems with the Internet, however, are its lack of organization and its abundance of questionable information. (These issues will be discussed further in skill sections #3, page 235, and #4, page 242.)

Other sources of information that can be used for research include *personal interviews, television, videos,* and *organizations*. Personal interviews can be of particular value when the person could be considered an expert in his or her field. Television programs and news shows often contain interviews and factual reports on a variety of topics, and videos are now available on almost any subject. Professional organizations publish brochures and other information on their special interests.

Location of Sources

Once you have identified the types of sources that will provide the needed information, the next step is to determine where these sources can be found.

Libraries. The most obvious place to begin research is at a library, but which one? *Public libraries* usually have resources that are primarily of interest to the patrons in their communities: bestsellers, books on tape, children's books, "how-to" books, encyclopedias, and other general resources; they may also cater to a professional and/or business clientele, if there is enough interest or need. *Academic libraries*, on the other hand, will focus on materials for research: nonfiction books, specialized reference books, and scholarly resources.

Virtually all libraries give their patrons access to the Internet and to periodical databases. Libraries provide periodicals in paper and on-line formats. Whereas the academic library will most likely have a greater number and variety of journals and specialized databases, the public library will have general interest magazines, newspapers, and on-line resources. If a library is lacking a particular book or periodical you need, it can acquire it for you through interlibrary loan, a cooperative arrangement that allows libraries to borrow from one another. With its on-line book catalog, periodical databases, reference section, Internet access, and reference librarian who can answer questions and guide you in your research, the library—either public or academic, depending on your needs—is an excellent place to start your research.

A word on *company libraries*: Some large companies or businesses have libraries available for their employees' use. These libraries vary depending on the size of the company and its field of business. Law firms and hospitals, for example, often have in-house libraries, as do state and federal government agencies. Generally, these libraries contain useful materials that focus on the specialization of the company; if you are looking for information on a topic outside that field, however, you will probably find a broader variety at a public or academic library.

Virtual Libraries. For researchers who are unable to go to "real" libraries, the Internet provides us with a "virtual" library. From your home or work computer, you can now access almost any library's on-line book catalog. (However, you still will probably have to go to a regular library to sign out the book.) A number of books, magazines, and government documents are published in their entirety on the Internet. Organizations, businesses, educational institutions, and individuals have web pages devoted to their special interests.

Virtual libraries are especially useful for locating on-line reference and subject research sites. Some especially useful virtual libraries and reference sources include:

- A Collection of Special Search Engines
  http://www.leidenuniv.nl/ub/biv/specials.htm

- The Federal Web Locator *http://www.infoctr.edu/fwl*

- Infomine *http://infomine.ucr.edu*

- The Internet Public Library *http://www.ipl.org*

- The Library of Congress *http://lcweb.loc.gov*

- LibrarySpot *http://www.libraryspot.com*

- Ready Reference Using the Internet
  http://www.winsor.edu/library/rref.htm

- Thor+: The Libraries of Purdue University
  http://thorplus.lib.purdue.edu/index.html

- The Webliography: Internet Subject Guides
  http://www.lib.lsu.edu/weblio.html

- The WWW Virtual Library *http://vlib.stanford.edu/Overview.html*

People: Experts in the field you are researching are often overlooked as sources of information. The personnel officer in a company or organization, for example, will have a great deal of knowledge about hiring practices and regulations; a marketing director can tell you about business trends and selling techniques; a workforce development officer will have material on career opportunities and training strategies. It is a good critical thinking tactic to make good use of a professional's expertise.

Time Needed

Once you have determined the types of sources you need and their locations, it is a sensible idea to estimate the amount of time necessary to do the research and complete the project. Think realistically and critically about the nature of the assignment, its length, and where the information you need is located. Make a chart with dates and deadlines. As mentioned earlier, try to do your research at a local public or academic library; if your material is not available there, they can get it for you through inter-library loan. Be sure to allow time for this; it can take from one to three weeks, depending on the materials needed.

Summary of information literacy skill #2: To locate appropriate information, a critical thinker must continue to use a search strategy and:

• Identify the types of sources needed based on the information requirements of the project or assignment.

• Determine where these sources can be found.

• Estimate the amount of time necessary to complete the research.

···················· EXERCISES ····················

1. List five types of locations where you can locate information on the topic: "Physical Fitness on the Job." Discuss the advantages or disadvantages, if any, of each type.

_____

_____

_____

_____

_____

_____

_____

_____

(continued)

2.   Return to exercises #1 and #2 in the previous section. Now discuss the strategies you would use in locating the information for your classroom projects.

_____

_____

_____

_____

_____

_____

_____

_____

_____

_____

3.   Assume you are planning a family vacation to Italy this summer. Discuss the strategies you would use in locating information on this topic.

_____

_____

_____

_____

_____

_____

_____

_____

_____

_____

SKILL #3: ACCESSING THE INFORMATION EFFECTIVELY

Once you have identified the types of sources you need, the next step is to locate and access the information. In order to do this, you must recognize the variety of systems for organizing information and use these systems to find the appropriate information.

To locate information, you need to use an **access tool**—an information source, such as a catalog, periodical index, or bibliography that leads you to information. Most of your searching in the library will take place at computer workstations, which connect you to the library's resources. These computers include on-line book catalogs, periodical indexes and databases, and Internet access. (As stated earlier, many of these tools can now be accessed from your home or work computer.)

Book Catalogs

In virtually all libraries, the card catalog, which indexes the books and other materials in the library, has been replaced by a computerized **on-line catalog**, also called an OPAC (on-line public access catalog). The on-line catalogs in a library are connected to a central *server* (computer), which contains a *database* (electronic collection) of the *records* (publication information, etc.) of each of the books and other materials in the library. These records are composed of *fields* (items such as title, author, subject headings, contents, notes, etc., for each book). These fields become the *access points* (places in which you can look up something—titles, authors, etc.) in your search.

When you search for a book, you can generally search in the on-line catalog by title, author, subject heading, and keyword.

Searching by Title or Author. If you know the title of your book, simply enter it into the computer. On-line catalogs don't even require you to capitalize the words. If you don't know all the words in the title, just type in the words you do know, in any order. The catalog will search its database for records with those words in the title field. When conducting an author search, however, word order is important, so be sure to type in the author's last name first.

Searching by Subject Heading or Subject Keyword. In a subject heading or subject keyword search, you will be searching the subject field of the book record. The subject headings in this field are a controlled vocabulary; they have been determined by the Library of Congress, which put together a list of standard, acceptable headings into which all books are categorized. (This list is published in a four-volume set of reference books called *The Library of Congress Subject Headings*, available at most academic libraries, which use the Library of Congress Classification System; most public libraries use the Dewey Decimal Classification System.)

Now is the time you will need your list of subjects and related terms. Enter the subject you are looking for into the computer. The catalog will search its database for books that have that word or phrase in the subject heading field, often giving you a list of subjects and subtopics that will help you further narrow your search. When you get your list of books, use relevant terms listed in the subject heading field of each item to do other searches for related books.

What if the search terms you enter into the on-line catalog are not Library of Congress subject headings? The newer on-line catalogs will give you a cross reference to the official subject heading along with some additional headings. Choose from these and try your search again.

Searching by Keyword. Now that library catalogs are computerized, keyword (free-text) searching has proven to be very effective in locating information. When you use this method, the computer looks for your search term not only in the subject field but also in *all* fields of the book record; this includes title, author, contents, and notes fields. If your keyword is in any of these fields, that book record will be listed on the screen. Naturally, this will give you many more results than a search which only searches the subject heading field; but the results you get will not be as precise as searching by subject heading, because you will be locating items in which the term may be used differently or incidentally.

Keyword and subject searching also allow using multiple search terms so you can broaden or restrict your results. This is called using **Boolean searching** (a modern interpretation and application of classical logic), named for British mathematician George Boole. In Boolean searching, you can combine your search terms specifying that the computer will find results with *all* or *some* of the concepts you list. By using the operators *AND, OR,* or *NOT*, Boolean searches can narrow or broaden your search (as in a genus-species breakdown).

The connector "and" narrows a search because it retrieves only the records that contain *all* the search terms (keywords) listed; this helps you focus your search. The more keywords you enter, the narrower your search becomes.

For example: leadership *AND* business

"Or" expands a search because it retrieves records that include *either or both* of the search terms that are listed; this allows you to use synonyms to describe your topic. The more keywords you enter, the broader your search becomes.

> For example: personnel management *OR* human resources management *OR* manpower management

"Not" excludes records from a search. This allows you to eliminate irrelevant contexts of your topic.

> For example: teamwork *NOT* sports

You can even combine operators for a more specific query.

> Example: teamwork *AND* business *NOT* sports

As you can see, Boolean searching helps you to define a topic precisely so that you will get more useful results.

Most computer catalogs also support **truncation**, a technique in which you replace the ending of a word with a truncation symbol, usually an asterisk (*) or a question mark (?). This enables you to search for a term when you are not sure of its exact spelling or when you are not sure which form of the word to look for. The computer will search for all forms of the term that have that particular root.

> For example: administrat* would retrieve any words beginning with those letters, such as administrator, administration, etc.

Recently, many computer databases have begun to allow these symbols to be used even in the middle of words to replace unknown letters. Read the database's searching instructions to learn what features it supports.

Periodical Indexes and Databases

Libraries now provide computerized periodical indexes and databases in addition to the traditional print indexes. Some examples of these databases include InfoTrac, Dialog, FirstSearch, and Proquest. These electronic indexes can be found either on CD-ROMs or on-line subscription services. Because electronic indexes are a relatively new development, however, you may find that only the last few years of publications are included; for older material, you may need to use the library's print indexes such as *The Readers' Guide to Periodical Literature* or the *New York Times Index*.

There are a variety of periodical indexes. Some cover specific subject areas, such as business or health, whereas others focus on general or popular periodicals, and still others cover primarily scholarly publications. Different indexes or databases also give differing amounts of information. Some only give a basic *citation* (title, author, and publication data) or an *abstract* (short summary of the article), whereas others contain the *full text* of the article. Be sure to read the description of the database (usually on the screen or posted nearby) or consult a reference librarian if you have questions about the coverage or content of a database.

These databases can be searched in much the same way as the on-line book catalog—by author, title, or subject keywords. Boolean searching can be used to its best advantage in periodical databases. You can search just part of the article record (citation and abstract) or the entire full text of the article. Once you find an appropriate article, you can retrieve it by printing it there at the workstation, if it is available in full text; finding it in the library's periodical section, in paper format (hard copy) or microform-microfilm (rolls) or microfiche (sheets) of film; or sending for it through inter-library loan, if the library does not have it. Additionally, many databases offer you the option of downloading the article to a disk or e-mailing it to yourself. The library usually provides a printout of the titles it owns, along with a listing of dates and formats. Critical thinking here involves using the library's services and materials to your best advantage. Don't accept your first or preliminary investigation into the topic. Keep digging for information from a broad spectrum of resources.

Bibliographies

A bibliography, a list of materials on a given topic, is also a useful access tool. Libraries often have book-length lists of materials on a single topic. These lists, compiled by experts or researchers in the field, could include essays, periodical articles, books, pamphlets, or videos that are available on that particular subject. Bibliographies can usually be located by searching the on-line book catalog.

Internet

You can access the Internet in almost any library as well as from your home or office computer. The Internet is a "network of networks," linking the user to an unbelievable amount of information from all over the world, and new sources are added daily. The easiest way to use the Internet is via the World Wide Web, a graphical interface that presents information in a format that allows you to explore the countless on-line sources ("web sites") that are available.

Before we go any further, it is important that you understand that there is a difference between Internet sites and the periodical databases discussed earlier. The periodical databases are resources subscribed to by the library; they are usually available in CD-ROM or in on-line form. Although the on-line form comes to the library via the World Wide Web, it is *not* a web site. The articles are from "real" periodicals; they have been compiled by the database provider and, for a fee, are made available to the library's patrons. Internet sites, on the other hand, are put on-line by anyone who wants to publish a web page.

An efficient way to find information on the Internet is to use Internet search tools, such as a *subject directory* or a *search engine*. A directory categorizes thousands of home pages under a relatively small number of subject groups, such as education, health, news, etc.; these are listed on the directory's home page. Directories allow you to find relevant sites without searching the entire Internet because you are restricting your results to those listed in the appropriate subject areas. A disadvantage, though, is that you may miss relevant sites that are categorized under a different subject. Directories are useful for locating information on general topics or when you want to browse. Yahoo! is a good example.

A search engine catalogs web resources and allows you to use your own search terms to locate web sites with those words; it works like an electronic index to Internet sites. Some popular search engines are Google, Hotbot, Infoseek, and AltaVista, but there are many more. They all work in the same basic way, but some scan the entire text of the web sites they cover; others only check certain parts such as the title and first paragraph. Search engines are useful for specific search terms, although the amount of information, much of it irrelevant, returned by a simple search can be overwhelming. Boolean-type searching can be very helpful here, but because the commands and symbols vary among search engines, directories, and databases, be sure to check the help screen of the resource you are using to suggestions to formulate your search.

Web addresses for commonly used search engines and subject directories include:

• AltaVista *http://www.altavista.com*

• Excite *http://www.excite.com*

• Google *http://www.google.com*

• HotBot *http://www.botbot.com*

• Infoseek *http://www.infoseek.com*

- Lycos *http://www.lycos.com*

- Northern Light *http://www.northernlight.com*

- Snap *http://www.snap.com*

- Yahoo *http://www.yahoo.com*

For a comparison of search engines, their features and options, go to "Finding Information on the Internet," a tutorial sponsored by the Library at the University of California, Berkeley; its web address is

http://www.lib.berkeley.edu/TeachingLib/Guides/Internet/FindInfo.html.

At times it is very frustrating and time consuming to use the Internet. There is slow response time during busy times of the day, there's lots of junk to sift through, and some web sites are here today and gone tomorrow. There are few books and periodicals, and everything must be screened very carefully. You must remember, though, that the Internet is still a "work in progress"; its full capability has yet to be explored and developed fully. There is an incredible amount of potential information available on the Internet, but you must use a critical eye and evaluate it thoroughly (skill #4, page 242).

There are many books that will help you utilize the Internet effectively. Some useful titles include:

- *Authoritative Guide to Web Search Engines* by Susan Maze, David Moxley, and Donna J. Smith. NY: Neal-Schuman, 1997.

- *Best Bet Internet: Reference and Research When You Don't Have Time to Mess Around* by Shirley Duglin Kennedy. Chicago: American Library Association, 1998.

- *The Extreme Searcher's Guide to Web Search Engines: a Handbook for the Serious Searcher* by Randolph Hock. Medford, NY: CyberAge Books, 1999.

- *The Internet for Dummies* by John R. Levine, Carol Baroudi, and Margaret Levine Young. Foster City, CA: IDG Books Worldwide, 1997.

Summary of information literacy skill #3: To locate and access information, a critical thinker must:

- Use appropriate access tools such as an on-line book catalog, periodical index/database, bibliography, or the Internet.

- Read the directions and help screens for each access tool.

- Use appropriate access points such as title, author, subject, or keyword.

- Formulate search terms carefully; use the search tips and directions offered by databases, directories, and search engines.

- Narrow or expand a search by using Boolean operators; see help screens or use advanced search options.

- Review the result list and adjust a search based on these results.

- Use several different periodical databases; they may index different periodicals.

- Use several different Internet subject directories and search engines; they index different web sites.

- Evaluate sources using the criteria discussed below (see skill #4).

EXERCISES

1. Describe a frustrating experience you had in effectively accessing the information for a school, work, or home project.

_____

_____

_____

_____

_____

_____

_____

_____

_____

(continued)

2. How would the strategies discussed in this section help in effectively accessing the information?

_____

_____

_____

_____

_____

_____

_____

_____

SKILL #4: EVALUATING THE INFORMATION AND ITS SOURCE

Evaluation is not a step that should be left to the end of your research; it should be an ongoing process. As you do your research, you will locate many potential sources for your assignment or project; you will not have time to read through all of them, so you must be discriminating in selecting from the vast number of resources available to you. It is up to you to select a reasonable number of sources on which to spend your time. (see also skill #5, page 247.)

As you go along, you must do some preliminary evaluation of the information for its usefulness and suitability for your purposes. The title will often give you clues to a book's or article's usability. A date may show whether a book or article is up to date or too old for consideration; an abstract (if available) can help you decide if an article is appropriate to your level of comprehension and to your topic.

Once you have found a promising resource, preview it critically to see if it is worth a closer look. For books, check the author's credentials on the flyleaf, scan the table of contents and index, and skim through the book to check for style, vocabulary level, charts, etc. For periodicals, consider the reputation of the periodical, check the type of publication (scholarly journal? general interest magazine?) for level of language and depth of scholarship, and skim through the first paragraph of the article. For Internet sites, consider the relevancy and depth of the contents, check for a current publishing or revision date, and look for a reputable author and/or sponsor. (Because Internet sites require a whole new concept in evaluation technique, we will discuss how to further evaluate web sites in detail later). Once you have completed these previews with a critical eye, you will have narrowed your research materials to a reasonable set of resources from which you can derive useful information.

Evaluating Traditional Sources

Most book and periodical publishing companies have strict guidelines for what they will publish. Editors and experts in the particular subject areas read, verify the accuracy of, and evaluate manuscripts that are submitted for publication; librarians who purchase the materials for their institutions also review these sources. Although you should apply the criteria discussed below to all prospective sources of information, when applicable, your part in evaluating traditional books and periodical articles primarily involves checking for appropriate content and currency. Evaluating Internet resources, however, calls for more critical thinking and analysis. Information found on web pages does not have the editorial and selection filters mentioned above; the author puts whatever he or she chooses directly on the Internet, so you must be even more cautious in examining each information source.

Evaluating Internet Resources

So much can be found on the Internet, but how much of it is valid, useful information? Because the Internet lacks the quality control of print sources, the following criteria—authority, objectivity, currency, content, accuracy, quality, style, and functionality—can help you evaluate on-line sources carefully and critically (Figure 10-4).

Authority. Determine the author of the page. What are his or her qualifications for writing on this subject? Is there an e-mail address or professional affiliation? Look at the bottom of the web page or go to the home page for author information. It is often possible to find the home page, where the credentials are usually located, by "peeling back" the URL (Internet address) by level (separated by "/") to get to the root address of the site. If no author is indicated, or only a first name is given, be skeptical of the content.

Objectivity. Determine the purpose of the page or site: entertainment, business/marketing, reference/informational, news, advocacy, personal page. Does

FIGURE 10.4 *An incredible source?*

the site represent an organization that wants to sway your opinion? What are the goals of the organization? Is only one point of view presented? Does the site want to sell you products or services? Who is the publisher or sponsor?

Check the "root domains" of the URL to find the type of group responsible for the web page: .edu (educational), .gov (governmental), .com (commercial), .org (organizational), .net (network), or .mil (military). The symbol ~ in front of a name may mean a personal home page. Again, peel back the URL to find the home page of the site. Don't accept the information presented at face value. Take the web site's underlying intent into account.

Currency. Determine the currency of the web page or web site. Is the date of publication clearly labeled? How recently was the web page revised? Is it up to date? The date is usually noted at the bottom of the page, or you may have to peel back the URL to the home page of the web site to find out when it was published.

Content. Determine if the content of the page fits your needs. What topics are included in the page? Are the topics explored in depth? Is the language used at the appropriate level of scholarship? Be sure that the kind and level of information are suitable to your research project.

Accuracy. Determine the accuracy of the information. Are the sources of information given? Are they reliable? Is the information verifiable elsewhere?

Keep a critical mind and question the sources. Use additional print materials to complement and confirm the information.

Quality, Style, and Functionality. Determine the site's presentation. Is it laid out clearly and logically with well-organized subsections? Is the writing style appropriate for the intended audience? Are the grammar and spelling correct? Do the links work and are they current? A reliable, professional site is accurate, organized, and functional.

Remember, most Internet sites have not been reviewed or checked for accuracy by experts in the field. Anyone can put anything on the Internet and call it "information." It is up to you to critically evaluate the material you find before using it in any kind of research project.

Summary of information literacy skill #4: To choose appropriate, accurate information for a project, the critical thinker must:

• Evaluate sources and information as an ongoing process during all stages of research.

• Evaluate sources and information by using the criteria of authority, objectivity, currency, content, accuracy, quality, style, and functionality.

EXERCISES

1. Select any controversial topic that has at least two clearly opposing sides. Then locate at least three internet sites on this topic. Choose two of the sites where their points of view conflict on this topic, one pro and one con. Describe in detail (by providing specific examples) how the information presented conflicts.

_____

_____

_____

_____

_____

(continued)

_____

_____

_____

_____

_____

_____

2. Evaluate the sources above for their currency, objectivity, style, and authority.

_____

_____

_____

_____

3. Compare the methods used in evaluating Internet sources with the methods used in evaluating information in periodicals and books.

_____

_____

_____

_____

4. Compare the criteria for evaluating the credibility of scientific information discussed in Chapter 9 with the criteria discussed in this chapter.

_____

_____

_____

_____

SKILL #5: ORGANIZING AND APPLYING INFORMATION EFFECTIVELY TO ANSWER QUESTIONS OR SOLVE REAL-LIFE PROBLEMS

Once you have collected the information you plan on using in your paper, the next step is to organize and synthesize what you have found and choose what is important to answering your research question.

Organizing Material

After you have gathered information and before you begin writing your paper, presentation, or project, you should decide on a tentative thesis and compose a preliminary outline. A **thesis** is a one-sentence statement of the central theme of your research; the thesis statement is like a hypothesis used in solving a problem. Your thesis statement will answer the research question you posed at the beginning. For example, the research question "What is the best way to delegate responsibilities?" might now lead to the thesis statement "The manager's ability to delegate responsibilities effectively plays a crucial role in keeping an organization running smoothly." A brief, tentative outline would include the major points of your verification of this statement; it reflects the structure of the argument you will use to "prove" your thesis. The pieces of information you gather are the premises; the thesis statement is the conclusion.

As you look over what you have found, organize your information and categorize it into your outline. This tentative thesis and outline will guide you in your organization, but, as a critical thinker, be sure to remain flexible; be prepared to modify the focus of your research, depending on the material you choose.

Choosing Material

How do you choose which information to use? One of the central tasks of critical thinking is determining if information is acceptable. In the previous skill section, we discussed criteria for evaluating materials we found while researching. There are, however, also common sense factors we take into account as we encounter information. We generally accept information if it doesn't conflict with our background knowledge or observations and if it seems to come from a credible, unbiased source.

Background knowledge is information we have accumulated through experience and observation. We naturally tend to weigh new information against what we already believe is true. Generally, we can trust our background knowledge and so we challenge information that is contrary to these beliefs. As critical thinkers, however, we should not automatically rule out information completely just because it conflicts with our background knowledge. For example, because of a bad experience at a previous workplace, we may have a negative view of unions, so when we read about a new union-approved contract, we might tend to dismiss it as being unfair. Our past experiences and/or observations may be inaccurate or not directly applicable to the information in question. Critical thinkers keep an open mind and investigate thoroughly any new information. They also read widely and maintain an inquiring mind so that their base of background knowledge is broadened.

A *credible, unbiased source* is a knowledgeable person who has no reason to be biased on a subject. A person's knowledge or expertise is usually based on his or her education, training, or experience in a given field. We naturally tend to accept information from an expert. However, we should realize that the expert's knowledge should only be applied to his or her relevant area of expertise. An expert in personnel issues would not necessarily give factual information on marketing strategies, even though both these areas are part of the business world. We should also take into account the objectivity of the expert. Does he or she gain an advantage from providing the information? Critical thinkers evaluate the credentials of experts and investigate any possibilities of bias in their information. Sort out conflicting claims by weighing the evidence and examining ideas thoroughly. Once you have established connections among the ideas, examine *how* these ideas "fit" the thesis and general research question you are answering. Having designed an argument, examine its implications for other ideas.

Once you have organized, evaluated, interpreted, and synthesized the material, you can use the information to answer your research question and accomplish a specific purpose, whether that is to create a research paper, develop an oral presentation, or solve a real-life problem.

Summary of information literacy skill #5: To organize and apply information effectively, a critical thinker must:

• Organize material by constructing a thesis statement and an outline.

• Choose information by keeping in mind the common sense evaluation techniques of background knowledge, observation, and credibility.

• Combine, interpret, and apply information to create a final product.

• Examine the implications of the information to explore connections to related ideas.

EXERCISES

1. Compare developing a thesis statement in this section with developing a preliminary hypothesis in a causal analysis in Chapter 9.

   _____

   _____

   _____

   _____

   _____

2. Using materials from the exercises in skills 2, 3, and 4, collect and interpret the data on the subject of pay equity and gender. Then describe how the data can be organized in a coherent inductive argument.

   _____

   _____

   _____

   _____

   _____

   _____

   _____

   _____

   _____

   _____

SKILL #6: ACCESSING AND USING INFORMATION LEGALLY AND ETHICALLY

The branch of law called **intellectual property** is based on the idea that original works, including publications, cannot be used without acknowledgment or permission. This is the foundation of the copyright regulations that govern the legal use of materials created by others. Using another person's words or ideas without giving credit is called **plagiarism**. This theft of written materials is a serious offense with academic consequences that can involve failing the assignment, failing the course, or even being dismissed from the institution.

Plagiarism can be committed in several different ways: by failing to use quotation marks around quoted material, by failing to cite words and ideas borrowed from others, and by failing to use your own words when summarizing and paraphrasing material.

Most people realize that they must cite direct quotations used in their research, but often they assume that if they summarize or put the ideas from the material in their own words, no citation is necessary. This is incorrect! You need to include a citation to the sources you use because you take ideas from them, even if you combine these ideas with your own. The only time a citation is not needed is when the material is *common knowledge*. Deciding what constitutes common knowledge, however, can be tricky. Famous names, dates, and places are usually considered common knowledge, as well as common sense information and information referred to in many sources. If you are not sure if something is common knowledge, consult your instructor or other knowledgeable person in the field.

Many cases of plagiarism occur by careless note taking and record keeping. To avoid plagiarism, be careful when taking notes. If you write down the exact words from a source, put those words in quotation marks on your note cards. When paraphrasing or summarizing, use your own words to restate the author's meaning. Because one of the purposes of the citation is to allow the reader to find the source you used, record your source of information: author, title, publication information, and page numbers. You will need these data for your citations and for your bibliography list.

As a serious researcher it is up to you to acknowledge your sources of information accurately in your research. This is called *documenting* your sources. It usually involves giving credit both within and at the end of your paper. As you use information in your text, you must use a citation to show exactly where the information originated. Then, at the end of your paper, you must have a list (variously called a bibliography, works cited, or references) of all the sources used.

There are several different styles of documentation that are acceptable in research projects, depending on the academic discipline involved. The most common are the Modern Language Association (MLA) format, used for history and the humanities, and American Psychological Association (APA) format, used for social sciences such as psychology, sociology, and business. The Chicago style and Council of Biology Editors are other, less frequently used documentation styles. Even though the order in which the elements of a citation are presented and the punctuation and capitalization within the citations may differ for each style, each entry requires the basic, universal components of a citation: author, title, and publication information. If in doubt about which style to use, consult with your instructor, or consider using the same format as in the sources you are citing. In any case, be consistent: once you choose a style, stay with it.

Books and web sites for documentation styles include:

- *MLA Handbook for Writers of Research Papers* (5th ed.) by Joseph Gibaldi. New York: Modern Language Association of America, 1999.

- *Publication Manual of the American Psychological Association* (4th ed.). Washington, DC: American Psychological Association, 1994.

- *The Columbia Guide to On-line Style* by Janice R. Walker and Todd Taylor. New York: Columbia University Press, 1998.

- Research and Documentation On-line
  http://www.bedfordstmartins.com/hacker/resdoc

- Bibliography Style Handbook
  http://www.english.uiuc.edu/cws/wworkshop/bibliostyles.htm

- MLA Style: Documenting Sources from the World Wide Web
  http://www.mla.org/set_stl.htm

- Electronic Reference Formats Recommended by the American Psychological Association *http://www.apa.org/journals/webref.html*

- Basic Columbia Guide to On-line Style
  http://www.columbia.edu/cu/cup/cgos/basic.html

- On-line Resources for Documenting Electronic Sources
  http://owl.english.purdue.edu/Files/110.html

Summary of information literacy skill #6: To access and use information legally and ethically, a critical thinker must:

• Recognize and avoid plagiarism by citing words and ideas borrowed from others.

• Acknowledge sources accurately by using a standard, appropriate documentation format.

···················· **EXERCISES** ·····················

1. Assume you are writing a report for work or for a class project. Explain by way of example how you would use material assumed to be common knowledge in your field. Now explain how you would use material in your field that would require appropriate citation. Provide specific examples.

   _____

   _____

   _____

   _____

   _____

2. Write an MLA or APA citation for a textbook, periodical article, and an Internet source on any subject relating to the benefits of corporate community involvement.

   _____

   _____

   _____

   _____

Summary

IN THIS CHAPTER WE:

- Discussed how information literacy leads to lifelong learning

- Explored six information literacy research skills

Exercises

1. List six critical thinking skills you can use to become information literate.

2. Discuss how you would use each of the search skills in investigating the "right" college for a prospective high school graduate.

Writing from Experience

Write a brief essay discussing the research strategies you would use in investigating a possible career change either within your organization or within a totally new field.

TOPIC COVERED IN THIS CHAPTER

- Definition of moral reasoning and its relevance to critical thinking

- Three ethical theories: utilitarianism, duty theory, and virtue theory

- Application of moral reasoning and moral theory to business ethics case studies

- Moral syllogisms

- Individual role in moral decision making

- Applying moral reasoning skills to "real-life" situations

Chapter

11

CRITICAL THINKING AND MORAL REASONING

KEY TERMS

categorical imperative

descriptive claims

prescriptions

utilitarianism

values

In the commercial world, honesty in business is a service, not merely and mainly to the other parties of the transaction. Fidelity is an act of loyalty to the general confidence of man upon which the whole fabric of business rests.

– Josiah Royce, Philosophy of Loyalty

Some of the most difficult decisions we face at work have little or nothing *directly* to do with business. For example, how many of us have agonized over decisions such as telling a supervisor that a colleague has arrived thirty minutes late three out of five days every week for the past two months; that a coworker spends half the morning playing solitaire on his or her computer; that a manager and employee have an intimate relationship where favorable treatment is offered at work; that a new job offer arrived and a response is due in less than two weeks; that a product your boss approved meets legal guidelines but is still defective. These difficult personal decisions involve moral dilemmas faced every day on the job. Although they may be ultimately related to the success of the organization, they seem far removed from business decisions concerning matters like the bottom line, profit margins, market share, and the global economy.

In this chapter we will clarify the nature of moral reasoning and examine specific examples of how critical thinking is applied to moral decision making. Although no hard and fast solutions to the moral dilemmas are offered, this chapter provides general guidance on how to approach these difficult decisions.

Moral Reasoning

Moral reasoning is commonly defined as reasoning about what is right and wrong and good and bad. However, according to our criteria for good definitions, this is vague, untestable, and lacks explanatory power. More important, determining what is good or bad or right or wrong is the difficult task. We need to analyze this concept more critically.

As social animals, we are constantly faced with questions about what we ought to do in certain circumstances, what doing the right thing is, and what course of action we should recommend to our friends, family, and coworkers. Discussions about matters of morality touch us more deeply than others, and they often evoke strong emotional reactions. Yet, moral reasoning is basically no different from reasoning about other matters, with one key difference: Conclusions of moral arguments express values; they tell us how we *ought* to conduct ourselves.

Some philosophers argue that if we gather all the facts and apply logical thinking, we should have no difficulty in reaching conclusions in any argument, including moral arguments whose conclusions express values. Others have argued that moral decision making is merely a function of calculating the most pleasure produced by an act, subtracting the pain that might be caused by that act, and then figuring out the balance. If the balance of pleasure is more than pain, then we should promote that act. But as we know, when agonizing over personal moral dilemmas, it's just not that simple.

The Language of Morals: Description and Prescription

The specific language we use in moral discourse is of the utmost importance. Even the slightest shade of meaning can influence an audience because each word or phrase can convey moral condemnation or approval. The tone of expression, the connotation, and nuances in language can make a big difference in what is conveyed. That fact that we are often passionately concerned about moral issues demonstrates how important the language is that we use to express ourselves in these contexts.

DESCRIPTIONS

Descriptive claims are simply statements of fact (or purported facts). They convey information about some past, present, or future event and are claimed to be either true or false. They purport (or propose!) to offer an objective accounting of what occurred or might occur, and do not express evaluative judgments about those events, assuming that it is possible to eliminate personal bias, perspective, and cultural contexts, which of course, is questionable. For example, "Total sales figures for all products for last year were 10 percent higher than the total figures for the year before" is a descriptive statement that is either true or false. Descriptive statements are intended to be morally neutral. For example, the statement, "There are six chairs in this boardroom" conveys no emotional, evaluative, or moral component, and is purely descriptive. Descriptive claims are verifiable by observation, experimentation, and testing.

PRESCRIPTIONS

Prescriptions are statements about how things *ought* to be or *should* have been. They ascribe value to events or actions, asserting judgment or assessment of the action or event. Prescriptive statements also ascribe *norms* or standards, a set of acceptable behaviors agreed to in a society, to our actions. In short, they prescribe some action that you ought to perform; that action is deemed good or bad, right or wrong. For example, "Lying to your coworkers about the new incentive program is wrong" expresses a negative value and is prescriptive. The statement, "Loyalty to your management team is a quality we admire" prescribes a positive value. These kinds of claims are not generally verified in the same way as factual claims, that is, by observation, experimentation or testing. Rather, they are assessed by measuring them against a set of principles and norms of a society.

NONMORAL PRESCRIPTIONS AND FACTUAL JUDGMENTS

Not all prescriptions express *moral* judgments or standards. Sometimes we recommend (prescribe) an action that has little or nothing to do with morality. For example, "Brand X toner is good for this type of copying machine" expresses a value judgment about product X and implicitly suggests that we ought to use that brand. But the judgment and implicit recommendation are not intended as moral prescriptions. They are intended as *practical* recommendations, procedures, or practices.

These practical statements take on the role of a description because they depict the copier's qualities (a good toner is one that makes darker copies, produces less mess, etc.). "Good" in this case can be determined factually, through observation and testing but without appeal to social norms and moral principles. Moral assertions, on the other hand, express value judgments that are not based solely on their practical value. The statement about the toner is unlike the purely descriptive "there are six chairs" but also unlike the moral admonition, "lying is wrong." It is a prescription that expresses non-moral value.

RELEVANCE TO CRITICAL THINKING

In Chapter 2 we saw how certain linguistic expressions affect our intended meaning and reactions to what is said. This is especially true in assessing moral arguments. In many instances, determining the precise meaning may involve determining which statements are intended as moral value judgments and which are intended as factual statements and which are intended as merely practical recommendations. Getting clear on the kind of dispute we are engaged in is an essential first step in resolving the dispute. Is the disagreement about a factual matter, a moral issue, or a practical suggestion, or some of each?

EXERCISES

I. Determine which of the following are descriptive and which are prescriptive. Then state which express nonmoral value. (Some of these exercises are intended to stir debate.)

1. Deceiving a customer about the defect in the product, no matter how minor, is wrong.

   _____

   _____

2. Informing the customer about the minor defect will decrease sales of that item.

   _____

   _____

3. The company has never told us what a "minor" defect is.

   _____

   _____

4. It is company policy to inform supervisors in advance if you know you will be late.

   _____

   _____

(continued)

5. Maria should tell her supervisor when she is going to be late.

_____

_____

6. Being late week after week shows that Louis does not have his life in order.

_____

_____

7. The company's new day care center was a good idea.

_____

_____

8. I don't like the idea that the company charges each employee per child for day care use.

_____

_____

9. You should always check the fax machine for messages before leaving the office.

_____

_____

10. Going to the cafeteria for lunch is a bad idea.

_____

_____

II. In the following passage, identify the statements that are intended to be descriptive, prescriptive, or practical nonmoral judgments.

Katrina, an activist for women's rights in her organization, was celebrating a recent decision to award salary adjustments to women who were discriminated against over the years by her company. A colleague, Joshua, suggested sarcastically that she continue her battle with the company. "Why stop now?" he said. "Sue for back pay, why don't you?"

He added, "If you are adjusting salaries for women, then you should know that salaries have been out of line for some time. You've been here for ten years, haven't you? According to your own statistics, you've been losing $1,500 a year, or $15,000 over ten years." Katrina replied, "Good idea. Why not? Shouldn't I and others who endured past inequities be reimbursed?"

Some of her colleagues agreed that they ought to receive back compensation. Others thought that because they made their point and were now on equal footing, they should simply accept the decision as is. Besides, they argued, if it's expensive for the company, we could see layoffs.[1]

_____

_____

_____

_____

_____

_____

_____

III. Develop a brief essay discussing which aspects of the above case are best decided on factual considerations and which on moral grounds.

_____

_____

_____

_____

_____

_____

_____

_____

·······WRITING FROM EXPERIENCE·······

Briefly describe an ethical dilemma you have encountered at work. Discuss which aspects of the conflict were (should be) decided by becoming clear on the factual matters and which aspects were decided on becoming clearer on the moral issues.

_____

_____

_____

_____

_____

_____

_____

_____

_____

_____

_____

_____

_____

_____

_____

_____

_____

_____

Ethical Theories

Most moral decisions are made within a framework or set of principles that help guide us in the decision-making process. These frameworks or theoretical models provide fundamental assumptions that form the background against which we test individual decisions. In western philosophy there have been many such theories. In this section we will examine two ethical theories popular in American culture.

UTILITARIANISM

Jeremy Bentham (1748–1832) sought an objective basis for making value judgments that would provide a common, publicly acceptable measurement tool for determining social policy and social legislation. He believed he could accomplish this by examining polices in terms of their beneficial and harmful consequences. He assumed that the benefits and social costs of actions could be measured on a common numerical scale and then added or subtracted from each other. The outcome could be determined quantitatively as a matter of weighing benefits against costs. If the consequences of an act resulted in benefits outweighing costs, then that would be the right act to follow, because that act produced the most happiness for the most people.

Sometimes called "The Greatest Good Theory," **utilitarianism** is built on the proposition that we measure overall happiness in terms of the pleasure and pain produced by the actual or potential consequences of an act or rule. The act that produces the most overall happiness (pain or pleasure) for the greatest number of people is the morally good course of action. Modern versions of utilitarianism are especially attractive to business situations because they use concepts such as "cost-benefit analysis," "outcomes" and, of course, "utility." Due to its reliance on economic measurements of success for happiness and concerns for usefulness, some philosophers have gone on to say that utilitarianism is merely a practical guide for business decisions and not an ethical theory at all. More on this later.

Case Study

THE FORD PINTO CASE

1

Let's make this clearer by example. One of the most well-known case studies in business ethics is the Ford Pinto case.[2] In the 1960s Ford Motor Company's position in the automobile market was dwindling due to heavy competition from fuel efficient, Japanese-made cars. The company desperately tried to regain its market share by designing and manufacturing a low cost, subcompact, lightweight car. The company felt pressure to produce the car within two years instead of the normal four-year time frame. Hence, design changes usually made before production would have to be made during production. The urgency led the company to focus on design features geared toward the marketplace and to compromise some of its testing requirements regarding engineering. The resulting design dictated that the gas tank would be located behind the rear axle, leaving it vulnerable to punctures in cases of rear-end collisions. In preliminary crash tests the company found that when struck from the rear at 20 mph or more, the tank would rupture and gas would spray out into the interior compartments. The spray might spread to passengers and ignite in real accidents at higher speeds.

Ford decided to proceed with production nonetheless. The design met government standards applicable then for gas tank safety and, according to their own cost-benefit studies, the cost of modifying the design would exceed the profits they might make if they delayed production.[3] Their studies estimated that the modified gas tank for a projected 12.5 million cars would eventually cost about $11.00 per unit, totaling $137 million. Ford would add the cost of the modification to the car, passing on that cost to consumers.

CASE

1

Their statistical projections showed that there would be about 180 deaths and 180 serious burn injuries and 2,100 burned vehicles out of 12.5 million cars. At the time, the government calculated that human life had a compensatory value of $200,000; insurance data showed that burn injury awards were $67,000 and $700 for the value of a subcompact car in salvage.

If Ford paid out the claims, it would cost (180 × $200,000 + 180 × $67,000 + 2,100 × $700) $49.15 million dollars. If they did not modify the car, consumers would be asked to pay costs of $49.1 million instead of $137 million, resulting in a greater cost to society at large (potential consumers) for leaving the design as is and going ahead with production. Eventually, Ford phased out the Pinto, but sixty people died and at least 120 people suffered severe burns due to exploding gas tanks.

This kind of reasoning, that is, cost-benefit analysis, fits the utilitarian model because it measures the costs (damage, medical expenses, lost income, and future income) against gains in benefits, even though the calculation is in purely economic terms. Although Bentham did not measure social costs solely in such terms, one can see how this theory could be expressed in this way. Nonetheless, Ford used this reasoning in arguing that their policies were justified and socially responsible based on cost-benefit analysis.

Alternative Rationale

Not all applications of utilitarian analyses result in the negative outcome of the Ford Pinto case. Ford could have used a utilitarian rationale by showing how negative publicity resulting from deaths due to a faulty design would affect future sales, which, in turn, would outweigh redesign costs. In fact, recent automotive marketing strategy emphasizes design safety as a major selling point of their cars. This emphasis has resulted in benefits for both consumers and increased sales of safer cars for automakers. Of course, the real troublesome issue in this case is setting a fixed amount of money to the worth of a human life. Whether $200,000 or $2 million, setting the value of life in terms of dollars causes concern.

Personal Applications

Although the case focuses on decision making at the top level of a corporation, one could easily imagine moral dilemmas occurring at all levels of the company. One such dilemma that comes to mind immediately involves "whistleblowing."

A whistleblower is someone who sounds an alarm from within the organization, aiming to bring attention to abuses or dangers that threaten the organization and its members and/or the public interest. When internal alerts fail, whistleblowers often go outside the organization to protect themselves from retaliation or to protect the public interest.[4]

.... **EXERCISES** ....

Suppose you were a Ford employee and had knowledge that the gas tanks were placed in a potentially perilous position. When you brought this to the attention of your supervisor, you were told to leave the concerns to the engineers and upper management. "If it were really a problem," your supervisor said, "they would fix it." However, you wanted to pursue the matter further, so you brought it to the attention of higher level management and received a similar response. At some point, you decided to blow the whistle on the project, but not without a great deal of personal risk. Even though new legislation has been enacted to protect whistleblowers from possible intimidation or retaliation, you were still very concerned about your future in the company. Further, your colleagues would question your loyalty to them and to the company.

In a brief essay, provide a utilitarian argument that would defend your going outside the company to draw attention to the potentially dangerous design. Identify which premises characterize the argument as utilitarian. Identify which statements express moral judgments, especially the conclusion.

_____

_____

_____

_____

_____

_____

_____

DUTY THEORY

Although the Pinto case lends itself conveniently to a cost-benefit, utilitarian analysis, many ethical dilemmas fit more easily into other theoretical ethical models. As we shall see in this section, the role we play in moral decision making determines to a great extent which approach is most appropriate. Moreover, as we saw in the Ford Pinto case, utilitarianism, as a consequentialist theory, has its problems.

An alternative, nonconsequentialist theory offered by the German philosopher Immanuel Kant (1724–1804) is concerned with moral rights. Kant argued that we possess moral rights regardless of utilitarian benefits and are obligated to certain duties irrespective of their utilitarian outcomes. His theory is based on the maxim that every human being should be treated as a free person equal to everyone else, and everyone has an absolute right to such treatment. All human beings have a moral duty to treat others in this same way simply because they are fellow human beings, no matter what the individual's circumstances.[5] Utilitarian principles, on the other hand, base moral rights on maximizing beneficial consequences, which differ from circumstance to circumstance. According to Kant, utilitarian principles cannot become universal moral *laws* (Kant called them categorical imperatives). Moral laws, he says, must be universal, applicable to all human beings without exception and without sole regard to contingencies or individual personal preferences or benefits.

The foundation of Kant's moral theory is the **categorical imperative**: One ought to act in such a way that the maxim for acting should become a universal law (i.e., it is categorical, without exception). Stated in another way, a person should act in a way that he or she would recommend that act for *everyone* in a similar situation, and for the same reasons. In this sense, the act must be "universalizable" to all humans. The principle is akin to the Biblical injunction "Do Unto Others" in that it requires you to treat others as you would want to be treated yourself, but further requires that acting toward others is not based on benefits that might accrue from the act. Rather, it is always based on "pure" motives, never treating others as tools or means for some other purpose. The test for a moral law is to ask: Would I *will* (i.e., chose, recommend) this act for *everyone* in the same situation?

Application of Kantian Reasoning

An example of Kantian reasoning is applied to the following. Suppose you are a human resource manager in a small organization. You advocate a policy that requires hiring people who, like yourself, are interested in tennis, fine cigars, and are male. For this rule or policy to be universally acceptable, you would have to be willing to accept that if you were a woman, nonsmoker, nonathlete, you would advocate this same policy, something that presumably you would be *unwilling* to do. The policy would fail the test for becoming a universal moral law and, therefore, cannot be applied as a moral duty.

In the Ford Pinto case, the company decision makers knew that the product had serious safety risks and that consumers were ignorant of this fact. In a Kantian analysis, they would have to be willing to advocate marketing the car even if they themselves were in the position of an uninformed consumer buying a Pinto. If not, marketing the car would fail the test of universal acceptability and fail the test of becoming a moral maxim. The moral law tells you what you ought to do—it provides the rule of duty you must follow.

Moral Arguments

The trouble with theories like utilitarianism, some say, is that statements of fact-descriptive claims, including statistical and mathematical calculations of cost versus benefit, cannot imply prescriptive claims attributing moral values. That is, we cannot infer what *ought* to be the case from statements about what *is* the case. Prescriptions cannot follow logically from descriptions.

> For example: Susan is a single working parent of young children. Therefore, Susan ought to provide adequate day care for her children.

The argument on the surface is fairly convincing. But on careful logical examination we discover it is missing a premise. The fact that Susan is a single working parent does not *by itself* imply anything about her moral obligations. Jumping to the conclusion based on this fact commits the naturalistic fallacy because there is nothing in the descriptive statement that morally obligates Susan. The argument lacks the implicit moral premise that contains the obligation: "One ought to provide adequate care for one's children."

Now we can form the deductive argument:

> All parents ought to provide adequate care for their children.
> Susan is a parent.
> Therefore, Susan ought to provide adequate care for her children.

Statement 1 expresses a categorical moral prescription, statement 2 a fact, and statement 3, the conclusion, a moral judgment. Without the moral prescription about caring for children we could never reach the conclusion, no matter how many factual claims we make about the benefits of adequate care for children.

The argument takes the form:

> All P (parents) are A (adequate providers).
> All S (Susans) are P.
> Therefore, All S are A.

You might object to this analysis by noting that the additional premise is unnecessary because it is trivially true. Obviously, one ought to care for one's children. Or, you might claim that because "adequate care" already contains the moral prescription, the extra premise is not needed. But the objection that the phrase already contains a prescriptive element begs the question. For the meaning of "adequate care" to convey a moral prescription, one must have already decided on what was moral *before* constructing the argument.

Elements of the Moral Arguments

The following scheme summarizes the above analysis of the moral deductive argument.

> Moral Standards, Maxims, Principles (premise)——>
> Factual information, descriptions of behavior (premise)——>
> Moral judgments about the rightness or wrongness of the behavior (conclusion).[6]

In ordinary arguments, the sequence of these elements need not be presented in this order (the conclusion might be stated first, the factual information last). When assessing a moral argument for its validity or strength, you use the same strategies you applied in evaluating all arguments. For example, you could attack the factual claims, showing which ones lack support or contradict known information, or are inconsistent with other claims in the argument. You could attack the moral prescription showing that other individuals or institutions can or should provide care for children, not just a parent. Or, you could construct a counterargument by analogy (see Chapter 5). But if you accept the premises unchallenged, then the conclusion follows.

The above analysis also shows that even though one cannot deduce an "ought" from an "is," the factual information contained in the argument is not only *relevant* to the resolving the conflict, it is essential to it. Even if Kant is right—facts alone do not settle a moral dispute—the facts are *necessary* ingredients. Whether we can indeed infer a moral judgment from factual information is still debatable in philosophical circles, but the debate is beyond the scope of this text.

Here are some additional moral arguments with moral premises supplied.

1. Louis promised to work late to complete the team project. (One ought to keep one's promises.) So, Louis should work late.

2. The advertising strategy to sell pellet guns to teenagers deceived people into thinking the guns could not penetrate human skin. So, we should either discontinue selling to teenagers or alter our advertising. (Intentional deception is morally wrong.)

3. The organization collects from married employees for insurance premiums more than double that of two non-married employees. (All people ought to be treated equally.) The company should charge married employees the same as non-married employees.

4. I have a new job offer. The headhunter wants a response immediately. With such short notice, I should turn it down.

EXERCISES

I. For each of the following, a moral principle must be added to make the argument valid. Supply the missing principle.

1. The company's safety policies prohibit female employees from working in hazardous duty areas. Therefore, they are not allowed opportunity for extra compensation for hazardous duty.

_____

_____

2. Maria filled in for Cindy on her project twice this week. The least she could do is return the favor once in a while.

_____

_____

3. Affirmative action based on quotas is illegal. Our company sets aside fifteen spaces in its training program for minority candidates. This practice should be stopped.

_____

_____

4. If you bring drugs to work, you'll lose your job.

_____

_____

5. The company's CEOs promised more diversity in their training programs. We should see some results.

_____

_____

6. The company's president was seen taking bribes. He should resign immediately.

_____

_____

7. Ahmed stayed late three times this month. He should get some kind of compensation even if he is a salaried employee.

_____

_____

8. The married couple in the next office suite voted on each other's request for promotion. They should have at least abstained.

_____

_____

II. Case Study: The Megaliter: Caveat Emptor

Television Advertisement:

> Hey kids! Want a monster thirst quencher? Ask the Mega Monsters—They drink the new Choco-Blaster. The new extra energy megasize chocolate drink! A thirst-blasting taste in a full-size liter bottle. Not your ordinary size soft drink. Try it now!

Let's assume that this fictional television advertisement appears during prime viewing hours for young children and uses favorite cartoon characters promoting the "megaliter." The drink appears in larger-than-life pictures with larger-than-life cartoon characters.

(continued)

However, a liter is a standard unit of measure of liquid capacity. Thus a megaliter in this context is exactly the same as a standard liter. It is no larger than any other liter and contains the same amount of drink as a standard liter. The prefix "mega," in a technical sense, also means "a thousand." Thus, the ad could be misleading in this sense as well. However, recent popular usage understands the meaning of "mega" as "large," "great," or "powerful."

Let's also assume that a recent survey claims that 50 percent of children believe that a megaliter is larger than a standard liter.

The research also shows that a significant number of those who thought a megaliter contained more soft drink also live in poor neighborhoods with low literacy rates and in neighborhoods with a large elderly population, many of whom have vision problems.

The decision makers in the company selling the drink are split over the policy of marketing this product to children with the potentially misleading label. Some executives say it is deceptive advertising and could cause trouble with federal regulators or consumer advocacy groups; others say it's just good business. Both sides express concern for the potential loss of jobs in the community if the marketing strategy fails.

1. In a brief essay, develop a utilitarian argument defending the policy of marketing giant quarts. Include in your argument a rationale for marketing this product to poor and senior citizen communities.

    _____

    _____

    _____

    _____

    _____

2. In a brief essay, develop a Kantian argument defending the prohibition of such marketing. Which statements in your argument characterize it as a nonconsequentialist defense?

    _____

    _____

    _____

    _____

    _____

    _____

3. In a brief essay, develop your own argument either defending or attacking the marketing strategy. Construct a diagram of the argument.

_____

_____

_____

_____

_____

_____

Individual Role in Moral Decision Making

Most of us occupy more than one role in life. These various roles affect the decision-making process because the position or status you occupy determines to a great extent the approach you use in moral reasoning. For example, the decisions you make as an employee, supervisor, manager, or consumer will involve different reasoning processes, depending on the level of responsibility and the individual roles you play in these situations. Moreover, the reasoning processes you use at work will differ from ones you use at home as a parent, citizen on local committee, or officer on a local board of directors. An example from politics demonstrates how role plays an important factor in decision making.

> It is well known that former New York governor Mario Cuomo would defend both his belief in the right to life as a Catholic and his duty as governor to uphold the laws of the state allowing abortion.

Assuming that we can separate our personal and professional lives as clearly as Mr. Cuomo, we can see how the role we play in the moral decision-making process can affect the outcome of the decisions. (Do you think Kant would take issue with this?)

Summary

IN THIS CHAPTER WE:

- Defined moral reasoning

- Showed how moral reasoning is similar to and different from other types of reasoning

- Examined the language of moral reasoning, especially the distinction between prescriptive language and descriptive language, and demonstrated its relationship to critical thinking

- Explored two influential theoretical models of moral reasoning with case studies on how these models apply to real situations

- Compared moral syllogisms with other types of syllogisms

- Discussed how various roles in life influence strategies used in moral reasoning

- Examined closely a case study by applying the principles of critical thinking learned in earlier chapters

Exercises

I. Putting Your Skills to Work

Ethical Conflicts at Work: Whistleblowing and Company Loyalty—Point-Counterpoint

Instructions:

The following arguments focus on the conflict between company loyalty and whistleblowing. The first argument, presented by Professor Sissela Bok, characterizes the conflict as a "lesser of two evils"—whistleblowing always shows disloyalty, and the whistleblower experiences extreme negative consequences for blowing the whistle, even though the act is sometimes necessary and justified. Professor Robert Larmer argues that although there are circumstances when whistleblowing may be seen as breach of loyalty, it need not be. In fact, whistleblowing can actually be the "highest" form of company loyalty.[7]

1. Construct an argument in your own words defending Sissela Bok's position on whistleblowing.

    a) Explain the merits and deficiences of this practice in utilitarian terms.

    b) Describe how Immanuel Kant would react to your argument.

2. Construct an argument in your own words in defense of Robert Larner's position criticizing the practice of whistleblowing.

    a) Explain the merits and deficiences of restricting the practice of whistleblowing in utilitarian terms.

    b) Describe how Immanuel Kant would react to your argument.

3. Diagram both arguments.

4. Which argument do you believe is stronger? Defend your answer.

TOPIC COVERED IN THIS CHAPTER

- Applying critical thinking strategies to management decisions

- Identifying obstacles to critical thinking in management

- Working toward solutions: Four approaches for analysis

- Communication analysis

    - Inductive reasoning

    - Information-based reasoning

    - The logic of consequences

APPLYING CRITICAL THINKING TO MANAGEMENT DECISION MAKING

One thing is clear in the study of managerial work: the manager plays the major role in the unit's decision-making system. As its formal authority, only the manager can commit the unit to important new courses, only the manager has full and current information to make the set of decisions that determines the unit's strategy.

– HENRY MINTZBERG, *MANAGING WITH PEOPLE IN MIND*[1]

The aim of this chapter is to apply the principles, techniques, and strategies examined in the text to real-life case studies you might encounter at work. Four case studies are presented, each one analyzed in the context of a different critical thinking strategy. The first case involves applying informal reasoning and communication analysis discussed in Chapters 3 through 7. We will focus on how emotively charged language contributes to a conflict among employees. The second case focuses on the general critical thinking strategies of inductive reasoning examined in Chapters 8 and 9. The third case applies the strategies and techniques for conducting information research, which were discussed in Chapter 10. The final case involves integrating several approaches but focuses on the "logic of consequences."

It should be clear by now, however, that no one strategy should be applied at the expense of another. In some situations one approach is more effective than another as a *primary* strategy, but in most situations the best solution is to take into consideration a variety of approaches. Open-mindedness is essential to critical thinking, including the approaches to critical thinking itself. A comprehensive, integrative approach will be discussed at the end of the chapter.

Case Study

1

STRATEGY: ATTENTION TO LANGUAGE

In this case, confusing, unclear, and emotively charged language contributed to an existing conflict between two groups of employees. The problem, which requires a management-employee solution, is exacerbated by poor communication between the groups. Hence, our approach will focus on language as an obstacle to clear thinking. We will also analyze the overall structure of the problem.

BACKGROUND

Marcel Rabeau owns and operates fourteen lawn, garden, and household equipment sales and service stores. The stores are located within a hundred-mile radius of each other, but most of the service and repair work is done in a large service center located in Marcel's hometown, where the first store opened thirty years ago. The service center and warehouse are adjacent to the flagship store, which he manages. Marcel grew up in the business, starting with repairing lawn mowers, snow throwers, and small gas engines. Eventually, he bought the business and has been running it ever since.

Although many of the products Marcel sells are national brands, he has service contracts to repair all items sold in his stores and those in competitors' stores. All parts for national brands are shipped to the service warehouse where an inventory control system monitors stocks of supplies and materials. The service and repair staff share space in the parts warehouse building.

The repair and service end of Marcel's business, although profitable in itself, is seen by store managers as supporting the retail sales end of the business. Sales staff and store managers handle all requests for repairs and service and then pass the requests along to the service center for processing and disposition. The company has achieved success based on a reputation for both quality service and competent, friendly sales staff. The company motto is "Quality service with quality products." The sales staff rely on the high level of support from the service people to clinch sales and maintain an edge on their competitors.

The service center also runs its own service van to pick up items for service or repair. The cost of running the van (driver, insurance, gas, etc.) does not come out of either the stores' budgets or the service department's budget. However, the service department hires and trains drivers as well as supervises the daily operation of pickup and delivery.

CASE

1

THE CONFLICT

The view that the service department's role in the company is to support the sales staff is not shared by all employees in the company, particularly those in the service department. Tension among store managers, sales staff, and service center staff has increased over the years to the point where Marcel felt compelled to call several problem-solving meetings. He asked store managers, sales managers, and service managers to try to come to some resolution by the end of the fiscal year. So far, after three meetings, no real solutions have emerged. The tension is mounting as resentment builds. Marcel hopes the situation will not deteriorate to the point where it affects the quality of service and attitudes toward customers.

The service department sees the conflict as one of fairness. From their perspective, there are two issues underlying the debate: inadequate recognition and appreciation for their work and unequal compensation for their time and effort. The retail people see the problem as timeliness of service and inadequate recognition for their work.

Details from the Service Perspective

When urgent requests for repairs or service come in to the stores, the urgency is passed along to the service department. In order to accomplish a quick turnaround, the service department must rely on nonconventional mail operations and specialty carriers such as overnight delivery services, same-day delivery, and internal and external courier services. This increases the cost to the department, which operates on its own budget. Equally important, service staff must work late on Fridays and most of the day on Saturdays in order to return the repaired items back to the store by closing time on Saturdays, if possible. This incurs overtime expenses and increases staffing problems.

Because the service department must show a profit, the staff complains each time they are billed for added expenses passed on to their department. They argue that the sales staff and store managers should absorb some of the costs of extra expenses incurred for rush orders in their budgets. Or, the stores should charge customers for work completed after 5 P.M. on Fridays and on Saturdays. In addition, they contend, all staff should tell customers to place their requests for service earlier in the week to avoid the weekend time crunch. In other words, if customers want work done in a hurry, they should either plan ahead or pay more. At the very least, the service department shouldn't have to pay for the extra expenses out of its budget. There must be some way to charge customers or the stores for added expenses. The stores should build this into their budgets, or the company should find a better way to calculate department net profits.

The second issue is related to the first. Many of the service people resent working on weekends, even with overtime pay. Moreover, many of them give up lunch hours or stay late working on last minute repair orders, sometimes without extra pay. Most store managers leave at the close of the day, even though they work Saturdays and Friday evenings. "Besides," say the service people "store managers make a lot more money than the hourly wages paid to service staff. The whole issue for us is fairness."

The salespeople rotate weekend responsibility, coming in every other Saturday and Friday evening. Service staff rarely have the option to work weekends. However, sales commissions on the weekends are nearly double the amount of what they earn during the week. So, few salespeople complain about weekend work. Most take a day or two off midweek anyway.

Details from the Sales Perspective

The sales staff, on the other hand, argue that customer service is essential for successful sales, the ultimate goal of the company. They can't tell a customer, who decides on Thursday, that he should have thought about repairs a lot sooner than on Friday or Saturday. Nor do they want to be put in the position of saying, "To have this lawn mower fixed in the next two days will cost you 20 percent more" and then ask the customer if he or she is interested in buying a new hedge trimmer. Raising the price of the equipment in general to accommodate increased costs for servicing the equipment is not the answer either. Most salespeople claim, "The service department should realize that their work helps sales, and that's the only concern—it's the bottom line. Their budget problem is not our concern." Some add, "Look, the main issue is an accounting matter as to which budget gets charged. Besides, it's about time the service people earned their keep."

CASE

1

THE DEBATE

The manager of the service department, Helena Feurstein, approached Mr. Rabeau as follows.

> I keep hearing that the stores appreciate all we do for them but the workload is getting out of hand. My department has to show a profit or we get in trouble. This affects our yearly performance evaluations. That stinks! They keep demanding that service be done on weekends, late evenings, and after normal hours, and so on. Do you know what that costs us? Then they whine and moan when it takes a week to service their equipment. Every time I use FedEx® or an overnight delivery service it costs me a minimum of $16 to send the item back. If I use an independent courier service, it costs me up to $60! It's killing us and it's just not fair.

> On top of it all, do you know what I have to pay my repair crew to work on weekends and Friday nights, even if I can find someone? We get penalized for doing extra work! The more we do on weekends, the more customers expect they can just walk in and demand to get their equipment repaired in one day. If the salespeople had any guts, they would tell the customers that we can't work miracles here. At the end of the year, the service department has to scramble to show a profit when all the added expenses are figured in.

They're a bunch of wimps anyway. They're interested only in the commissions they can earn. Store managers are interested only in the bottom line—their store's profit margin. Either they charge customers more or they quit complaining. Those are the only options.

Mr. Rabeau passed along Helena's complaints to store managers in nearly the same language in which it was conveyed to him. He mentioned modest price increases on some items and larger increases in service charges for most items as one way to solve the problem.

The store managers decided to meet on their own to elect a spokesperson to speak with Mr. Rabeau. First, they met with their salespeople to make sure they had the information they need to plead their case. The store managers sent Ralph Lowman to represent them with their concerns. They want to convince Mr. Rabeau to avoid price increases of any kind, which would take them out of competition with rival companies, especially the new megastores. One thing they have going for them over the large chain stores is speedy, high-quality, low-cost service.

Mr. Lowman begins the discussion with Mr. Rabeau as follows:

We have been telling the service people for years that they do a good job. What else do they want? They're paid well for their work. For people without a lot of education they do OK in the repair business. And they're not always that speedy. Some of the equipment comes back from repair almost two weeks after we put in the order. Sometimes I'd like to tell them either put up or shut up. That's the way it goes in business. The customer is always right. They know that the option of increasing prices will hurt everyone. The service people must be mad, but they should think this thing through rationally.

Mr. Rabeau calls a joint meeting one more time between both groups. His comments are as follows:

Look, you're both acting like a bunch of babies. Can't we do something here? Can't we resolve this? The way I see it

CASE

1

is that I am going to institute some changes. First, the stores will be financially responsible for shipping items to the center, and the center is responsible for costs associated with shipping them back to the stores. That way, the salespeople will think a little harder about the real costs for servicing equipment. Second, my office will be entirely responsible for the company vans. That means I will supervise transporting items between the stores and the center. I have asked for one of the assistant service managers to help me with tracking costs and running the van. His salary will come out of my office. This will cut down on some of the workload for the service department. Third, we will hold bimonthly meetings between both groups to discuss how this plan is working out. Lastly, I will appoint an assistant manager of the main store so I can get out more to the other stores to see what's going on. I will also routinely visit the service center to see how things are working out there, too. OK? Now let's all be nice to each other so we can continue our good reputation and maybe even earn a little more next year with increased sales and service revenue.

············ **EXERCISES** ·····················

I. First, in a brief essay describe:

1. What you perceive are the major problems causing the conflict

_____

_____

_____

_____

2. What the service people perceive are the major problems

_____

_____

_____

_____

3. What sales and store managers perceive are the major problems

_____

_____

_____

_____

4. What Mr. Rabeau perceives are the major problems

_____

_____

_____

_____

II. For each of the previous questions discuss:

1. Whether the dispute involves disagreements over facts or disagreements in attitudes toward the facts. If both, then discuss to what extent it is either one or the other. Make a list of both facts and opinions expressed by all sides of the debate.

_____

_____

_____

_____

_____

_____

_____

_____

_____

_____

_____

_____

2. Do you believe the various positions on the issues can be reconciled? If so, how?

_____

_____

_____

_____

III. Identify emotively charged language in Ms. Feurstein's comments. Specifically,

1. Identify slanters, innuendo, stereotyping, loaded questions, and other persuasive techniques.

_____

_____

(continued)

_____

_____

_____

2. Identify vague and ambiguous language.

_____

_____

3. Translate as much of her emotive response as possible into emotively neutral language.

_____

_____

4. Identify any informal fallacies in the response.

_____

_____

IV. Repeat Exercise III for Mr. Lowman's response.

1. Identify slanters, innuendo, stereotyping, loaded questions, and other persuasive techniques.

_____

_____

_____

_____

2. Identify vague and ambiguous language.

_____

_____

3. Translate as much of his emotive response as possible into emotively neutral language.

_____

_____

4. Identify any informal fallacies in the response.

_____

_____

V. Repeat Exercise III for Mr. Rabeau's response.

1. Identify slanters, innuendo, stereotyping, loaded questions, and other persuasive techniques.

_____

_____

_____

_____

_____

2. Identify vague and ambiguous language.

_____

_____

3. Translate as much of his emotive response as possible into emotively neutral language.

_____

_____

4. Identify any informal fallacies in the response.

_____

_____

VI. If the company had established formal channels of communication between management at all levels and employees at all levels, the risk of a prolonged and damaging crisis could be avoided. In a brief essay, propose a formal system of communication among employees that would improve all aspects of communication.

_____

_____

(continued)

_____

_____

_____

VII. Do you believe Mr. Rabeau violated Ms. Feurstein's confidentiality in repeating to Lowman her response? How would you have handled the situation in conveying the service department's concerns to store managers?

_____

_____

_____

_____

VIII. Summarize Ms. Feurstein's argument in less than twenty-five words. Next,

_____

_____

1. Identify the premises and conclusions.

_____

_____

2. Diagram the argument.

_____

_____

3. Construct your own argument in defense of Ms. Feurstein's position.

_____

_____

4. Construct a counterargument in opposition to her position.

_____

_____

IX. Repeat Exercise VII for Mr. Lowman's argument.

_____

_____

1. Identify the premises and conclusions.

_____

_____

2. Diagram the argument.

_____

_____

3. Construct your own argument in defense of Mr. Lowman's position.

_____

_____

4. Construct a counterargument in opposition to his position.

_____

_____

X. In a brief essay of approximately two pages, describe how you would resolve this conflict. In your essay, you should:

1. Describe what steps you would take to gather more information.

2. Construct an argument to convince both parties of what the "best" course of action is.

3. Diagram your argument at the end of the essay.

_____

_____

_____

_____

(continued)

········WRITING FROM EXPERIENCE········

Describe an experience at work or at home where ineffective and emotionally charged communication contributed to a conflict. Discuss how the problem was resolved. Discussed how clear communication played a role in solving the problem.

_____

_____

_____

_____

_____

_____

_____

_____

_____

_____

_____

_____

_____

_____

_____

_____

_____

_____

Case Study

2

STRATEGY: APPLYING INDUCTIVE REASONING

This case study examines four approaches to line supervision in a large warehouse distribution center. The case focuses on how management styles affect employee production and efficiency. We will describe each supervisor's approach separately and then analyze the style and content of their actions in the context of inductive reasoning strategies discussed in Chapters 9 and 10. However, the case study is not intended as a guide or a systematic analysis of management styles. Rather, it is merely a sample comparison of how supervisors actually interact with employees. Although we will apply inductive reasoning strategies, neither the application of them nor the case itself is a comprehensive review of approaches to management.

BACKGROUND

The D-B Shoe Company is a large distributor of shoes manufactured in foreign countries. They warehouse and ship low- to medium-priced shoes to department store chains throughout the United States. One of their distribution centers is located in a medium-sized city in the northeast. The warehouse operates twenty-four hours a day in three shifts. We will describe the management style of two day shift supervisors, one second shift, and one third shift supervisor.

THE PROBLEM

Senior management has become concerned about the efficiency of this particular distribution center. Approximately 2 percent of the materials shipped from the center had arrived at their destination stores in damaged condition. Most of the damaged material was returned and recorded as "lost merchandise." Moreover, production at the plant in terms of the total number of cases shipped lags behind other distribution centers of similar size. The center also accumulates more incorrectly filled orders than the other centers. Although 2 percent seems like a small figure, the loss amounts to millions of dollars to the company. Management believes that most of the damage loss and lower production rate are due to sloppy work habits, short-cut measures, and loosely and inconsistently enforced production procedures. The problem has persisted for nearly two years.

The company hired an independent observer/consultant to advise senior management on a strategy to rectify the situation. But first, the company needed to understand the causes of the problems. The observer not only watched employees in action; he also conducted extensive interviews with the supervisors and line people.

The Floor Workers (Order Fillers)

Orders from chain stores are processed in the central office of the warehouse and sorted into categories for various departments to fill. For example, orders for larger items like hiking boots and winter all-weather boots were handled by one department, which then divided them into adult and children's, men's and women's categories, etc. Smaller items such as sandals and shower shoes were handled by a different department, which then sorted them into smaller categories.

Some shift supervisors would collect the orders from the main office at the beginning of each shift and then parcel them out to floor workers to fill. Some supervisors liked to alternate the types of shoes filled by an order filler (floor worker) because they could avoid complaints from order fillers about working only with heavier and/or larger shoes. In addition, some fillers disliked working with rubber products because they carried an unpleasant odor and some created rashes when handled without gloves for extended periods of time.

Order fillers would receive their list of orders as soon as they punched in for work. Some supervisors arrived early to place the orders in the floor worker's company mailbox before the shift started. The floor worker could then review the order immediately and begin to plan how to fill the order most efficiently. For example, children's boots were located in large stacked bins next to women's loafers, men's boots next to men's sneakers, etc. The order filler would like to save time and energy by filling the orders according to some rational sequence in the warehouse's physical layout. The orders were filled by placing the shoes into cases, which were then loaded into larger crates. The larger crates were boxed in sealed metal containers for shipping. The filled order sheets were returned to trays and picked up by "runners" who would bring the sheets to the main office for tallying and processing.

A labyrinth of large and small conveyors carried the filled cases and crates into holding areas where they were again sorted according to store destination. The metal containers were then stacked onto pallets, which were loaded into trucks waiting at the loading docks.

The Day Shift Supervisors

Mike Intereri is a gregarious and likable person. He chatted most of the day with his floor crew, joked around with them, often at his own expense, and made his presence known throughout the shift. An easy-going guy, people

CASE

2

liked him and would defend him against criticism from upper level management. Management thought he was "soft" on employees.

Mike always arrived on the floor just before 7 A.M. with the day shift crew and chatted with them as they punched in. He chided them about having to "work their tails off" to beat the third shift's output. He added, "The night crew probably sabotaged the conveyors again and they'll probably go on the fritz for us like usual." He smiled and gave encouragement as they headed on to the floor.

He quickly surveyed the conveyors as he walked over to chat with the preceding shift supervisor. Both shifts milled about, one leaving their filled orders in trays while the other picked up their orders for the day. He asked Tom Barszak, the third shift supervisor, how things were going. Tom replied, "It was an uneventful evening, just a few log jams on the conveyors, and conveyor #23 near bin A-15 was slow because some of the wheels need grease or fine-tuning. Nothing drastic." Mike said, "OK, I'll keep an eye on 23 and I'll see if the jams were cleared." He headed for the conveyors.

On any given day, there would be minor breakdowns of the conveyors, dropped and spilled crates, incorrectly pre-sorted bins, and other minor mishaps. On rare occasions, a conveyor would shut down completely or a forklift would accidentally tip over a large bin. All too often, it seemed a major shipment of shoes to the warehouse would be delayed. The first two problems were attended to by a crew of trained maintenance workers and their helpers. The shipping delays, however, created a different problem. The delays meant blank spaces on the order sheets. This required extra work for the order fillers because they had to mark in the margins which shoes would be missing on the order. They then had to fill out a special form for a "back order" request.

If a conveyor malfunctioned to the point where it must be shut down, it held up production for an entire area until it was fixed. This affected a shift's output even if the cause did not occur on that shift. If cases jammed but did not cause a shutdown, they could damage the conveyor and/or slow down production. All equipment failures were reported immediately, and maintenance crews were dispatched as quickly as possible to fix the problem. Work stoppage and employee safety are the primary concerns of all supervisors.

Mike wanted to be prepared for what he might face that morning so he would attend to maintenance problems first. He always responded to problems early but rarely, if ever, inspected the equipment at the beginning or end of the shift for preventative measures. Nor did he conduct routine maintenance checks of the equipment such as greasing and cleaning movable parts. He felt that if things were running smoothly, he could attend to maximizing output. He wanted to make sure his people were working as efficiently and productively as possible. Even though each shift was not evaluated on its total output, there was definitely competition between them. Besides, he reasoned, it's maintenance's job to keep the equipment running smoothly.

He constantly reinforced the idea with his people that a safe, productive working environment is not only good for the company but good for employees. When it came time for raises and merit citations he wanted his people to be first in line. He also supported them by making sure that they knew he cared about their well being. He thought, "If they're happy, I'm happy."

Susan Daley also worked the day shift but on a different floor. She shared one thing in common with Mike—she was usually on the floor, making her presence known. Unlike Mike, she was shy, quiet, and engaged in banter only to reduce tension in a difficult situation. Even though she was a bit uncomfortable in that role, she tried to be outwardly pleasant most of the time. Most of the floor workers were neutral to her. They neither disliked her nor especially liked her. They saw her constant presence as tolerable. They appreciated the fact that she took her job seriously, even if some of them didn't.

As was her habit, Susan arrived a few minutes early so she could pre-sort orders and alternate the types of orders to be filled by the floor workers before they punched in. She wanted to leave time to chat with the preceding shift supervisor to discuss his impression of how things were going before she started her shift.

She asked the night shift supervisor about which conveyors were acting up with minor squeaking or rubbing noises and which needed more serious

CASE

2

attention. She considered preventive maintenance as a major concern even if it took time away from production. She reasoned that avoiding slow-downs and shutdowns would, in the end, save time and effort. However, she was not pleased with the fact that other shift supervisors left the preventive work for her. Maintenance always seemed to occur on her shift, which also did not endear her to the maintenance staff.

Another preventive measure she liked to implement was carefully monitoring sharp corner turns in the conveyors. That's usually where the jams occurred. If the day's work involved mostly large cases, she would even place a helper at that corner to prevent the backlogging of cases from jamming against each other and from falling on the floor. This also cut down on damage because the jams were the primary cause of spills. The spilled cases could damage the shoes when they hit each other or bounce on the floor. The maintenance department resented this "totally unnecessary" use of staff.

Because the preventive measures took time away from direct contact with order fillers, they felt she was more involved with equipment than with them. Also, these measures slowed down operations from time to time. This led to complaints from the floor workers that their output suffered due to her "overprotectiveness" of the equipment. And the maintenance people groused that her approach was "overkill," which took time away from more immediate jobs. Her conversations with employees were direct, cordial, and almost always about improving production. (Secretly, some gossiped that she should either "lighten up or get a life.")

As she paced the floor, she checked all the conveyors herself, making sure that they were in good operating condition and making sure the computerized "case counters" on them were working properly. The counters kept track of the number and types of crates packed in each shift.

The Night Shift Supervisors

Tom Barszak was energetic and well liked by his people. He covered the 11 P.M. to 7 A.M. third shift, a difficult task in itself. Many of the workers were new because the night shift had the biggest turnover in staff. The turnover was due to transfers to the day shifts. However, the union recently negotiated a contract that called for an extra 5 percent pay increase for the second (3 P.M. to 11 P.M.) shift and a 10 percent increase for the third (11 P.M. to 7 A.M.) shift. Despite the extra wages, there was still a big turnover of employees on these shifts.

Two other factors contributed to the difficulty in supervising the night shifts. First, there were fewer maintenance people available, which made repairs take longer to complete and little or no time for preventive measures. Second, more than a few of the night workers held other jobs, most worked part-time and a few full time. As a result, some avoidable errors could be traced to inattention due to tiredness and distractions from other jobs. The night shift had the highest error count in filling orders.

Tom held things together very well despite the inherent problems. He would spend time with the floor workers, listening to their complaints about "slackers" and "whiners" in his department. He avoided preventive maintenance because, like the night maintenance department, the shift was always short staffed because absenteeism also took its toll on this shift. This cut into his production schedule, which always fell short. It got so bad some evenings that he would tell his people not to fix the jams. They should take the cases off the conveyors to clear the jam and then place the blocked ones on the floor. If he found the time, he would later call maintenance helpers to fix very minor problems and ask them to replace the cases on the conveyors while they were there fixing the problem.

The second shift supervisor, Kelly Ward, worked her way up from order filler to supervisor on this very same floor. She felt empathy for her order fillers and came to their defense whenever possible. In return, they trusted her, worked hard, and appreciated her laissez fair attitude. She did her best to stay in the background while letting people know she was always available. She spent a good deal of time talking individually with employees, asking about their well being and trying to avoid personnel conflicts before they started. She believed that tension in the workplace led to stress, which in turn led to errors. Besides, as the newest supervisor in the company, and a two-year probationary supervisor, she did not want to alienate her people early in her career. She also wanted to make a strong

CASE

2

effort to increase production as much as possible. When it came time for employee performance evaluations, she wanted to be sure that her floor was the most productive of all the second shifts.

Like Tom, she believed that employee harmony and production output are the supervisor's primary concerns. She also told her people to place jammed cases on the floor for maintenance to take care of. She did not want to distract them from filling orders. Working the night shift was difficult enough, so keeping her people focused and concentrating on what they were supposed to do was her primary goal.

EXERCISES

For these exercises, consult Chapters 8 and 9 of this text.

I. In a brief essay of approximate 200 words, describe the main problems facing senior management of the company.

_____

_____

_____

_____

_____

_____

_____

_____

_____

_____

(continued)

_____

_____

_____

_____

_____

_____

_____

_____

_____

II. List four generalizations about each of the supervisor's management style.

_____

_____

_____

_____

III. List four necessary and four sufficient conditions that would lead to efficient production in this distribution center. Also list three necessary and sufficient conditions for error-free production.

_____

_____

_____

_____

_____

_____

_____

IV. List four common factors among supervisors' management styles that are directly related to efficient production.

_____

_____

_____

_____

_____

_____

_____

_____

_____

_____

_____

V. List five difference factors among supervisors' management styles directly related to efficiency and production and then five for error-free production.

_____

_____

_____

_____

_____

_____

_____

_____

_____

(continued)

VI. List five factors not directly related to management style that you believe affect efficiency and production. For example, the fact that some third shift employees were tired from working two jobs is related to errors might be a factor outside the shift supervisor's control (even though the supervisor could consult with upper management on developing company policies to address this problem).

VII. List in order of priority which common and difference factors have the greatest impact on production.

_____

_____

_____

_____

_____

VIII.   If you were the manager of the distribution center and had received the observer's descriptions of supervisors' styles, list the five most immediate actions you would take to address the causes of the problems in the center. Then list four long-range plans that would improve efficiency at the center.

_____

_____

_____

_____

_____

_____

_____

_____

_____

_____

_____

_____

_____

_____

_____

_____

_____

········WRITING FROM EXPERIENCE········

Describe the management styles of at least three supervisors you have had worked for. Then analyze their management styles in the context of common and difference factors.

_____

_____

_____

_____

_____

_____

_____

_____

_____

_____

_____

_____

_____

_____

_____

_____

_____

_____

Case Study

STRATEGY: APPLYING EFFECTIVE RESEARCH METHODS

This case focuses on strategies for gathering information. Specifically, the case examines how a budding entrepreneur must first develop a strategy for collecting, analyzing, and applying information to a decision-making problem involved in starting his own small business.

PRELIMINARY RESEARCH FOR A NEW BUSINESS

One of the first and most important steps in undertaking a risky adventure such as starting a new business in today's competitive market is collecting "good" information on which to base your decisions. An effective strategy for locating sources of information, and the ability to evaluate those sources, are essential for the success of any new venture. Once the information is collected, you must then organize it into a coherent format so that you can access and use it effectively in your decision making. For the first part of the case study we will focus only on locating the most suitable site for the business venture.

BACKGROUND[2]

Even though it was late, Kevin Nett felt a rush of excitement as he pored over the marketing research report on his desk. Working as an engineer had been satisfying to Kevin, but he had always wanted to be his own boss and manage his own business. Maybe this waterpark idea was the answer. The timing seemed right. Although Kevin was married with one small child, he had not incurred substantial debt after college. He had few immediate financial obligations, and his mortgage payments were reasonably small thanks to help from his parents. He was only 29, had several excellent business contacts in the community, and was anxious to make his mark in the business world. Besides, the next step in the company would be a promotion to a higher level of management, which would remove him from the hands-on work he liked so much, the source of his satisfaction in the job.

Kevin sat back in his chair and thought about all of the people he knew who loved water sports. While he was a young boy and all through his college years, he and his friends had made numerous trips to various types of amusement and theme parks. Many of his fondest memories were of his visits to waterparks. Unfortunately, there were only two within driving distance to Tuscaloosa. White Water, located north of Atlanta and Point Mallard, located in north Alabama near Decatur. Mr. Nett thought about all of the young people and families in the Tuscaloosa, Birmingham, and

Montgomery population centers and he envisioned a recreational facility that would be an immediate hit.

All of a sudden, this distant dream was beginning to move closer to reality. Kevin had begun to develop his plan. He proposed several design layouts for land and equipment needs. He also was able to locate construction firms who specialized in building amusement and theme parks and obtained cost and time estimates for actual construction as well as the water requirements needed to support various size parks. One of the major issues that needed to be addressed quickly was the basic decision on the makeup, size, and location of the park.

TYPE OF PARK AND LOCATION

Kevin is only interested in developing a waterpark and is only considering locations in or adjacent to Tuscaloosa, Alabama. The community's lack of water facilities has convinced him that such a waterpark would be an immediate hit in the local community. Kevin feels that the park would attract a broad range of single people and families.

The waterpark will be called Aquapark. Development is projected to be accomplished in three phases. Phase I will consist of a kiddie pool with slides and water toys, three combined water slides, free fall and speed slides, a river run, and sunbathing areas. There will also be a picnic and lounging area near the main building.

Phase II will consist of a wave pool, surf pool, and bumper boats. Phase III will feature an advanced river run and other possible future additions such as a party area, which would be reserved for birthday parties and family gatherings.

Land Sites

Three possible sites in the Tuscaloosa area have been recommended to Kevin. Based on his park configurations, the park will require approximately 35 to 60 acres to accommodate all three phases.

One location is near the Northport suburb, north of the Blackwarrior River and Highway 69. The site is 44 acres of wooded, rolling terrain. This location has a selling price of $4.8 million. Highway 69 is a major artery through Tuscaloosa. There is one factor that could decrease the value of this site. I-359 currently does not extend to that part of town, and the scheduled extension to be built includes no provision for an interchange near the waterpark site. This situation would have to be studied to determine the impact on the waterpark before this site could be selected.

The second location is at the south end of town on Highway 82. This site offers 85 acres of heavily wooded, flat, swampy terrain. The land sells for $13,600 per acre and can be subdivided for $20,000 per acre. A major racetrack and a national forest are located nearby so there is a moderate flow of tourist traffic in the area. Major earthmoving costs would be incurred in adapting this site.

The third location is on Highway 11, east of town. There are 52 acres of slightly rolling terrain available for $890,000. Mr. Nett felt he needed to do more research on housing and construction in the area. The city seems to be expanding in that direction. The location is three miles off of I-59, the major interstate highway linking Birmingham, Tuscaloosa, Meridan, Mississippi, and New Orleans.

At this time, Mr. Nett is considering only locations that are in close proximity to Tuscaloosa. He believes that a Tuscaloosa site would be a prime location sufficiently close to population centers and major interstate highways.

INFORMATION STRATEGY

As a critical thinker, he wants to make sure that he has considered all the relevant data before making his decision on the best location. The task before him is to develop a strategy to ensure that he has indeed considered all the relevant data. An information literate entrepreneur will have an edge on the competition and a sound, well-informed basis for an effective business plan.

EXERCISES

For the purposes of this case, you will examine only the issues directly related to site location. Obviously, other considerations are important, such as raising capital, staffing plans, marketing strategy, construction costs, and time available to devote to the project. As a parent, resigning his position from a financially secure employment situation is very risky. The longer Kevin devoted full time to this project, the longer he would be without an income.

I. As with every case study analysis, the first step is to define the problem clearly. In a succinct essay, describe the major problems in locating his park.

_____

_____

_____

_____

_____

_____

_____

_____

_____

_____

_____

_____

_____

_____

II. This exercise has several parts. It asks you to consider a comprehensive strategy for collecting relevant data on which to base your decision for the most suitable site for the park. In responding to the questions refer to the specific skills discussed in Chapter 10 of this text.

1. Skill #1. Recognizing the need for relevant and usable information has already been addressed to some degree in developing this case study. Your responses to the first question further defined the problem. Now the need for "good" information must be established. In the context of the problem, discuss the following information literacy requirements:

   a) Briefly describe the scope of the information required. That is, what are the tentative limits of your investigation? Remember, the longer you take to conduct the research, the longer it will take you to begin actual construction of the project. State the problem in the form of a research question—a topic you want to research.

   _____

   _____

   _____

   _____

   _____

   _____

   _____

   b) List the types of sources available to you for background information (for example, practical texts on "how to start your own business," would be a good place, among others, to begin you general inquiry). What other types of general background sources are relevant to the project?

   _____

   _____

   _____

   _____

   _____

   _____

   _____

_____

_____

c) List other related subjects you plan to research later on but plan to set aside the details for now. As you gather information on site location, you might come across other useful information for further analysis later.

_____

_____

_____

_____

_____

2. Skill #2. Strategies for locating the information are the next logical steps in researching your topic.

a) Explain in detail how you will explore at least six types of information discussed on pages 228–233 of this text. For example, if you decide to interview professionals in the field as a possible source, provide examples of the questions you might ask them. If you investigate government sources, what specific types of documents would you require (e.g., EPA rules and regulations, demographic information, housing trends, etc.)?

_____

_____

_____

_____

_____

b) List where each of these sources can be found.

_____

_____

_____

(continued)

c) Estimate the amount of time you think you will need to locate these sources. Explain how you arrived at this estimate.

_____

_____

_____

_____

_____

3. Skill #3. Accessing information effectively requires an assessment of the research tools immediately and easily (and in this case, inexpensively) available to you. Assuming that you have easy access to on-line search capability, and that academic and local libraries are available within a 30-minute drive, discuss in some detail how you will begin actually searching the types of information sources you have identified above. Include at least six types of research tools you would use in your description. Describe how you would use each tool.

_____

_____

_____

_____

_____

_____

_____

_____

_____

_____

_____

_____

4. Skill #4. Evaluating the information and its source is the next essential step in the process. Because you would be using government sources for a great deal of the data (e.g., for zoning regulations, environmental impact regulations, traffic patterns, and demographics, traffic and land development patterns, etc.) their credibility in terms of objectivity of this information is fairly well established. However, you should comment on some of the other criteria such as currency, relevancy, and scope. Evaluate the other sources you will use according to the criteria for skill #4 in Chapter 10 on pages 242–245. Discuss each criterion in detail as it applies to the data you will be collecting.

_____

_____

_____

_____

_____

_____

_____

_____

_____

_____

_____

_____

_____

_____

_____

5. Skill #5. For the last task in this exercise, step back from the material for a while to look at the "big picture." That is, you should now turn to organizing all data you have collected into categories. Then examine the various types of information by enumerating possible connections and relationships to each other and to related data. As recommended in Chapter 10, an outline with a research question is a good place to begin. Your research question might be "What is the most suitable location for an waterpark within a 50-mile radius of Tuscaloosa?"

(continued)

a) Construct an outline (or a schematic diagram) of the information you want to gather and have already gathered into categories. Examine the categories in view of your research question.

_____

_____

_____

_____

_____

b) Explain how the categories respond to the kind of information you are seeking. Your outline should show the connections among the pieces of information. That is, describe as best you can how all the pieces "fit" with each other and with your plan. Some information might be categorized as "for future consideration." For example, availability of water could be related to environmental impact studies. Even if there is an ample supply of water, there may be restrictions on its use.

_____

_____

_____

_____

_____

c) Prioritize the information into essential (necessary) and sufficient rankings. That is, which data are absolutely essential to locating the park and which are sufficient to locating the park.

_____

_____

_____

_____

_____

d) For imprecise information, such as the estimated time involved in conducting the searches, interpret the consequences for the various time estimates.

_____

_____

_____

_____

_____

6. Describe five examples in which your searches could lead to unethical or improper practices. Use the guidelines discussed in Chapter 11, skill #6 to complete this exercise.

_____

_____

_____

_____

_____

III. In a brief essay of approximately 300 words, discuss your strategy for gathering information on which to base your marketing plan for the waterpark.

_____

_____

_____

_____

_____

_____

_____

(continued)

Case Study

4

MANAGING A STAFF REDUCTION PLAN

It is always a difficult task to inform someone who has been a loyal, productive employee that his or her position is being eliminated. No matter how hard we try to look at this aspect of management in a critical, objective, and logical way, we can never eliminate the emotional side of this responsibility. In fact, management studies show that in addition to "bottom-line" considerations, human factors are critically important to all levels of management decisions. Nonetheless, it is often necessary to carry out decisions resulting in the elimination of an employee's job. This case examines both human factors and hard-line business decisions.

We will use an integrated approach in analyzing this case. However, the focus will be on the "logic of consequences," which is a decision-making process that assumes that current actions are based on (projected) future effects of our decisions. In addition, the logic of consequences also assumes that the desired outcomes are arranged according to a set of priorities or preferences.[3] The strategy has at least two other names—the "best alternative theory" and the "maxi-min theory," which requires that we maximize positive outcomes while minimizing negative effects.

CASE

4

BACKGROUND

Ms. Roberta Ratchett is the department head and director of a countywide education, counseling, and treatment program for alcohol and substance abusers. The program is primarily funded through grants from state human services agencies. Ms. Ratchett oversees four programs under the auspices of the Dutchess County Department of Mental Health and coordinates several education programs in cooperation with local school districts. The organization also jointly sponsors four community programs with the support of local businesses, the United Way, and with direct funding from county and city agencies. Each of the smaller programs is supervised by a program director or by a part-time program director/clinician.

When Ms. Ratchett was interviewed for the position, she was told in very clear terms that one of her first and major responsibilities would be to develop a short-term plan to reduce the agency's budget by nearly 50 percent. As with many human services programs, the bulk of the operating budget consists of personnel line item expenditures. Rent was subsidized through a separate grant, and supplies, travel, and other expenses were modest compared to the personnel side of the budget.

RATCHETT, THE HATCHET

She suspected that the agency wanted to hire a qualified "outsider" who had no personal attachments to the agency or its staff. She could then face the layoffs with the least amount of personal investment and personal relationships with the staff. The rumor mill had spread the word that the state wanted a hatchet man/woman to carry out a "massacre" in the agency. The unflattering phrase heard in the break room and in the hallways was "Ms. Ratchett, the hatchet."

CASE

4

Roberta was 30 years old at the time, married with two small children. She had an associate's degree in human services, a bachelor's degree in psychology, and was pursuing her master's in counseling at the local university. There were twenty-four staff members in the program—nineteen professional counselors, three clerical staff, and one paraprofessional. Some of the professional staff members were part-time employees under contract with other agencies for services rendered.

One of the most commonly heard complaints from staff members was their objection to the appointment of a new director who lacked advanced educational credentials to be a department head. Many of the professional staff possessed master's degrees, some doctoral degrees, and a few of the contracted consultants held medical degrees. Some staff groused, "How can she evaluate our work when she doesn't even know what we do. She doesn't even have the educational background [i.e., credentials] to work here, let alone supervise us. Yet she's the one who will decide where to let the axe fall."

TENTATIVE PLAN

Ms. Ratchett had been a very successful administrator in similar but smaller programs. She had a reputation for being fair, well organized, intelligent, and clear in communicating her goals and expectations. She was also known as a strong woman who handled difficult situations effectively and forcefully.

Ms. Ratchett thought long and hard about developing her management plan. However, as she did so she silently criticized the people who hired her and the state sponsoring agency for being shortsighted. The county should have had a crisis management plan already in place before the crisis fell on them. Her predecessor understood the different roles of employees, the stockholders of the decisions, the clients, and the agency's policies. He would have had an in-depth understanding of what could and could not be done. They must have known something was in the works before the final decisions were made. When all the dust settled after the new budget was in place, she would propose a management crisis plan for future administrators to use as a guideline. Once the guidelines were in

CASE

4

place, all employees would have some knowledge of the decision-making process. However, she now faced some difficult decisions for the immediate future with little preparation.

After careful review of the budget with her immediate supervisor, the director of Clinical Operations, and with state fiscal representatives, she tentatively concluded that a minimum of nine professional and one support staff positions must be eliminated. Even though she had little flexibility with regard to the exact number of positions marked for elimination, she did have considerable flexibility with regard to the outplacement of the people involved. The fact that she had a full year in which to develop and implement the budget reduction plan contributed significantly to the options available to her. Important relevant factors included the following:

• The state was willing to offer full college tuition reimbursement to any employee whose position was eliminated.

• The state would fully fund any employee who entered a training program for continuing education and/or a training program for new career exploration.

• There were three professional positions vacant in other departments within the county's parent organization. Qualified retrenched employees had preference for these vacancies. However, two positions were offered at lower salaries than current ones, some maintained seniority status, some did not. One position was a temporary leave replacement position.

• All staff would receive placement counseling and résumé services through the state employment office. Retrenched employees would receive preference for positions in other locations in the state.

• Although severance pay was not an option, the state would provide special temporary benefits for child care services for employees seeking new positions. These benefits were offered to supplement unemployment insurance and union benefits for those eligible.

• Clerical staff were members of the civil service union, professional employees were not unionized.

CASE

4

• Employee performance evaluations were uneven. A few employees had been "written up" by supervisors for various deficiencies and/or disciplinary actions. On the other hand, most employees had glowing evaluations.

• Full-time positions could be split into part-time positions. However, any position converted to less than half time would lose most benefits.

Ms. Ratchett decided she would meet with each employee as soon as possible to discuss the various options. She knew she had to be direct with them. She also understood from her own past experience that they deserved to be treated with dignity and respect. In the meantime, she would focus on the budget to determine exactly how many employees would be affected. Perhaps she could reduce other expenditures, seek special grant funding, or reduce other than personnel services. One thing she knew for certain is that once she gathered the information she needed, she would weigh the pros and cons of the possible consequences. To weigh all the alternatives, she needed to think about the relative importance of their effects.

THE FINAL PROPOSAL

To minimize the impact on personnel, Ms. Ratchett placed a "stop order" on all items other than personnel services. This meant canceling all unnecessary travel, holding all requests for new equipment and supplies, including office furniture, computers, and accompanying software, and urging all employees to use only the supplies absolutely necessary to carry out daily operations. However, these measures saved the equivalent of only one half of a professional line item. She needed to address eliminating or reassigning positions.

She believed she had all the relevant information needed to make her decisions, with one important exception—she did not know the preferences and personal circumstances of the individual employees, the human side of the problem.

She reasoned as follows.

> If I prioritize each position based on the potential conse-
> quences to clients, then I could better target which func-
> tions would have the least dramatic impact on the overall
> effectiveness of the program. If I then consider factors
> such as lowest seniority or weakest performance evalua-
> tions into the decision, I could better serve our clientele
> and maintain a sense of fairness. Lastly, if I take into
> account some of the personal circumstances such as who
> would prefer a part-time position, or prefer to take the
> opportunity to pursue college education, or prefer reloca-
> tion retrenchment, I could serve the staff as well as possi-
> ble under these difficult circumstances. The next step is
> to listen to the staff to learn more about their individual
> situations.

After an initial "ice-breaking" chat, Ms. Ratchett explained the situation to
each employee. Here are some of the personal factors she learned through
her interviews.

> Support Staff A: I've always wanted to be a counselor
> myself. I see what the people do here and I want to be in
> the helping profession myself. The problem is, I only have
> an associate's degree in secretarial science.

> Support Staff B: You probably don't know this but I am a
> single parent with three children at home. I need this job
> and the benefits that go with it. I just returned to work
> after my children entered school. I'm lowest on the sen-
> iority list with the least experience and education.
> Getting a new job won't be easy. Once unemployment
> ends, I can't survive on public assistance. I don't have a
> car, so commuting to a new job is going to be difficult.

> Support Staff C: Are there other support positions open-
> ing up in other areas? I could commute to Kingston if I
> had to. I am the most senior here but I would be willing
> to consider some other options.

CASE

4

Professional Employee A: Sure, everybody knows the trouble all human services programs are in with this slash-and-burn governor we have. Mr. Compassion, he is not. Personally, I can't wait to get out of this business. I'd like to start my own landscaping company. I've heard that there are courses in this at the community college. But I've got two small children at home, I don't think I can afford to lose this job.

Many of the conversations proceeded in much the same way with the remaining professional staff. She listened carefully and took notes for each interview. She would study them along with the various positions and needs of the programs.

•••••••••••••••••••• EXERCISES ••••••••••••••••••

I. As succinctly as possible, summarize the main problem facing Ms. Ratchett.

_____

_____

_____

_____

_____

II. Based on the information available to you about this case, discuss your strategy for downsizing the program. Specifically, list in order of priority the factors described on pages 322–323 that you consider the most important. Provide a rationale for the rankings on your list. Your rationale should take into consideration the consequences of each factor.

_____

_____

_____

(continued)

_____

_____

III.   Discuss to what extent the priority of each of the factors on your list is based on personal considerations, which are based on strictly fiscal considerations, and which are based on both.

_____

_____

_____

_____

IV.   Do you think Ms. Ratchett should address the gossip about her academic credentials? Do you believe she should address the rumors about being a hatchet person? Defend your answers in the form of convincing arguments. Identify the premises and conclusions of your arguments.

_____

_____

_____

_____

V.   In a brief essay of 300 words, explain the decisions you would take if you were the program administrator. Justify your decisions.

_____

_____

_____

_____

_____

_____

Summary

IN THIS CHAPTER WE:

- Applied four critical thinking strategies to case studies in management decision making

  - Communication analysis: removing ineffective, confusing and inflammatory language.

  - Inductive reasoning: examining generalizations, identifying fallacies, evaluating inductive arguments, and establishing causal connections.

  - Information-based reasoning: identifying information sources, accumulating data, evaluating data, evaluating sources, and organizing information.

  - The logic of consequences: evaluating the consequences of decision making in the context of the "best alternative" theory.

- Applied these strategies toward removing obstacles to clear thinking and leading toward well-informed, clearly reasoned solutions to management problems

- Integrated and applied the techniques studied in the text to real-life problems

- Included the opportunity for you to apply these strategies to your own personal circumstances

Glossary

A

access tool – An information source, such as a catalog, periodical index, or bibliography, that leads you to information.

ad hoc premise – A phrase that is used to characterize a hypothesis in an argument. It usually means that the premise was added after the fact and was invented specifically for the purposes of the argument in which it functions. It has little or no testable consequences.

ad hominem – An informal fallacy in which a statement or argument is directed at a person's character or special circumstances rather than the content of what is said by the person. The statement or argument is directed at the source.

ambiguous statement – A statement that could be interpreted in more than one way and the precise intended meaning is unknown. Its intended meaning is made clear by context.

amphiboly – An ambiguity caused by loose, ungrammatical, or awkward phrasing of words, which leads to alternative meanings of a statement. The intended meaning is made clear by correct, clear, or precise phrasing.

analogy – A comparison between two or more entities or events.

appeal to anecdotal evidence fallacy – A fallacy in which reasonable, relevant evidence is ignored in favor of one or two experiences offered as examples to support an argument.

appeal to authority fallacy – An informal fallacy in which reference is made to an expert or noted author in support of an argument. The author's area of expertise lies outside the area under consideration in the argument.

appeal to common belief fallacy – A fallacy in which the evidence in support for an argument is based on commonly held or majority opinions. It has the form, "This is true because everybody (or most people believe) believes that it true."

appeal to common practice – A fallacy in which the evidence in support of an argument is based on commonly held or majority practices. It has the form, "This practice is acceptable because everybody (or most people do) does it."

appeal to force fallacy – A fallacy in which the arguer's support of a statement is based on a veiled or implied threat for not accepting its truth.

argument – A collection of statements in which some of them are offered in support of some other. The statements offered in support of others are called premises and the statements supported are conclusions.

argument by analogy – An argument based on the comparison of two or more events or entities.

B

background knowledge – The body of knowledge assumed relevant and antecedent to an investigation. It is also the body of knowledge generally accepted as true and against which statements under investigation are tested and measured. This body of knowledge includes factual knowledge based on our own personal experiences and experiences of others.

begging the question fallacy – A fallacy in which the conclusion and premises of an argument assert essentially the same thing. An argument whose conclusion contains or restates the premises. Sometimes called circular argument.

Boolean searching – A method of searching data that produces more precise results by compiling search terms using the operators, "and," "or," and "not."

burden of proof fallacy – A fallacy in which the responsibility (burden) for establishing the truth of a conclusion or for proving a point is placed on the wrong party.

C

categorical imperative – A term used by Immanuel Kant for a moral absolute. It is a universal moral statement that entails moral duty.

causal arguments – Arguments based on inductive reasoning which establish a causal connection between premises and conclusions.

causal laws – An inductive generalization in which the causal relationship between entities or events has been proved true.

causal relationships – A relationship in which two or more entities or events are connected in such a way that one is said to be the cause of the other.

common causal factor – In individuals, an entity or event that is present and is presumed causally related to some effect. In groups, entities or events that when present will result in more occurrences of the effect.

conclusion – Statement in an argument supported by the premises.

concomitant variation – A pattern of inductive reasoning in which the occurrence of one event or entity varies consistently with some other event or concurrence, and it is concluded that the events or entities are causally related.

connotative definition – A definition that asserts the sense of a word or phrase, sometimes referred to as its conventional meaning.

critical thinking – A process in which a person evaluates ideas and information and their sources; arranges them according to their reasonableness and coherency; assesses them for their implications; and considers alternative sources and makes connections to other facts and ideas.

D

decision method criterion – An objective and generally accepted method used to verify the truth of statements.

deductive arguments – Any argument whose premises provide conclusive grounds for its conclusion.

denotative definition – A definition that is given by identifying the objects of a class to which the term being defined refers. A list of objects offered as examples of the word or phrase being defined.

dependent premises – Any set of premises wherein two or more premises must be taken together to support a conclusion.

descriptive claims – Statements offered as objective, value neutral, and stated as the "facts" in a case.

difference factor - In causal analysis, the factor among necessary and sufficient conditions that made the difference between the occurrence and nonoccurrence of some event.

E

emotive force - The impact or expression of feelings, sentiments, attitudes, or emotions.

euphemism - An inoffensive, sometimes pleasant phrasing of statements that are substituted for more offensive or unpleasant statements.

explanation - A collection of statements offered in response to the question "why?" An elucidation and/or illustration of difficult or unclear concepts stated in familiar terms.

F

fallacies - An argument in which the premises purport to but do not provide grounds for the truth of the conclusion.

fallacy of composition - A type of grouping fallacy in which an inference is erroneously drawn from the characteristics of the parts or the individuals in a group to the characteristics of the whole or to the group itself.

fallacy of division - A type of grouping fallacy in which an inference is erroneously drawn from the characteristics of the whole group of individuals or of a complex entity to the individuals in the group or to the parts of the complex entity.

fallacy of equivocation - An argument that contains an ambiguity whose meanings are confused in the course of drawing the inference to the conclusion.

formal fallacy - A fallacy resulting from an error in reasoning whereas it is possible for the conclusion of an argument to be false and the premises true.

G

generalization - A statement that asserts a connection from particular events or facts to general events or facts.

grouping fallacies (ambiguities) - Fallacies resulting from an ambiguity in meaning. The ambiguity occurs when it is unclear whether the intended referent of a word or phrase is a group consisting of individuals or a single individual.

H

hidden premises - Implicit statements in an argument that are assumed as premises.

hyperbole - A gross exaggeration or overstatement.

I

independent premises - Premises that individually support the truth of the conclusion without the support of other premises.

inductive generalization - An inductive statement that asserts a generality from particular events or facts.

informal fallacies - A fallacy in which the premises do not support the conclusion due to confusion in the language in which it is expressed rather than due to the structure of the argument.

information literacy - The ability to identify, locate, evaluate, and effectively use information.

innuendo - Statements or phrases used to insinuate or imply something without stating implicitly or directly.

intellectual property - The ideas, publications—electronic or printed—and communications of others.

L

law of contradiction – A term used to describe two statements having necessarily opposite truth values. If two statements are contradictory, one of the statements is true and the other must be false.

loaded question – A question that relies on one or more unsupported assumptions. Sometimes called "rhetorical question," it assumes additional facts related to a desired answer as part of the question.

M

metaphor – An often colorful figure of speech in which one thing is spoken of as if it were another.

N

necessary condition – An object or event without which another object or event could not exist or occur. In causal arguments, the set of circumstances whose absence would prevent the effect's occurrence.

O

objectivity – The lack of bias or prejudice.

on-line catalog – An electronic file of the records of books and other materials in a library's collection, called the OPAC (on-line public access catalog.)

ostensive definition – A definition in which the objects referred to are referred to by pointing or gesturing in some way to them.

P

persuasive comparison – Persuasive language in which one uses a comparison or analogy as its basis for persuasion.

plagiarism – Using another person's words, ideas, phrases with giving credit or obtaining permission.

post hoc **fallacy** – A fallacy in which one concludes from the occurrence of two events in sequence that one of the events caused the other.

premises – In an argument, the statement that is offered in support of some other statement, the conclusion.

prescriptions – Statements that contain value judgments. They assert what ought to be rather than what is.

prevailing factors – See "difference factor."

R

research question – The purpose for researching a project presented in the form of a question.

S

scientific explanation – An explanation based on inductive reasoning and set in the context of an accepted inductive theory.

search strategy – A plan or method of conducting a search for information.

semantic ambiguity – An ambiguous statement whose ambiguity rests on at least two clear and accepted meanings of the same word or phrase. Contrasted with syntactic ambiguity.

simple arguments – Arguments with only one premise and one conclusion.

skeletal outline – The underlying structure of a piece of written or oral communication expressed as an argument. The outline shows only the connections between premises and conclusions, and includes only those essential aspects needed to formulate the piece into an argument.

slanters – A linguistic devise used to influence opinions, attitudes, and behavior.

stereotyping – A generalization about a group based on oversimplified characteristics of the group and ignoring the characteristics of the individuals in the group.

stipulative definition – A definition in which a new meaning is arbitrarily introduced and attached to a word or symbol for specific explanatory purposes.

structure (for an argument) – The underlying design of an argument showing only the connections between premises and conclusions, and the logical flow of ideas from one to the other.

subjectivist fallacy – A fallacy in which the premises are based on the personal opinions and experiences of the arguer without regard to accepting or rejecting an opponent's argument.

sufficient condition – In causal reasoning, a set of circumstances that comprise all the necessary conditions taken together and whose presence results in producing the effect under investigation.

syntactic ambiguity – An ambiguity that occurs as a result of confusing, ungrammatical, or misleading language or sentence structure.

T

thesis statement – A one-sentence statement of the central theme of one's research. It is like a hypothesis used in solving a problem.

truncation – A search technique in which you shorten a word, replacing the ending of a word with a truncation symbol, usually an asterisk (*) or a question mark (?). The computer will search for all forms of the term that have that particular root.

U

utilitarianism – An ethical theory based on the principle that one should promote as much happiness as possible for the greatest number of people affected by the action while weighing the possible harm created by such action. Often called the "greatest good" theory, it attempts to measure the amount of good (happiness) consequences that might result from any action or rule against any harm that might result from that action or rule.

V

vague statements – Imprecise statements that could be made more precise in the context in which they are expressed.

values – In moral contexts, the norms, principles, and entities that a society deems worthy of maintaining.

Bibliography

"A Progress Report on Information Literacy: An Update on the American Library Association Presidential Committee on Information Literacy: Final Report," published by the Association of College and Research Libraries, March 1998. <http://www.ala.org/acrl/nili/nili.html>, 6 June 2000.

American Management Association. *Training Manual*. New York: American Management Association, 1998.

Anderson, Robert L. *Managing Small Businesses*. Minneapolis/St. Paul: West Publishing Co., 1993.

Bazerman, Max H., and Margaret A. Neale. *Negotiating Rationally*. New York: The Free Press, 1992.

Beard, Henry, and Christopher Cerf. *The Official Politically Correct Dictionary and Handbook*. New York: Villard Books, 1992.

Berkeley, George. "Three Dialogues between Hylas and Philonous" In *Berkeley, Hume, and Kant*, edited by T. V. Smith and Marjorie Grene. Chicago: University of Chicago Press, 1940, 1957, p. 9.

Bettis, Richard A., Stephen P. Bradley, and Gary Hamel. "Outsourcing and Industrial Decline," *The Executive* 6, no. 1 (1992): 7–22.

Beauchamp, Tom L., and Norman E. Bowie, eds. *Ethical Theory and Business*. Englewood Cliffs, NJ: Prentice-Hall, 1979.

Braverman, Jerome D. *Management Decision Making*. New York: AMACOM, 1980.

Brookfield, Stephen. *Developing Critical Thinkers*. San Francisco: Jossey-Bass Publishers, 1987.

Cantor, Jeffrey A. *Delivering Instruction to Adult Learners*. Toronto, Ontario: Wall & Emerson, Inc., 1992.

Carnap, Rudolf. *Meaning and Necessity*. Chicago: University of Chicago Press, 1947, 1956.

Chronicle of Higher Education Almanac. Washington, DC: Chronicle of Higher Education, 1999.

Corridan, Kara. "Solutions: How a Small-Business Owner Found Inventive Ways to Deal with Work/Family Conflicts," *Working Mother* (March 1999): 23.

Descartes, Rene. *The Philosophical Works of Descartes*. 2 vols. Translated by Elizabeth S. Haldane and G. R. T. Ross. Cambridge: University Press, 1968.

Kant, Immanuel. *Foundations of the Metaphysics of Morals*. Section 41. Translated by T. K. Abbott, 1785.

Kelley, David. *The Art of Reasoning*. 3rd ed. New York: W. W. Norton & Co., 1998.

Kimbal, Bruce. *Orators & Philosophers*. New York: Teachers College Press, 1986.

Leonard, Bill. "Recipes for Part-Time Benefits." *HR Magazine* 45, no. 4 (2000):56–62.

March, James G. *A Primer on Decision Making*. New York: The Free Press, 1994.

Meyers, Chet. *Teaching Students to Think Critically*. San Francisco: Jossey-Bass Publishers, 1986.

Mintzberg, Henry. *Managing with People in Mind*, Harvard Business Review paperback reprint # 90085, 1991. Boston, MA: Harvard Business School Publishers, 1991.

Moore, Brooke Noel, and Richard Parker. *Critical Thinking*. London: Mayfield Publishing Co., 1998.

Moore, George Edward. Principia Ethica. 1903. In *Philosophic Problems: An Introductory Book of Readings*, edited by Maurice Mandelbaum, Francis W. Gramlich, and Alan Ross Anderson. New York: Macmillan, 1957.

Newton, Lisa H., and Maureen M. Ford, eds. *Taking Sides: Clashing Views on Controversial Issues in Business Ethics and Society*. Guilford, CT: Dushkin Pub. Group, 1990.

Paul, Richard W. *Critical Thinking: What Every Person Needs to Survive in a Rapidly Changing World*. 3rd ed. Edited by Jane Willsen and A. J. A. Binker. Santa Rosa, CA: Foundation for Critical Thinking, 1993.

Random House Dictionary of the English Language. College Edition. New York: Random House, 1968.

Romain, Dianne. *Thinking Things Through: Critical Thinking for Decisions You Can Live With*. Mountain View, CA: Mayfield Publishing Company, 1997.

Ruggiero, Vincent Ryan. *Becoming a Critical Thinker*. 2nd ed. Boston: Houghton Mifflin, 1996.

Scudder, Samuel H. "Take This Fish and Look at It." In *Readings for Writers*, 9th ed., edited by Jo Ray McCuen and Anthony Winkler. Fort Worth, Texas: Harcourt Brace College Publishers, 1998, 205–208.

Shaw, William H., and Vincent Barry. *Moral Issues in Business*. 7th ed. Belmont, CA: Wadsworth Publishing Company, 1998.

Sleigh, Robert C. *Necessary Truth*. Englewood Cliffs, NJ: Prentice-Hall, 1972.

Velasquez, Manuel G. *Business Ethics: Concepts and Cases*. 4th ed. Upper Saddle River, NJ: Prentice-Hall, 1998.

References

PREFACE

1. *Chronicle of Higher Education Almanac* (Washington, DC: Chronicle of Higher Education, 1999).

CHAPTER 1

1. Vincent Ryan Ruggiero, *Becoming a Critical Thinker*, 2nd ed. (Boston: Houghton Mifflin, 1996), 5.

2. American Management Association, *Training Manual* (New York: American Management Association, 1998), 2-5.

3. Ruggiero, 5.

4. "Discourse on Method," Rule 1. In *The Philosophical Works of Descartes*, vol. 1, trans. Elizabeth S. Haldane and G. R. T. Ross (Cambridge: University Press, 1968), 7.

5. Brooke Noel Moore and Richard Parker, *Critical Thinking* (London: Mayfield Publishing Co., 1998), 13.

CHAPTER 2

1. Jerome D. Braverman, *Management Decision Making* (New York: AMACOM, 1980), 8.

2. Rudolf Carnap, *Meaning and Necessity* (Chicago: University of Chicago Press, 1947, 1956), 7.

3. George Edward Moore, Principia Ethica, 1903, in *Philosophic Problems: An Introductory Book of Readings*, Maurice Mandelbaum, Francis W. Gramlich, and Alan Ross Anderson, eds., (New York: Macmillan, 1957), 398.

CHAPTER 3

1. Dianne Romain, *Thinking Things Through: Critical Thinking for Decisions You Can Live With* (Mountain View, CA: Mayfield Publishing Company, 1997).

2. James G. March, *A Primer on Decision Making* (New York: The Free Press, 1994), 1-2.

3. Ibid., vii.

4. *Random House Dictionary of the English Language*. College Edition (New York: Random House, 1968).

5. Jerome D. Braverman, *Management Decision Making* (New York: AMACOM, 1980), 2.

6. Robert C. Sleigh, *Necessary Truth* (Englewood Cliffs, NJ: Prentice-Hall, 1972), 53.

7. Braverman, 8.

8. George Berkeley, "Three Dialogues between Hylas and Philonous," in *Berkeley, Hume, and Kant*, ed. T. V. Smith and Marjorie Grene (Chicago: University of Chicago Press, 1940, 1957), 9.

9. Bruce Kimbal, *Orators & Philosophers* (New York: Teachers College Press, 1986), 7.

CHAPTER 4

1. Henry Beard and Christopher Cerf, *The Official Politically Correct Dictionary and Handbook* (New York: Villard Books, 1992).

2. Moore, Brooke Noel, and Richard Parker. *Critical Thinking*. (London: Mayfield Publishing Co., 1998).

3. Richard A. Bettis, Stephen P. Bradley, and Gary Hamel "Outsourcing and Industrial Decline," *The Executive* 6, no. 1 (1992): 18.

4. Bettis 18.

5. Ibid. 18.

CHAPTER 5

1. Kara Corridan, "Solutions: How a Small-Business Owner Found Inventive Ways to Deal with Work/Family Conflicts," *Working Mother* (March 1999): 23.

CHAPTER 6

1. M. Garrett Bauman, *Ideas and Details: A Guide to College Writing* (New York: Harcourt Brace, 1992), 191.

2. Kara Corridan, "Solutions: How a Small-Business Owner Found Inventive Ways to Deal with Work/Family Conflicts," *Working Mother* (March 1999): 23.

3. David Kelley, *The Art of Reasoning*, 3rd ed. (New York: W.W. Norton & Co., 1998).

4. James G. March, *A Primer on Decision Making* (New York: The Free Press, 1994), 96.

CHAPTER 7

1. Bill Leonard, "Recipes for Part-Time Benefits," *HR Magazine* 45, no. 4 (2000): 56.

CHAPTER 8

1. Mandelbaum, 531.

2. Jerome D. Braverman, Management Decision Making (New York: AMACOM, 1980), 7.

CHAPTER 9

1. Samuel H. Scudder, "Take this Fish and Look at It," in *Readings for Writers*, 9th ed., by Jo Ray McCuen and Anthony Winkler (Fort Worth, Texas: Harcourt Brace College Publishers, 1998), 208.

2. David Myers, *Social Psychology*, p. 20.

3. *Webster's New World Dictionary*

4. Helen Longino, *Science as Social Knowledge* (Princeton, NJ: Princeton University Press, 1990), 13.

CHAPTER 10

1. American Library Association, "A Progress Report on Information Literacy: An Update on the American Library Association Presidential Committee on Information Literacy: Final Report," published by the Association of College and Research Libraries, March 1998,(6 June 2000) <http://www.ala.org/acrl/nili/nili.html>.

2. Ibid.

CHAPTER 11

1. William H. Shaw and Vincent Barry, *Moral Issues in Business*, 7th ed. (Belmont, CA: Wadsworth Publishing Company, 1998).

2. Manuel G. Velasquez, *Business Ethics: Concepts and Cases*, 4th ed. (Upper Saddle River, NJ: Prentice-Hall, 1998).

3. Velasquez, 71.

4. Shaw and Barry, 360.

5. Immanuel Kant, *Foundations of the Metaphysics of Morals*, Section 41, trans. T. K. Abbott (1785).

6. Ibid.

7. Lisa H. Newton and Maureen M. Ford, eds., *Taking Sides: Clashing Views on Controversial Issues in Business Ethics and Society* (Guilford, CT: Dushkin Pub. Group, 1990).

CHAPTER 12

1. Henry Mintzberg, *Managing with People in Mind* (Boston, MA: Harvard Business School Publishers, 1991), 11.

2. Robert L. Anderson, *Managing Small Businesses* (Minneapolis/St. Paul: West Publishing Co., 1993). **This case study was adapted from "Case 2: Aquapark" with permission from publishers.**

3. James G. March, *A Primer on Decision Making* (New York: The Free Press, 1994), 2.

Index